The Joy of Stats

The Joy of Stats

A Short Guide to
Introductory Statistics
in the Social Sciences

ROBERTA GARNER

broadview press

Library and Archives Canada Cataloguing in Publication

Garner, Roberta
    The joy of stats : a short guide to introductory statistics in the social sciences / Roberta Garner.

Includes bibliographical references and index.
ISBN 1-55111-691-X

    1. Social sciences—Statistical methods—Textbooks.   2. Statistics—Textbooks.
I. Title.

HA29.G37 2005   300'.1'5195   C2005-901663-9

Broadview Press, Ltd. is an independent, international publishing house, incorporated in 1985. Broadview believes in shared ownership, both with its employees and with the general public; since the year 2000 Broadview shares have traded publicly on the Toronto Venture Exchange under the symbol BDP.

We welcome any comments and suggestions regarding any aspect of our publications — please feel free to contact us at the addresses below, or at broadview@broadviewpress.com / www.broadviewpress.com

North America
Post Office Box 1243,
Peterborough, Ontario,
Canada K9J 7H5
Tel: (705) 743-8990
Fax: (705) 743-8353
customerservice
@broadviewpress.com

3576 California Road,
Post Office Box 1015,
Orchard Park, NY
USA 14127

UK, Ireland, and
Continental Europe
NBN International
Estover Road
Plymouth, Devon PL6 7PY
United Kingdom
Tel: +44 (0) 1752 202300
Fax: +44 (0) 1752 202330
Customer Service:
cservs@nbninternational.com
orders@nbninternational.com

Australia and
New Zealand
UNIREPS
University of
New South Wales
Sydney, NSW, 2052
Tel: + 61296 640 999
Fax: + 61296 645 420
info.press@unsw.edu.au

Cover design and typeset by Zack Taylor, www.zacktaylor.com

The author has made every effort to locate copyright holders of material published in this book and would be pleased to hear from any party not duly acknowledged.

Printed in Canada

For Zeke and Rafael, and in memory of Renée,
who encouraged me to write this book.

Myths

Statistics probably was invented by the ancient Egyptian god Thoth, a being with the head of a baboon or an ibis. Thoth was the patron of writing, mathematics, astronomy, geometry, science, games, gambling, and the occult.

The ancient Greeks believed that even the Olympian Gods were subject to Tyche, whom the Romans later called Fortuna and we call Lady Luck. She is represented as a charming and unpredictable woman, holding the Horn of Plenty or the Wheel of Fortune. But Tyche was a sister of the Moerea, the Fates, three hideous hags who spin, measure, and cut the Thread of Life. Behind her capricious smile, Tyche is inexorable and unalterable. All four sisters were children of Zeus and the Titaness Themis ("Law"), who personifies the order of the world.

Contents

List of Figures and Tables   13
Acknowledgments   15
Preface   17

Chapter One: Basic Concepts   29

Part I: Variables   29
   Level of Measurement   31
   Dichotomous Variables   35
   Operationalized Variables   39
   Independent (IV) and Dependent (DV) Variables   40
   Causality   41
   Units of Analysis: Individual and Place-level Data   43
Part II: Thinking about Procedures   45
   Descriptive and Inferential Statistics   45
   Difference   48
   Observing and Estimating   51
Conclusion   53
Key Terms   53

Chapter Two: Describing Distributions   55

Part I: Frequency Distributions   55
Part II: Summary Measures   58
   Measures of Central Tendency (Mean, Median, Mode)   58
   Measures of Dispersion   64
   Categoric Variables: Index of Diversity and Index of
      Qualitative Variation   67
Part III: Graphing and Visual Displays of Distributions   70
Part IV: Standardized Scores or Z-scores   80
   The Mathematical Imagination: The Magic of Z-scores   81
   Math Interlude: Chebycheff's Inequality   83
Conclusion   85
Key Terms   86

Chapter Three: Statistical Inference 87

Part I: Thinking about Statistical Inference 87
Statistical Inference: What Are We Trying To Do? 87
Variability 95
The Mathematical Imagination: A World Without
Variability 105
The Normal Curve 106
Sampling Distributions and the Normal Curve 109
Sampling Error: Variability of the Sampling Distribution 111
The Central Limit Theorem 111
Math Thoughts 114
Underlying Distributions and Sampling Distributions 118
The Sampling Distribution of a Proportion 121
Part II: Doing Statistical Inference 127
The Logic of Statistical Inference 127
Confidence Intervals 129
Hypothesis Testing (The Null Hypothesis and *T*-tests) 134
Conclusion 149
Key Terms 149

Chapter Four: Relationships Among Variables 151

**Part I: An Overview—Thinking About Variable
Relationships** 151
Four Types of Data Analysis Techniques 154
Beyond Bivariate Analysis: Adding Variables and Staying
Alert 157
Part II: Data Analysis Techniques 163
Section One: Regression Analysis 164
Math Interlude: The Natural Log Transformation 164
Section Two: Crosstabs 189
Section Three: ANOVA 201
Section Four: Logistic Regression 206
Conclusion 216
Key Terms 218

Conclusion 219

Contents

How To? 221

Choosing a Data Analysis Technique 221
Regression Analysis 222
    Pearson's Correlation Coefficient 222
    The Bivariate Regression Equation 224
    Coefficient of Determination (aka "R-squared") 228
Crosstabs and Related Procedures 231
    Computing Chi-Square 231
    Joint and Marginal Distributions 233
    More about Running Percentages 235
    Measures of Association 237
ANOVA and the F-test 241
T-tests 244
    One-Sample T-test 244
    Independent Samples T-test 247

Exercises 249

Questions 250
Answers 261

Math Refresher 283

Tips for Studying Math 283
    Estimating 284
    From Common Sense to Formula 286
The Number Line 287
Greater and Lesser 287
Absolute Value 289
Fractions and Other Proportions 290
    Decimal Fractions 291
    Percent 292
    Comparing Fractions 294
    Computing Percent Change and Percentage Point Change 295
Operations 296
    Addition 296
    Multiplication 296
    Subtraction 297
    Division 297
    Word or Story Problems 300

Squaring, Higher Powers, and Square Roots   301
  Squaring   301
  Higher Powers   302
  Square Roots   303
  Scientific Notation   304
Manipulating Formulas   304
The Coordinate Plane, Ordered Pairs, and Functions   308

Appendix   315

Tables of Probability Distributions   315
  Table 26: Critical Values for the Z-distribution   316
  Table 27: Critical Values for the T-distribution   318
  Table 28: Critical Values for the Chi-Square Distribution   320
  Table 29: Critical Values for the F-distribution   322

Bibliography, Reading Suggestions, and Works Cited   327

Index   331

List of Figures and Tables

FIGURES

Figure 1: Pie chart—Respondents' highest degree (GSS data)   71

Figure 2: Bar chart—Respondents' highest degree by count (GSS data)   72

Figure 3: Bar chart—Respondents' highest degree by percentage (GSS data)   72

Figure 4: Bar chart displaying two variables—Respondents' degree and use of e-mail   73

Figure 5: Histogram for a continuous variable—Respondents' age (GSS data)   74

Figure 6: Displaying a continuous variable—Stem and leaf plot of age of respondents   76

Figure 7: Displaying a continuous variable—Boxplot and percentiles for age of respondents   77

Figure 8: Histogram for distribution of samples means   91

Figure 9: Histogram of the probability distribution of the sum of the upturned faces of two dice   104

Figure 10: The standardized normal curve   108

Figure 11: Sampling distributions of means of samples $N = 2$, $N = 4$, and $N = 30$ from three different types of populations   117

Figure 12: Educational histograms   119

Figure 13: Third variables and 0-order relationships   160

Figure 14: A strong positive correlation   165

Figure 15: A weak positive correlation   166

Figure 16: A strong negative correlation   167

Figure 17: A weak negative correlation   167

Figure 18: A 0-correlation   168

Figure 19: Thinking about R-squared   175

Figure 20: Regression analysis—Distance and commuting time to campus   177

Figure 21: Regression analysis—Literacy and infant mortality in six Central American countries   182

Figure 22: Multiple regression—A model using doctors and hospital beds to predict male life expectancy   185

Figure 23: Crosstabs—Total family income in quartiles by college degree, with chi-square and gamma (GSS data)   198

Figure 24: ANOVA—Hours per day watching TV by college degree (GSS data)   204

Figure 25: ANOVA—Family income in dollars by astrological sign (GSS data)   205

TABLES

Table 1: Variable—Eye colour for a class of 40 people; $N = 40$ 56

Table 2: Variable—Height (ordinal level of measurement) for 40 people; $N = 40$ 56

Table 3: Variable—Number of Siblings; $N = 20$ 56

Table 4: Continuous Data in Intervals   57

Table 5: Variable—Truck ownership among Greasy Bob's customers   60

Table 6: Displaying a continuous variable—Descriptives   75

Table 7: Acceptance by gender and department   162

Table 8: Adult literacy and infant mortality rates   181

Table 9: Reading enjoyment by gender (counts)   190

Table 10: Reading enjoyment by gender (percents)   190

Table 11: Expected values (counts) under the null hypothesis   193

Table 12: Logistic Regression Predicting Suicidal Thoughts, Add Health, Wave 1, 1995, (N=3103)   214

Table 13: GPA by drinking habits—Distribution of each variable separately   233

Table 14: GPA by drinking habits—The null hypothesis   233

Table 15: GPA by drinking habits—Low drinkers are good students   234

Table 16: GPA by drinking habits—Low drinkers are good students   234

Table 17: GPA by drinking habits—High drinkers are good students   234

Table 18: The counts   235, 239

Table 19: Correct percentaging, in the direction of the IV   236

Table 20: Incorrect percentaging, by dependent variable   236

Table 21: Selecting Measures of Association   237

Table 22: Weight by Height   238

Table 23: Illness by vaccination   241

Table 24: Gender ideology by sex category—Observed values   278

Table 25: Expected values for the null hypothesis   278

Table 26: Critical Values for the Z-distribution   316

Table 27: Critical Values for the T-distribution   318

Table 28: Critical Values for the Chi-Square Distribution   320

Table 29: Critical Values for the F-distribution   322

Acknowledgments

I would like to thank all the people who encouraged me and made this book possible: My colleagues at DePaul University; the students in my statistics classes who endured my weird cartoons; my mom Renée, who in her nineties told me that statistics is vital in today's world and urged me to develop the project; my son Michael, who shares my fascination with the meeting of mathematics and social reality; the reviewers of early drafts of this book; and all my editors at Broadview Press—Michael Harrison, Anne Brackenbury, Barbara Conolly, Tara Lowes, Zack Taylor for the spirited design, and—for her wonderful work—Karen Taylor.

Preface

Statistics is an exciting field of knowledge, useful in scientific research and everyday life and entertaining in its basic ideas. Mastery of statistics contributes to an understanding of nature and human societies. Statistics enables us to focus on key features of nature and society, to organize our thinking, and to see through false and misleading claims that we often encounter in the media and everyday life. Confidence about statistical and quantitative reasoning makes us more aware, selective, and critical about the flood of information and misinformation we face in our complex, globalized world.

This short book is designed to help the beginner enter the conversation of statistical reasoning. It explains the purpose and logic of the procedures and concepts of elementary, applied statistics. "Elementary" means that it is for beginners. "Applied" means that we are primarily interested in using statistics to understand information about the natural and social world. Instead of getting into the details of formulas and statistics software, the book keeps our minds on the basic questions in applied statistics: Why are we using this procedure? What is the point of this concept?

I was fortunate to have been a teen guinea pig for the development of the New Math curriculum at University of Illinois High School in the 1950s and came to love math as a playful practice of the imagination rather than as tedious calculations and rote memorization. I would like to share that sense of fantasy and discovery with you.

STATISTICS FOR PLEASURE

"Joy" sounds like a mischievous reference to sex manuals, and, indeed, statistics has a pleasurable side where fantasy enhances technique and the mathematical imagination takes us to strange places. It is believed that, in the left-brain, centres of math activity lie close to regions of joy and relaxation. So the association between statistics and pleasure, fun, curiosity, and relaxation is quite reasonable, even if it may seem a little surprising at first.

PURPOSES

Joy of Stats is a guide that helps you read other kinds of statistics texts. It can accompany texts that are mathematically challenging and rigorous because it provides a quick overview of the logic of statistical reasoning, summarizes mathematical procedures in words as well as mathematical symbols, and presents intuitive motivation for proofs and formulas. It can provide background for texts that are focused on data analysis, large data sets, and computer software for statistical applications; *Joy* explains the underlying logic of the techniques and provides the basic formulas (which computer-oriented texts sometimes don't include). Finally, *Joy* can accompany comprehensive texts; *Joy* offers a "bird's eye view" of the terrain—of the forest—that can help you find your way through the intricate details covered in the long textbooks—the trees. It can be used as a preview to prepare for reading more comprehensive books and as a review to refresh memories of statistics learned long ago.

NEW WAYS OF THINKING

Quantitative reasoning and applied statistics stimulate new ways of thinking, as we go back and forth among mathematical concepts, formulas that precisely express these concepts, and real world research, data, and observations. Bringing these different types of mental activities together is an exciting challenge.

Chapter One introduces the concept "variable" which is essential for understanding the quantitative and logical work that follows. Chapter Two explores distributions of variables, one at a time, beginning with familiar procedures like finding averages and making tables. It then proceeds to a key topic in statistics, the description of variability. Chapter Three develops the logic of statistical inference, using samples to draw conclusions about populations. This logic is complicated and is at the heart of statistics. Chapter Four presents several major data analysis techniques for finding relationships among two or more variables. It is followed by a "How To?" section that summarizes the basic procedures for these techniques. At the end of the book, you will find a "Math Refresher," a short review of math concepts. You can begin your work by skimming the "Math Refresher" to make sure you remember this material, or you can just consult it as needed. The book ends with an annotated bibliography for exploring statistics in more depth.

Statistical reasoning connects three distinct types of thinking. First of all, it involves formulas and calculations, "math" in the traditional and narrow way in which most people use the term. Second, it applies these mathematical tools to real-world, empirical situations encountered in research or addressed in public policy debates. Third, it develops and uses a conceptual vocabulary for talking about quantitative information and, above all, probabilistic logic. Statistics provides the concepts we need for talking about uncertainty and risk.

The challenge is to connect all three of these ways of thinking, to break through the "fire walls" in our minds that separate "math" (assumed to be formulas and calculations) from "concepts" (which are actually the fundamental part of mathematical thinking) and "observation of the real world." In teaching statistics, I have often found that students can work through calculational formulas, but have difficulty talking about what they are doing. This book will connect symbolic manipulation and calculation to words that refer to ideas, concepts, and logic. In applied statistics, both the formulas and the math concepts have to be used to interpret and make sense of real-world, empirical observations, and public issues.

Throughout the text you will find five tools for making these connections among math procedures, concepts, and applications.

- The first is the **algorithm**, precise step-by-step verbal instructions for computing or finding a number that matches a math concept like the mean.

- Algorithms are usually associated with **formulas**, which express the same concept in math symbols rather than in a sequence of steps expressed in words. It's important to talk about the formula using the words and concepts of the algorithm in order to create a connection between the formula (the symbols and calculations) and the ideas. The algorithm helps us to connect the formula in symbols to the concept in words.

- Another type of mental connection is formed by linking concepts to **examples**. Some of our examples will be very simple ones designed to illustrate a technique. We will also work through examples of actual data analysis, based on real research, in order to illustrate statistical concepts and techniques.

- The fourth approach to concepts is presented in inserts called **"the mathematical imagination."** They are little vignettes that encourage thinking about a new concept and provide intuitive motivation for ideas whose proofs are too advanced for this book.

- To help the reader remember the concepts I provide a **key term list** at the end of every chapter. A main idea of this book is that quantitative and statistical reasoning requires learning a new vocabulary in which concepts are precisely matched with formulas or procedures, and the key-term lists are quick ways to review the vocabulary.

HOW TO READ STATISTICS: "TAKE IT SLOW AND EASY."

As you work through this book, keep in mind that reading a math-related book is not like reading a novel or an exciting tale of true-life adventure. It requires a different pace of reading, more akin to savouring than devouring. Here are a few tips:

- Put yourself in a relaxed yet intensely alert mood—calm, playful, and highly focused. Make sure that you have plenty of time and don't feel rushed. If you start feeling anxious and stressed, rather than alert, curious, and receptive, take a break.

- Read slowly, trying to visualize concepts using math ideas such as the number line and the x-y plane. Make little drawings or graphs, and use your visual skills to enhance your understanding of concepts.

- Talk about the formulas and ideas to yourself or friends. After completing a step of a calculation say out loud what you have just accomplished. Imagine a mean pest who challenges every step of your calculation: "Why are you dividing by that? What is the point of the addition?...." In your conversation with this imaginary wise guy, explain what you are doing and why you are doing it. Don't just say, "Because the formula tells me so...," but talk about the overall purpose of the formula as well as the meaning of each step.

- Work through very simple examples with whole numbers.

- Think about real situations that could be used to illustrate what you have just learned and make the abstract concepts relevant and connected to your life or social issues you care about.

- Create a science fiction movie inside your head that takes a math concept to the extreme, forming an imaginary world in which bizarre things happen.

- Combine old-fashioned rote learning techniques with your playful imagination. Recite definitions out loud. Make flash cards with a formula on one side and, on the other side, an algorithm in words, a definition, and/or a note about the purpose of the formula.

- Don't hesitate to go back to an earlier point in the text to reread or review an idea—math reading is not linear, and it is usually very helpful to read backwards as well as forwards, as new ideas deepen and change your understanding of earlier material.

- Finally, be persistent and mentally adventurous. Never avert your eyes from a page of numbers or symbols; overcome the desire to flip the rock of avoidance back over those loathsome symbols swarming across the page. Don't be afraid or ashamed to ask questions of friends, tutors, and instructors. Curiosity, courage, and energy are essential to learning math!

Math Review

Here is a little math you need to review before starting in on elementary statistics. If you feel a bit rusty when you see the list, don't worry; you'll have an opportunity to refresh your skills, and in fact learning statistics may help you appreciate these concepts more after seeing them put to use. You can review more intensively by using the "Math Refresher" section of the book.

USING FRACTIONS, ESPECIALLY IN THE FORM OF PERCENTAGES

Fractions express a proportion. For example, $\frac{36}{100}$ means if we cut a pie into 100 pieces, we get 36 of those pieces.

- The "bottom" is called the denominator, and it names the pieces; the "top" is called the numerator and tells us the number of pieces we have. If fractions give you trouble, think of Mom or Dad cutting up pies and passing out the slices.

- Fractions can also be expressed in decimal form. To convert a top/bottom fraction into a decimal fraction, divide the top (numerator) by the bottom (denominator). In other words, divide the bottom into the top.

- A percentage is just another way of writing a fraction. We set the total amount (the whole pie, the entire federal budget, all students at York University, the price of a coat, etc.) equal to 100 pieces and then the percentage tells us how many of those 100 pieces we're dealing with.

- Percentages are typically used to express proportions of a collective object like dollars in a budget, prices in dollars, or people in a country or institution. They are also used to express rates such as mortgage rates and other types of interest rates, tax rates, and increases in quantities.

- Converting a regular fraction into a percentage is easy. Divide the bottom into the top to turn it into a decimal fraction; then move the decimal point 2 places to the right. You should be able to convert the most common fractions into percentages and vice versa:

$$\frac{1}{2} = 50\%; \frac{1}{4} = 25\%; \frac{1}{5} = 20\%; \frac{2}{5} = 40\%; \frac{3}{4} = 75\%;$$
$$\frac{1}{10} = 10\%, \text{ etc.}$$

This conversion, in both directions, should be memorized and become automatic.

GRAPHING IN THE X-Y COORDINATE PLANE

- The x-y coordinate plane is a two-dimensional plane. A point in the plane has an x-coordinate and a y-coordinate, written like this: (x, y).

- The x values are plotted along the horizontal axis and the y values along the vertical axis. The "origin" or (0,0) point is right in the middle of the plane, and there are four quadrants:

   Upper right: positive x, positive y.
   Lower right: positive x, negative y.
   Upper left: negative x, positive y.
   Lower left: negative x, negative y.

- Usually we think of y "as a function of x" so that when we are given an x, we have a formula for finding the matching y.

- A straight line is one function of this type (the one we will be most concerned with here), with the equation **$y = a + bx$**. In this equation, **b** is the slope (rise over run) and **a** is the y-intercept or constant term (the place where $x = 0$ and the line crosses the y-axis).

ALGEBRAIC FORMULAS AND ALGORITHMS

A formula is a precise, shorthand way of writing out a sequence of operations. In this book, we will think of an algebraic formula as a way of expressing a concept in a precise sequence of steps.

Many statistics concepts are based on common sense ideas; but common sense is vague, ambiguous. And wordy. We want to make our concepts as precise as possible, so we define each concept as a series of steps that must always be completed in a definite order. These steps can be expressed in words and then summed up more efficiently in a formula. These series of steps are called **algorithms** and are a key element in writing computer software. (By the way, algorithm and algebra are both words of Arabic origin. Hindus invented our numerals with place notation and a 0. Arabs then added new concepts and procedures and introduced the basics of calculation to Europeans around the end of the European Middle Ages; otherwise, Europeans might still be trying to divide MCCX by CLIV. So "al" is just the Arabic word for "the," and it appears in a number of math terms that Arabs introduced to the West.)

Sometimes there are several different formulas for the same concept. There may be a conceptual formula that expresses the basic ideas behind the concept and a calculational formula that provides the shortest way of doing the computation by hand. The calculational formulas were very important in the bad old days before computers, but nowadays we can devote our energy to understanding conceptual formulas and let the computer enjoy doing calculations.

Two more tips about algebraic expressions:

- A capital Sigma (which is a Greek letter), Σ, means "sum up everything that follows."

- Remember that there is a correct order to arithmetical operations; for example, anything in parentheses has to be done first. (See "Math Refresher" for more.)

ESTIMATING ANSWERS FOR CALCULATIONS

It is always a good idea to estimate answers to problems before doing them. Always think about the "ballpark" in which this answer will end up. What kind of a number should it be? What do I expect it to look like? What is the largest it might be? The smallest? Is it in units of some kind? Is it a percentage/proportion or not? Can it be negative? If the answer I get is very different from my estimate, what went wrong: did I miss a step, make a computational error, or misunderstand the concept?

A FEW EXERCISES TO REFRESH MATH MEMORIES

Take a quick look at the following topics and exercises. If they look familiar and you feel comfortable setting them up and solving them, mostly without a calculator, just proceed to Chapter One. Calculators are handy for longer problems, but they slow down the solution of simple problems. If you feel a bit shaky with these problems, take a look at the "Math Refresher" section. Remember that you can always return to the "Math Refresher" when you need it.

Fractions:

Convert each fraction into a decimal fraction (divide bottom into top) and into a percentage (move decimal point two places to the right).

a) $\dfrac{1}{2}$ b) $\dfrac{1}{3}$ c) $\dfrac{2}{3}$ d) $\dfrac{1}{4}$ e) $\dfrac{3}{4}$

f) $\dfrac{1}{5}$ g) $\dfrac{2}{5}$ h) $\dfrac{3}{5}$ i) $\dfrac{4}{5}$ j) $\dfrac{1}{10}$

These conversions should be memorized and "going back and forth" among the fractions, decimal fractions, and percentages should be automatic.

A percentage is a type of fraction that is often used when the "totality" (the whole pie) is not a single object, but a collection (people, money, etc.).

Percentaging a distribution:

Percentage the following distributions to the nearest percentage point. (Hint: you first have to add up the numbers to get the total; the total is then used as the "bottom" (denominator) for the fractions; divide to get the decimal fraction and move the decimal point over two places to the right for the percentage).

1. In one week at Bill's Bar and Grill, customers drank 340 Buds, 213 Bud-lites, 170 Labatt Blues, and 110 Goose Island Ales

2. At Decatur Community College, there are 750 LAS majors, 200 Graphic Design majors, 300 majors in Computer Tech, and 105 majors in Early Childhood Development.

3. In a study of social class, the researchers found that 300 people responded they are "working class," 365 said they are "middle class," 65 said "upper class," and 30 said "lower class."

Stop!
Before you do the calculation, eye the distribution and estimate the percentages! Then go ahead and use a calculator.

Operations with fractions:

Do the following problems without a calculator:

A. $\frac{1}{3}$ times $\frac{1}{2}$

B. $\frac{1}{3}$ divided by $\frac{1}{2}$ (Remember: to divide by a fraction, invert the fraction you are dividing by and multiply.)

C. $\frac{1}{3}$ times $\frac{1}{4}$

D. $\frac{1}{3}$ plus $\frac{1}{4}$ (Convert to a common denominator.)

E. $\frac{1}{3}$ minus $\frac{1}{4}$

F. $\frac{1}{2}$ divided by $\frac{4}{3}$

Explain why your answers make sense; if necessary, resort to thinking about a pie cut into wedges.

Negatives:

Compute the following quantities:

a) 1 times –3　　　　b) –4 divided by 2　　　c) –6 times –7

d) –6 divided by –7　e) –7 plus 6　　　　　f) –4 plus –5

g) –4 minus –5

Comparing quantities:

1. Which is larger? Answer without a calculator:

a) –4 or –3　　　　　b) 75% or $\frac{3}{5}$　　　　c) .05 or .01

d) $\frac{350}{450}$ or $\frac{36}{45}$　　　　e) .01 or .001

2. If a number is expressed as a fraction, and we increase the top (numerator), what happens to the number? Does it get bigger or smaller?

3. If we increase the bottom (denominator), does it get bigger or smaller?

4. If we divide a whole number by a fraction that is less than 1, is the result smaller or larger than the original number?

5. If we square a number between 0 and 1, is the result larger or smaller than the original number?

6. If we square a negative number, is the result negative or positive?

This completes our quick, basic review. If you feel confident with these basic concepts and skills, go ahead and start reading the next chapter, planning to consult the "Math Refresher" as needed. If you feel a bit shaky, you may wish to spend a little time with the "Math Refresher" before proceeding.

Math Review: Answers

Fractions:

a) .50 or 50%
b) .333 or 33%
c) .666 or 67%
d) .25 or 25%
e) .75 or 75%
f) .20 or 20%
g) .40 or 40%
h) .60 or 60%
i) .80 or 80%
j) .10 or 10%

Percentaging a distribution:

1. 41% Buds, 26% Bud-lites, 20% Labatt Blues, 13% Goose Island Ales

2. 55% LAS, 15% Graphic Design, 22% Computer Tech, 8% Early Childhood

3. 39% working class, 48% middle class, 9% upper class, 4% lower class.

Operations with fractions:

A. $\frac{1}{6}$ B. $\frac{2}{3}$

C. $\frac{1}{12}$ D. $\frac{7}{12}$

E. $\frac{1}{12}$ F. $\frac{3}{8}$

Negatives:

a) −3   b) −2
c) 42   d) .86
e) −1   f) −9
g) 1

Comparing quantities:

1. a) −3   b) 75%   c) .05   d) $\frac{36}{45}$ e) .01
2. It gets bigger.
3. It gets smaller.
4. It is larger.
5. It is smaller.
6. It is positive.

Chapter One:
Basic Concepts

This chapter introduces basic terms and concepts in applied statistics and research design.

Part I: Variables

Statistics is about variables and distributions. When we do statistics, we pretend that everything in the world can be described by variables. The qualities of everything can be broken down into variables (characteristics that can take on different values) and we look at the distribution and relationships of the variables. You may feel that this is a goofy, anti-holistic approach to reality, but in areas like modern medicine and rocket science, it led to effective ways of understanding and changing the world. For example, early biomedical researchers looked at whether being vaccinated or not with cowpox led to different outcomes in terms of whether a person became sick with smallpox. The variable "vaccinated or not vaccinated" turned out to be related to the variable "became sick or did not become sick." Isolating key characteristics of a situation and looking at their relationships for a large number of cases led to effective vaccinations and medical treatments.

The first step of most statistical analysis is to look at the way in which **cases** are distributed among **values** of a **variable**. There are three fundamental terms here:

1. Cases: These are the units of analysis, things that have certain characteristics or properties. For example, the cases could be individual people in a statistics class, all residents of Chicago, hamburgers, or lakes. We want to reach a conclusion about their characteristics.

2. Variable: This is the characteristic or property in which we are interested. It is a characteristic that pertains to the cases. A variable must be able to take on different values for different cases. Variables include characteristics like people's GENDER, people's HEIGHT, the DEPTHS of lakes, lake TEMPERATURES, and whether a hamburger is COOKED rare, medium, or well-done. Often we look at two or more different variables at a time and ask whether they are related. For example, we might want to know if GENDER is related to HEIGHT among human beings or if TEMPERATURE is related to DEPTH for lakes.

3. Values: These are the possible outcomes for a single variable. They are different for different cases. Values can be numbers or named categories. For example, the variable GENDER typically has two values, "man" and "woman." Some people (cases) are men, and some are women. The variable hamburger COOKEDNESS applies to the cases of hamburgers and could have the values "rare," "medium," and "well-done." The values represent the possible answers to a waiter's question, "How would you like your hamburger cooked?" The values of the variable people's HEIGHT could be "tall" and "short" or the values could be numbers in inches or in meters.

Do not confuse the variable and the values! For example, if GENDER is the variable, the values are usually "man" and "woman." If the variable is HEIGHT, the values are the numbers of inches or metres.

Once we have specified our cases, variables, and values, we can look at the distribution of the variable and ask distribution questions such as:

- How many people in Canada are men and how many are women? This is a question about the distribution of the variable GENDER with the cases being people in Canada and the values usually being "man" and "woman."

- How tall are people in the Stats class? This is a question about the distribution of the variable HEIGHT in the class, with the cases being individual students, and the heights being specific numbers in inches or meters, or alternatively, categories like "tall" and "short."

- How many hamburgers at Greasy Bob's Bar and Grill are cooked rare, medium, or well-done? This is a question about the distribution of the variable COOKEDNESS with the cases being hamburgers prepared at Greasy Bob's.

Variables and constants: If a characteristic or property is the same for all the cases—if it can take on only one value—it is a constant, not a variable. All the students in the Stats class are human beings, so SPECIES is a constant for the class. If all crime statistics in a study were from the state of Texas, STATE LOCATION would be a constant in this particular study.

WHAT IS A VARIABLE?

We define the variables and identify their values. Are variables and their values real? They are actually concepts we use to model nature or society, concepts that represent real processes and features of the world. These concepts are mental constructs that we claim and hope capture certain essential features of reality. They do so in abstracted and partial ways. We select those characteristics that we think are important in our research. For example, if we want to understand the survival rates of fish in Scotland's lakes, we probably would look at variables such as lake temperature, level of pollution, and available nutrients, and not at a variable like "beauty of the surrounding landscape"—which would however be crucial for a study of tourists' selection of travel destinations.

In the social sciences, the variable-concepts are often based on socially constructed notions such as "gender" and "race"—constructs that are already considerably removed from any physical or natural basis. We have to be careful not to "reify" our variables, treating them as real things.

We need to be aware of this constructed quality of variables and the social characteristics to which they refer. For example, when biomedical researchers use the variable "race" or "race/ethnicity"—perhaps looking at "racial" differences in infection rates or health outcomes—they need to remind themselves that their variable "race" is only a shorthand way of referring to a large mix of characteristics, most of them socially defined and not genetically determined (Hernandez-Arias, 2004).

Level of Measurement

The values of a variable can be defined in a number of ways. For example, when someone asks you how tall a basketball player is you might say, "Oh, he's very tall," or you might answer a specific number of feet and inches, "six-foot-six." These different ways of breaking down a variable and specifying its possible values are referred to as "level of measurement." The same variable, HEIGHT, can be defined in different ways producing data measured at different levels of precision and quantification. It is important to understand the concept of level of measurement for two reasons. First of all, we need to make initial choices in a research design, specifying the level of measurement of our variables; secondly, once we have made these choices and collected data, the level of measurement of each variable has implications for how we analyse the data.

Often researchers use a three-way classification of levels of measurement:

1. Nominal: The values of the variable are named categories that have no particular order or ranking. For example, majors at a college are usually treated as nominal; the variable MAJOR has values like English, Sociology, Psychology, Commerce, Music, or Theatre. Racial/ethnic IDENTITY is usually treated as nominal; so is the variable RELIGIOUS AFFILIATION. There is no inherent order to categories like Buddhist, Christian, Hindu, Jewish, Muslim, and so on.

The categories of the variable must be exhaustive and mutually exclusive, meaning every case must fall into some category and no case can be in more than one category. This specification can present problems in defining the categories and force a researcher to develop new categories. For example, the large and growing number of individuals with a biracial and multiracial heritage in Canada, the United States, and Caribbean countries means that the old racial category systems have to be revised. While religions are often thought of as mutually exclusive identities, a friend from Trinidad says he is both a Christian and a Muslim. In Japan, many people participate in both Buddhist and Shinto ceremonies. These examples, in which the categories are not mutually exclusive, challenge us to rethink about the usual category system for the variable RELIGIOUS AFFILIATION.

2. Ordinal: The values of the variable are categories that have an order or ranking, but no definite numerical value. For example, for the variable HEIGHT, values might be "tall, medium, short." For the variable FREQUENCY of movie attendance, the values might be "often, sometimes, never." For the variable SOCIAL CLASS, the values might be "lower, lower-middle, upper-middle, upper." As with nominal data, the categories must be exhaustive and mutually exclusive.

3. Interval-ratio or scale: The values of these types of variables are definite numbers on a scale. These numbers refer to meaningful quantities in the real world; they are not just code numbers assigned to categories. For example, the variable HEIGHT could be defined as height in inches, the variable WEIGHT could be defined in kilograms, and the variable INCOME could be defined as the number of dollars a person or a family receives in a year. For these variables, we need to define a unit of measurement. An interval scale has equal intervals, while a ratio scale also has an absolute 0, such as 0 length, 0 assets, and 0 degrees Kelvin.

CATEGORIC AND CONTINUOUS VARIABLES

For purposes of analysing data, the variables' level of measurement is often split into two basic types, the **categoric** and the **continuous**.

1. Categoric: This level of measurement combines the nominal and the ordinal. The values of the variable are "qualities" or categoric pigeonholes, which may or may not be orderable. These categoric values can be given code numbers, but the numbers do not refer to a scale or to real quantities. Generally, we cannot compute a mean or other quantitative summary measures for the variable. The categories should be exhaustive and mutually exclusive.

2. Continuous: This level of measurement is like the interval-ratio level. The values of the variable are quantitative, definite meaningful numbers on a scale. Furthermore, we can think of them as points along a continuum that can be subdivided forever. Measuring length or distance with a ruler is a simple example of collecting data at a continuous level of measurement. It makes sense to compute a mean and other quantitative summary measures for these data.

This distinction is very important, because most of the time our choice of data analysis technique depends on whether the level of measurement of our data is categoric or continuous.

There is a bit of fuzziness in this distinction between continuous and categoric. There are several "in-between" levels of measurement that pose problems. Some variables are clearly categoric or continuous; others are not. For example, most researchers would agree that RELIGIOUS IDENTITY is a categoric variable. The categories are specific religious affiliations expressed in words such as "Buddhist, Christian,

Hindu, Jewish, Muslim, and Shinto." It is a little ridiculous to think of these identities as being measured on a scale in some type of meaningful units of measurement. We could assign code numbers to each religious identity, but the variable is not quantitative. The code numbers are just convenient substitutes for writing out the names of the religion each time. On the other hand, most researchers would agree that HEIGHT IN INCHES is a continuous variable. The units of measurement are clear, the lengths can be subdivided indefinitely, and a quantity—a number—expresses the value of the variable. However there are several types of measurement that are not clearly categoric or continuous. When we encounter these levels of measurement—or decide to use them in defining variables in our own research—we will have to make choices about what type of data analysis is appropriate. There are two main types of these "in-between" variables. Later we will see that many researchers group these "in-between" types of variables with the continuous variables, but this choice should not be made unthinkingly.

Discrete-numerical variables: These are quantitative variables whose values fall along a scale or metric, often with a true 0, but they are not really continuous. The units of measurement are whole numbers, and it makes little sense to indefinitely subdivide the units. Only a whole number makes sense for the value. For instance, generally people don't have a fraction of a sibling or a fractional number of body pierces—only whole numbers. These data are discrete, but notice that the numbers do refer to a real scale (not just code numbers), and most researchers end up treating them as if they were continuous data. It makes sense to compute a mean (and other quantitative summary measures). For example, we can talk about the "mean number of children born to women in the Yukon" and come up with a fractional amount although each woman has only a whole number of children.

Constructed-scale variables: Variables are often created by constructing a scale whose values represent different levels of responses or behaviours. The scores on an attitude scale or other kinds of constructed scales are not meaningful quantities, but more like code numbers assigned to categories of an ordinal variables. For example, respondents could be asked to respond to statements on the five-point scale (called a Likert scale) from "strongly agree" to "strongly disagree." These scales are based on choices of categories (made by the respondent or by an independent observer) and are not based on natural quantities like height or weight. It is not clear what the intervals on the scale mean, and unlike metres, kilograms, or inches, the units of measurement are not standardized. It is not clear that they refer to equal intervals on an interval scale nor that it makes sense to subdivide the scale as if it were a continuum. Yet many researchers treat the scales as if they were continuous and compute means and other quantitative summary measures for them. They also often create an "index," based on a number of scaled items grouped together. Treating a scale as continuous data is not good practice with a five point scale, and even questionable for a seven or ten point scale, but be aware that you will frequently see it done.

QUANTITATIVE ANALYSIS OF QUALITATIVE DATA?

Qualitative, categoric data can be analysed quantitatively. This statement may come as a shock, but qualitative data—data that fall into qualitative categories—have their own set of data analysis techniques. Even if we cannot compute a mean for the data, we can still count up the frequencies—how many cases fall into which categories—and this allows us to carry out a number of statistical procedures. The nice "qualitative" categoric variables seem more welcoming to the math-aversive than the nasty numerical/quantitative/continuous ones, but you'll see that the quantitative data are often easier to handle and interpret. The fact that we can compute a mean (and other quantitative summary measures) allows us to analyse data with greater precision.

Dichotomous Variables

Dichotomous Variables: Dichotomous variables have two values. (Sometimes they are called binary variables.) For example, GENDER in many cultures is usually defined with two values, "man" or "woman."

We can think of the values of dichotomous variables as **"some quality"** and **"*not* that quality."** We could represent the variable by a switch with an **on** and an **off** position. For example,

A person had measles or didn't have measles.
A person is happy or not happy.
A person is tall or not tall.

These values for a dichotomous variable can be coded 1 and 0.

> **Very Important!**
> Those fabulous dichotomous variables!

Dichotomous variables are very useful but a little bit tricky because they can be treated as if they were at three different levels of measurement:

1. They can be thought of as a nominal-categoric variable with two values (e.g., GENDER being "man" or "woman"). This is the most obvious and comfortable way of thinking about dichotomous variables. If we assign 0 to men and 1 to women, we are simply using the numbers as code numbers, not as representations of real amounts or quantities.

2. They can be thought of as an ordinal-categoric variable (GENDER could be thought of as an ordinal variable that represents two categories, one of less masculinity and one of relatively more masculinity, or vice versa, a lot of femininity and less femininity.) The categories are ordered in terms of some characteristic, such as masculinity or femininity.

3. They can be thought of as an interval-ratio variable with 2 scale points: 0 represents the absence of this quality and 1 represents its presence. Once we think of the dichotomy as two points on a scale, we can treat dichotomous variables as continuous variables and do a lot of math with them! We can actually compute a mean for them, which we cannot do for categoric variables.

THE MEAN OF A DICHOTOMOUS VARIABLE

Although we have not yet formally introduced the mean, many people have learned about means in middle school or high school, so we can go ahead and ask this question: Can we compute the mean of a dichotomous variable? For example, what do you think is the mean of GENDER for a class in which the values of the variable GENDER were coded with women = 1 and men = 0?

This seems like a mighty strange question, but here is how it's done: We do it like any other mean: Add up all the values we find for the cases in the class and divide by the number of cases. In this case, we add in a 1 for every woman and 0 for every man, and then we divide by the total number of students. The number we get is actually the proportion of the class who are women. The mean is the proportion of students who are women, the value that was coded 1. If we had decided to code "man" as 1 and "woman" as 0, when we compute the mean we would get the proportion of men in the class as our answer. You will discover that in general the mean of a dichotomy is equal to the proportion of cases for which the variable in question was coded 1.

TURNING MULTI-CATEGORY VARIABLES INTO A SERIES OF DICHOTOMOUS DUMMY VARIABLES

(Skip this section if you don't want to read it, and return to it when you are ready for regression analysis in Chapter Four.)

Neat Trick! Any categorical variable can be turned into a series of dichotomous dummy variables.

For example, let's say there are three ethnic groups at Aberdeen High: Aleutians, Alsacians, and Algerians. First we could define ETHNICITY as a three-category categorical variable, each category or value representing one of the three ethnic groups. Then we could define ethnicity by two dichotomous variables: ALEUTIAN (1 = yes, 0 = no); ALSACIAN (1 = yes, 0 = no). ALGERIAN does not have to be defined as a third dummy variable, but is rather a default condition for all who are not defined by the first two dummy variables.

Presto, a three-category nominal variable is turned into two dichotomous dummy variables, which are much easier to use in equations.

CHOICES: SELECTING THE RIGHT LEVEL OF MEASUREMENT

A variable's level of measurement is often our choice. It is not "given by Nature" but reflects a decision about what kind of data we want to examine in our research. It has to be appropriate to the research question we want to answer.

For example, in most studies, GENDER is treated as a two-category variable ("man, woman"). But if our research is specifically focused on people whose gender and/or sex category are ambiguous and people who are changing their sex category, we may want to define very different categories. We would not only have the values "men" and "women," but other sex and gender categories as well: inter-sexed people (perhaps further differentiated by whether they are inter-sexed in terms of chromosomes, hormones, and/or anatomical features), men transforming to women, and women transforming to men. We might want a further division of some of these categories in terms of where the person is in the process of change—pre-surgery or post-surgery.

Or let's take a different example for the same variable, GENDER. We could imagine a study of gender that might replace the conventional dichotomy ("man, woman") with a continuous multi-point scale for defining the variable. Focusing on psychological characteristics and self-perceptions, such a study might define GENDER by a masculinity-femininity scale, a continuous level of measurement with many points. A diversity consultant in Chicago leads classes and companies in an exercise based on a continuous scale; he draws a line on the floor, marks one end with an F for feminine and another with an M for masculine, and asks all participants to line themselves up in a single file, not according to sex category (though many of them will doubtless include that consideration in forming their line), but by their self-perception as a feminine or masculine person. The resulting jostling and discussion lead to remarkable insights about our self-images and our conceptions of gender.

So before rushing into the conventional choices of values and level of measurement for a variable, we need to think carefully about the goals of the research design and to question conventional wisdom about all our variables.

CUTTING UP CONTINUOUS VARIABLES

Continuous variables can be cut up into intervals and then into ordinal variables, but we lose information. For example, we can ask respondents in a survey an open-ended question about income that is filled in with a specific number—"What is your income?" Often, however, this question is formulated with pre-coded categories, such as $0-40,000, over $40-80,000, over $80-120,000, and more than $120,000. The data have thus been grouped into intervals. As a further step, we might give each of these categories a label ("low, low-middle, high-middle, high") and a code number (1 through 4). At this point, the data would have been converted to an ordinal level of measurement. Similarly, the variable HEIGHT in inches, a definite number for each case, could be split into three numerically defined intervals and then into ordinal categories called "short, medium, tall." At each step we are simplifying the data, but losing information.

Dichotomizing a continuous or multi-category variable is a very powerful operation, creating a sharp contrast and focusing our analysis on a key distinction. For example, our income data could be re-categorized into "rich" and "poor." But a lot of detailed information is lost when we turn an interval-ratio variable or multi-category variable into a dichotomous one.

In preparing our data for data analysis, we can reorganize or "recode" variables into a different level of measurement. It is always best to recode a continuous variable into intervals or categories in such a way that the original variable with specific quantitative information remains saved and available in the data file. If a categoric variable is recoded into a smaller number of categories or dichotomized, the original variable should be saved as well.

Notice that once the data are collected we can go from continuous data to grouped or interval data and from multiple categories to fewer categories, but we cannot do the reverse! If we ask survey respondents to check off "old" or "young" for their age, we cannot retrieve their age in years, as a specific number, from this questionnaire. But we can recode their specific numerical age as "old" or "young" if we want to do so later.

Again, the important thing to keep in mind is that the level of measurement of variables is, to a great extent, our choice in the initial research design. It has to be appropriate to our research question.

Operationalized Variables

Variables are often first thought of in an abstract, conceptual way. We want to know if Vancouver is a more fun city than Toronto—what do we mean by "fun"? We want to know if Minnesota is a wealthier state than Mississippi—what do we mean by "wealthy"? We want to know if Sweden or Bosnia has a higher quality of life—what do we mean by "quality of life"?

In order to answer these types of questions, we have to go from a conceptual variable (fun, wealth, quality of life) to a measurable variable, one that we can observe very precisely.

These measurable variables are often called **operationalized variables.** (In some fields, such as sociology and political science, they are also called "empirical indicator variables," but the term "indicator variable" has a different meaning in math and economics.) Operationalized variables make an abstract concept measurable. An **operational definition** of a variable specifies a procedure ("operation") of observation and measurement.

Operationalized variables must have two properties:

1. Validity: They have to measure a characteristic that is perfectly related to the conceptual variable. If our conceptual variable is INTELLIGENCE, it doesn't make any sense to use SHOE SIZE as the operationalized variable. It's true that shoe size is a lot less abstract and easier to measure than intelligence, but very few people would agree that shoe size is closely related to intelligence or has the same meaning as intelligence. Of course, most problems with the validity of operationalized variables are not quite as obvious as this silly example; the problems usually arise when the operationalized variable is indeed related to or associated with the conceptual variable, but is not quite close enough in meaning or when there are too many instances where the association breaks down. For example, we might want to measure the wealth of a country by the number of luxury cars, but a closer look might show that countries with a high proportion of people living in poverty can have a very wealthy elite that drives a large number of fancy vehicles. So the proposed operationalized variable turned out not to be close enough to the underlying concept. Problems of operationalized variables' validity are the downfall of many research studies! A critical reading of quantitative research and public policy research should always begin with a close scrutiny of how variables were operationalized.

2. Reliability: The operationalized variable has to be a consistent measure. It has to produce the same results in repeated uses and be consistent regardless of who is doing the measuring. For example, we might decide to measure "intelligence" by "alert, coherent answers in an interview situation" but this is not a very consistent measuring procedure and might also produce different results for different interviewers. Reliability is related to the concept of "objectivity"—that a characteristic exists independently of the point of view, experiences, bias, social position, or personal relationships of the person doing the measuring.

Independent (IV) and Dependent (DV) Variables

Most research focuses on more than one variable at a time. Research is often designed to find relationships among variables and especially causal relationships.

When a study includes two or more variables, the independent variables are seen as possible candidates for causing changes in the dependent variables. "Independent" means "autonomous" or not relying on something else. "Dependent" means relying on something else, influenced or formed by something else, and not autonomous. Thus the independent variables are seen as possibly influencing or affecting the dependent variables.

Sometimes it's pretty obvious which variable is independent and which is dependent. We can ask, "Does a person's gender influence choice of major in college?" However, only in very unusual cases would it make sense to ask, "Does a person's choice of major influence gender?" Clearly, GENDER is the independent variable (IV) here and choice of MAJOR the dependent variable (DV). We could ask whether region in the US is related to incidence of the death penalty, with REGION being the IV and number of prisoners on DEATH ROW (proportionately to population) being the DV. It wouldn't make much sense to pose the question the other way around.

In other cases, the IV and the DV seem arbitrary—either variable could be the IV or the DV. For example, we might ask whether a province's high school dropout rate is related to its poverty rate. A high poverty rate might cause many young people to leave school early, or conversely, if a lot of people fail to complete high school, the province might end up with a less skilled workforce, more unemployment and low-wage employment, and hence more poverty. In this example, either DROPOUT RATE or POVERTY RATE could be the IV or the DV.

Causality

The choice of IV and DV is closely related to the question of causality. This is a profound philosophical issue: What do we mean when we say something causes something else?

Only the IV is considered a candidate for the causal variable. But just because two variables are related does not mean that one causes the other. An IV can be considered a **cause** of changes in the DV only if three conditions are fulfilled:

1. **Association:** The two variables are correlated or associated; there is a pattern of relationship in their distributions.

2. **Time order:** Change in the IV precedes change in the DV; there is a time order in their relationship such that the causal variable comes first in time. (If a person had cancer before she started smoking, we can hardly conclude that smoking caused the cancer.)

3. **A non-spurious relationship:** The relationship is non-spurious; we can show that there is no third variable that produced changes in the other two variables. The number of fire-fighters at a fire is related to the amount of property damage caused by the fire—but the fire-fighters don't cause the property damage. The two variables here, number of fire-fighters present and amount of property damage, appear to be related only because both are results of a third variable—the size of the fire. Similarly, the presence of storks in a district and a high birth rate appear to be related, but the relationship is spurious because the presence of both storks and babies is a product of the rural character of the district. The third variable—"ruralness"—eliminates the apparent relationship between storks and babies.

Even if all three conditions are fulfilled, we probably want to show exactly how changes in the IV bring about the changes in the DV before we are prepared to use the word "cause."

In Chapter Four, we will consider examples of multivariate relationships that are more complex than the spurious relationship. We may find intervening variables, variables that "operate between" an IV and a DV and help explain the relationship. For example, the relationship between region in the United States and incidence of the death penalty is not a simple direct product of regional location but might be explained by complex intervening variables such as the history of race relations, religious traditions, and attitudes towards violence. Another complicated multivariate relationship is the "interaction effect" in which two variables are related differently depending on the condition of a third variable. In a famous historical example, the classical sociologist Emile Durkheim found that in Europe at the end of the nineteenth century in countries with strict divorce laws, married people had lower suicide rates than single people; but in countries with liberal divorce laws, marital status made little difference in suicide rates. STRICTNESS OF DIVORCE LAWS was a third variable that conditioned the relationship between MARITAL STATUS as the IV and SUICIDE RATE as the DV.

Units of Analysis: Individual and Place-level Data

Variables can be defined on individual cases or on places where the individual cases are located (sites, locations, territorial units). This distinction in the way data are collected leads to major differences in the analysis and interpretation of data.

Individual cases and places: The units of analysis, the cases, can be individual cases (people, hamburgers, bees) or places where the individual cases are grouped together (cities, states, nations, and college campuses for people; restaurants or meatpacking plants for hamburgers; hives for bees).

1. Categorical variables become interval-ratio or scale variables that can be treated as continuous and express proportions or rates. For example, look at what happens to gender. If individual people are our cases, the variable is conventionally categoric with values "man" and "woman." But when we switch to place—let's say, colleges—the variable becomes "percent female" (or "percent male"), a variable that can be treated as a continuous variable.

> **Warning!**
> When we switch from individual cases to places, weird things can happen!

2. The independent/dependent variable relationship can be reversed. For example, at the individual level, gender can influence choice of college major, but choice of college major does not influence gender, except in very rare cases. But when we switch to a place as the unit of analysis, the relationship could work either way. Colleges with a high female enrolment might offer different majors than colleges with a high male enrolment, but also vice versa, colleges with different types of majors might attract different percentages of men and women.

3. The ecological fallacy rears its ugly head. Just because two variables are related at the place level does not mean that they both characterize the same individuals. The ecological fallacy is the mistaken assertion that two place-related variables refer to the same individuals. For example, states with many newcomers have a high suicide rate, but it is not necessarily the newcomers that are more likely to commit suicide. In the 2000 presidential elections in the United States, counties that had a high percentage of Bush votes also had a high Buchanan vote, but it was not because

Bush voters were voting for Buchanan (it couldn't have been the same people!). The Bush and Buchanan votes were correlated because counties with a high percentage of conservative voters had high vote percentages for both candidates, not because the same individuals cast votes for both candidates.

Place-level correlations are generally "looser" than individual-level correlations. When we find a place-level correlation we have to be extremely cautious not to jump to a causal conclusion.

And time series correlations are the "loosest" or "weakest" of all! A lot of variables appear to be related when we plot a time series. Changes in two variables happen at the same time or the same pace. For example, you might find a great correlation between your age and the rising prices of martinis in Calgary, Alberta when you plot the time series. But we can safely conclude that your rising age did not cause the rise in martini prices. Or vice versa! This is why we must be extremely cautious about concluding that a rise or fall in something (crime rates, divorce rates, test scores, inflation, etc.) is closely related to a rise or fall in something else. These conclusions are often fallacious!

Part II: Thinking about Procedures

In this part of the chapter we introduce a number of terms that help us to think about the underlying purpose of procedures in applied statistics.

Descriptive and Inferential Statistics

Underlying the distinction between descriptive and inferential statistics is the difference between a population and a sample. Inferential statistics refers to the reasoning involved in drawing conclusions about a population from a sample.

A **population** is all the cases, all the units of analysis, in which we are interested. A population is the entire set.

A **sample** is a subset that we draw from the population in order to reach a conclusion because it is not feasible to look at the whole population.

Sampling is something we do constantly in everyday life, because it is not feasible to test the entire population. When we cook a batch of chilli for our guests, we don't eat the whole potful to test if it's correctly flavoured; we take out a spoonful to sample the mix. When we meet an attractive person, we usually don't get married on the spot to find out if our whole life together will be happy; we sample these moments by dating, courtship, or engagement, for example.

Notice that a set of cases can be considered a population for some purposes and a sample for other purposes. The people enrolled in a statistics class can be considered as a population, or it could be considered a sample of some population—of young people in the United States and Canada, students at our university, college students in North America, or human beings. It is unlikely that it is a good— representative—sample of all these populations.

Recently there has been a lot of controversy over the use of sampling in the United States Census since it is supposed to be based on a count of the whole population. A good sample study may, however, be more accurate than a bad population census. The US census tends to undercount racial/ethnic minorities, the urban poor, and undocumented residents of the United States. Careful, well-designed sample studies would probably provide a better estimate of their numbers than the census as it is currently carried out.

This brings us to the difference between descriptive and inferential statistics. Descriptive statistics are numbers and procedures used to represent the distribution of one or more variables for a set of cases. We will soon see that they include frequency and percentage tables, measures of central tendency, measures of dispersion or variability, and various visual or graphic displays. We can describe the relationships of two or more variables for a set of cases. Sometimes we are simply interested in describing the numerical characteristics of the set of cases. But much of the time in research, we are looking at a sample, a set of cases from which we are trying to infer the characteristics of a population.

When we think of an entire population, we refer to the numerical values that sum up its characteristics as population parameters and represent them by Greek letters. When these numerical values refer to data from a sample they are called sample statistics and are represented in an algebraic expression by a Latin letter.

Inferential statistics are procedures used to generalize from a sample to a population when it is not feasible to study the whole population. We use the sample statistics to infer or estimate the population parameters. For example, if we want to see how North Americans respond to questions on social issues, it is too expensive and time consuming to ask everybody. If we want to test a new medication we cannot possibly test it on all people with the disease, and a new vaccine cannot be tested on everyone who might at some time be exposed to a disease. Thus we have opinion polls and clinical trials.

In statistical inference we use the sample data—the sample statistics—from the opinion poll or clinical trial to reach a conclusions about the population, that is, to make accurate estimates of the population parameters.

For example, if 58% of the sample supports a candidate in the poll, can the candidate conclude that she will win a majority of votes in the election? If a vaccine reduces the rate of infection in clinical trials, can we conclude that it will be generally effective?

The basic problem in generalizing from a sample is worrying about having drawn a sample that will produce an extremely misleading conclusion about the population. For example, the vaccine may be effective in the sample but turn out to be worthless for the population. The sample results for the political poll could turn out to be completely different from the actual election results.

There are two reasons why the sample observations might be misleading, **biased sampling** and **sampling error**, which are completely different problems although they sound alike.

Biased sampling is bad sampling that was not done correctly but in such a way that the resulting sample differed from the population in systematic ways that led to bad estimates. For example, if the opinion poll had been carried out by the candidate asking only her friends whom they would vote for, it is likely that the results would not be very good.

To avoid biased sampling, we ideally draw a **simple random sample.** This sample is taken based on a procedure in which random chance determines which cases are included and which are not. Each case in the underlying population has an equal probability of being selected for the sample and each case is selected independently of the others. These conditions mean that not only are all cases equally likely to be in the sample, but all sets of N cases (where N is the given sample size) are equally likely. Every sample of a given size has the same probability of selection. (There are other kinds of probability samples, which we will discuss briefly in Chapter Three; however, the simple random sample is the simplest and most important type for understanding statistical inference.)

Sampling error, random error in a correct sampling process, is a very different type of problem. Even if we drew a simple random sample (SRS), there is still a chance that the sample data—the sample statistics—might be misleading as we try to infer the population parameters. This reason is inherent in the sampling process. We might draw a sample with a perfectly designed sampling procedure, but, by the (bad) luck of the draw, end up with a sample that has an outcome that is extremely different from the true situation in the population. This error has to do with probability, luck, chance, randomness, and math, and is precisely what we will be concerned about in our discussion of statistical inference.

Here is what we are worried about: Did we draw a random sample that just happened to have an "odd" outcome compared to the population, even though our sampling procedure was perfectly correct and unbiased? Pretend we are trying to estimate the proportion of smokers among women students at a university by drawing a sample of 200 women rather than by asking all the women. Let's say only 100 women at DePaul University smoke among the 10,000 women enrolled, but randomly, by the luck of the draw, we happened to get all 100 of them in our sample of 200 women, leading to a completely mistaken estimate of the percent of women who smoke at this university. Using the sample data, we would infer the population parameter for the proportion of smokers to be 50%, when it is really closer to 1%. Is this sample proportion likely? No, but it is **possible** in random sampling. Or in a clinical trial, our random sample included by chance a lot of people with a natural immunity to Ebola fever, leading to a mistaken claim about the value of our new vaccine. Notice that this could happen by bad luck even when our random sampling procedure is fine—unbiased. We would have no way of knowing that we were coming to the wrong conclusion from our data This unpleasant possibility is exactly what inferential statistics is all about.

Here is another simple example to get us thinking about statistical inference. Let's say there are large and equal numbers of red and blue tickets in a jar, whose contents we can't see. We draw a random sample of 10 tickets from the jar, and they all happen to be red. This is certainly possible, although not terribly likely. It would lead to a very mistaken estimate about the distribution of tickets in the jar (the population). We will look more carefully at inferential statistics in Chapter Three. In the meantime, these examples should present a challenge to think about.

Difference

Underlying many discussions in applied statistics is a profound idea about the world—the concept of difference. When can we say that one thing (or condition or situation) is **different** from another one?

Often in research we are interested in differences. We want to know if a medication or surgical procedure really raises patients' survival rates. Does the intervention make a *difference* in the survival rate? Or are the survival rates the same, whether or not the intervention takes place? We want to know if a new reading curriculum makes a *difference* in children's reading ability. We might be concerned whether standardized test scores this year are *different* from those of last year. Is there improvement, decline, or no *difference*?

In more abstract terms, we often want to know if there is an independent variable that can serve as a predictor of a dependent variable because differences in the dependent variable are associated with differences in the independent variable. For example, is the SAT score a good predictor of students' academic performance in college? In other words, are differences in SAT scores associated with differences in variables used to measure academic performance, such as GPA or college graduation? If differences among students in their SAT scores cannot predict differences in their GPAs or their college graduation, SAT scores may not be valuable information in college admissions.

The basic problem is the question of how much difference must there be in order for us to decide that the difference is meaningful or significant? The real world is full of small differences that we believe we can ignore or that we ascribe to randomness. For example, my cholesterol level is not identical day after day and year after year. At what point should my doctor and I decide that an observed difference is a cause for concern? When children in a school take a standardized test year after year, it would actually be surprising if the average score was identical every time. We expect it to fluctuate a little bit, varying with small, apparently random factors. We are concerned about a decline or delighted by an improvement only if the average score has changed dramatically. If survival rates are only a fraction of a percentage point better after surgical intervention in an experimental group of patients than they are among a control group with no intervention, are we justified in concluding that this intervention works? Can we generalize this very small improvement to the whole population of people with this condition? What do we mean by "dramatic," "major," "meaningful," and "significant" differences?

Doctors ask patients to obtain a "baseline" reading for measures such as cholesterol levels, blood sugar, bone density, and so on. As the patient ages, doctors compare current levels to the baseline reading, looking for differences that might signal the onset of a problem such as diabetes. Small changes would not be considered significant; for example, cholesterol rising from 205 to 206 over the course of a year would not be considered very different and would not be a cause for concern, while a jump to 280 might be. Some "differences" might fall into an "indeterminate" range where further tests will be arranged.

These examples alert us to the difficult question of identifying difference that exists over and above small fluctuations. Small fluctuations can be thought of as "measuring error"—slight variability in making measurements of a quantity that is in fact quite stable. They could also be thought of as reflections of small, unknown factors. For instance my blood sugar level might be up a bit because I ate a chocolate mint the day before. These factors are not really random, but often they are unknown and therefore have the appearance of randomness. Finally, small differences may be reflections of "sampling error"—of just happening to have drawn a sample that is a little different from the overall population. The patients on whom we tested our new surgical procedure are not identical to all the people now and forever more who may have this condition. Sampling error is not a mistake in sampling; it is the variability that is inherent in sampling, a true randomness that produces small differences in sample outcomes.

Scientific research in general and statistical inference in particular are, in large part, efforts to distinguish small differences that don't mean much and arise from measurement error, sampling error, small unknown factors, and random fluctuation from those differences that are significant.

In a few cases, the presence of a significant difference manifests itself "in nature"—as a "phase transition." Splashing through puddles at 19 degrees Celsius is not much different from splashing through them at 20 degrees Celsius, but, as we approach 0 degrees Celsius, the puddles turn to ice. A few degrees difference makes a big difference. Unfortunately, the degree of difference found in most research situations is ambiguous, less "objective" than a puddle freezing over and more a matter of applying our own decision rule about what we mean by "difference." As statistics was developed as a field of applied mathematics in the first part of the twentieth century, these decision rules or tests of significance were invented.

Three clues to thinking about this problem can be noted here and will be taken up later.

First, the bigger the difference is (relative to the scale we are using to measure it), the more likely we are to think it is significant. A drop of 20 degrees Celsius is more impressive than a drop of 2 degrees. We are more likely to notice it and wish we had brought a warmer jacket. In the scale of human weights, a gain of 50 pounds is more significant than a gain of 5 pounds, and considerably more noticeable!

Second, the larger the sample for which we observed the difference, the more likely we are to think it is significant. If a new medication improves the health of 10,000 people we would be more confident that it is efficacious than if we tried it out on only two people with good results.

Third, the more variable the situation is in the first place, the harder it is to decide if a difference is significant. If my blood sugar level had been very stable and then suddenly took a jump, I would probably be more concerned than if it was always "all over the map." If my weight fluctuates a lot, a gain or loss of 5 pounds is less noteworthy than if it has been absolutely stable all my adult life.

Chapter Three will focus on how we decide that a difference or discrepancy is **significant** rather than the result of fluctuations that can be considered random.

Observing and Estimating

In the preface, I encouraged you to estimate answers always before doing calculations or working a problem so that the precise answer you calculate can be checked against your overall understanding of the situation and the procedure. In other words, make an educated "ball-park" guess. This educated guess is what we mean in everyday speech by the word "estimate" as in, "The estimated driving time from Chicago to Toronto is ten hours."

There is a related but more technical meaning to the term "estimate." An estimate is a guess or prediction derived from a mathematical model. It may or may not be close to an observation, a piece of data derived from empirical exploration of the real world. When we collect data, the observations are the actual values (numbers or categories) that we have found in our research. We are interested in how well we can describe their distribution with a mathematical or conceptual model—whether we can create a model that allows us to estimate the values of the observations accurately. If we can, then our model may be generalizable to other real situations. We may be able to predict the phenomena in question—poverty rates might be a predictor of incarceration rates in countries or states, vaccines may lower the rate of illness, and so on—and sometimes this means we can alter and improve the situation.

So at various points in the discussion, I will refer to **observations:** these are usually real data, real values for variables as they are collected and recorded by empirical methods for all the cases in a distribution. Examples would be test scores, heights, or each person's gender, wealth, or religious identity as this information is collected from real people. For cities or countries we might collect more "constructed" variables like homicide rates or literacy rates. At other times, I will use the term **estimates,** and this refers to the values that we predict from a conceptual or mathematical model, a model that we have created—often on the basis of generalizations from data observed in the past. For example, I might guess, after looking around, that most people in my stats class are two meters tall, but when we measure our actual heights, we would find that the observations are not very close to my guess. I might instead, on the basis of past data from university classes, estimate that the mean height of the class is about 66 inches or 167 centimetres, and this estimate would probably closely match the observed data in the current class.

Conclusion

In this chapter, we introduced concepts that allow us to apply statistics to research and real world issues. **Variable** is a key concept; we explored a number of terms that pertain to constructing, classifying, and thinking about variables. At the end of the chapter, we encountered three very broad ideas that probe the "nature of things"—sampling, randomness, and statistical inference; the concept of significant differences and discrepancies; and the idea of observing, estimating, and testing models.

Key Terms

variable

values

cases

level of measurement

nominal

ordinal

interval-ratio

categoric

continuous

dichotomous

discrete-ordered, discrete-
  numerical

dummy variables

operationalized variables

validity

reliability

independent variable

dependent variable

causality

units of analysis

  individual-level data

  place-level data

statistical inference

samples

random samples

difference/discrepancy
  (significant?)

estimates and observations;
  models

Chapter Two:
Describing Distributions

In this chapter, we will be concerned with understanding, summarizing, and displaying the distribution of one variable at a time for a complete set of cases. These procedures are usually called univariate descriptive statistics. In this chapter, we will not be concerned with inference from samples to populations.

There are many ways of describing a distribution. Often the researcher faces a choice: Keep all or most of the original information, at the cost of simplicity, or simplify the data, making it easier to reach conclusions, at the cost of losing some of the information.

Part I: Frequency Distributions

Usually we begin with a **frequency distribution**, a table that displays the data and shows how many cases there are for each value of the variable.

The frequency distribution of a categoric variable: If the variable is categoric—nominal or ordinal—creating a frequency distribution table is fairly simple.

- We list the values of the variable—all the possible categories—in the leftmost column of the table, and then we show the frequencies for each value in the next column, moving rightwards. The frequency for a value is the number of cases that fall into the category and is also called a "count."

- In the next column of the table, still moving to the right, we can display the relative frequencies, the proportion (always expressed as a percent) of the total number of cases that falls into each category.

Here are two simple examples:

Table 1: Variable—Eye colour for a class of 40 people; $N = 40$

Categories/values	Frequency	Relative Frequency (%)
Brown	20	50%
Blue	10	25%
Green	5	12.5%
Hazel	5	12.5%
Total	40	100%

Table 2: Variable—Height (ordinal level of measurement) for 40 people; $N = 40$

Categories/Values	Frequency	Relative Frequency (%)
Short	10	25%
Medium	20	50%
Tall	10	25%
Total	40	100%

Discrete-numerical (quantitative) with a small number of possible values: If the variable is discrete but numerical/quantitative with a limited number of possible values, usually whole numbers, the frequency table can also be simple. However, it can look tricky because it is easy to confuse the frequencies (the numbers of cases) with the numerical values (numbers that "belong to" the cases). The frequencies and the values are numbers that can be in the same range, but they refer to completely different things! Look carefully at the next example, the distribution of siblings in a psychology class with twenty students.

Warning!
Make sure you understand the difference between discrete/quantitative values of a variable and **frequencies** in the frequency distribution of the variable. (Think of examples for yourself—number of cars owned, number of body pierces, etc. for data sets of different sizes.)

Table 3: Variable—Number of Siblings; $N = 20$

Value: How many siblings?	Frequency: Number of cases	Percent
0	4	20%
1	8	40%
2	4	20%
3	2	10%
4	2	10%
Total	20	100%

Interval-ratio continuous data: This type of data is the most messy and difficult for a frequency display. We could show the number of cases (frequency) for every possible value in the data. However, if the range of values is large and the subdivisions fine (like income in dollars for families in the US or heights to the nearest $\frac{1}{10}$ of a centimetre for Manitoba residents), the table will get very long. To avoid a monster table and make the data easier to read, even at the cost of losing information, we typically group continuous data into intervals, as in this example.

Table 4: Continuous Data in Intervals

Age Interval	Frequency	Percent
0-20	200	20%
20+-40	200	20%
40+-60	300	30%
60+-80	200	20%
80+-100	100	10%
Total	*1000*	*100%*

In setting up the intervals, we have to decide whether to put the endpoints (like 20 years in the example) in the interval "above" or "below." Here we are putting the endpoints in the interval "below" and the little + shows that the next interval begins above the indicated value. Usually we use no fewer than 5 and no more than 10 intervals for displaying this type of data.

Part II: Summary Measures

Warning!

Most of this section of the chapter applies only to quantitative data, whether it is genuinely continuous, or numerical-discrete, or constructed scale data that we are treating as continuous interval-ratio data. In any case, the data have to be at the interval-ratio level of measurement for many of these summary measures. Several of these summary measures cannot be used for nominal and ordinal categoric data. Dichotomous variables can "swing either way" as noted previously, when we mentioned that the mean of a dichotomy is the proportion of cases coded 1.

Instead of looking at a frequency table, we can sum up a distribution with two very powerful types of measures: **measures of central tendency** and **measures of dispersion** (variability).

Central tendency tells us something about the average of the distribution, the middle of the distribution, about its point of similarity, about what the data "have in common," about what is typical of the data, and/or about what we can expect from the data.

Dispersion tells us about differences in the data, about variability and variation, about diversity, about spread, about inequalities, and/or about possible surprises.

These two types of measures should always be reported together. Unfortunately, most people learn a little about averages in school, but nothing about dispersion, so that very few media report a measure of dispersion along with the average. This lopsided reporting can be very misleading, and one effect of it is to mask inequalities.

Measures of Central Tendency (Mean, Median, Mode)

Most people refer to these as "averages." The most common are the mean, median, and mode. They are very different from each other; they are found in different ways and convey different information about the distribution. For this reason, their use can be manipulated to put a "spin" on the interpretation of the distribution.

THE MEAN

The mean is the arithmetic average of the distribution. Every value, for every case, has to be included in a sum; then divide by the number of cases.

Formula:

$$\overline{X} = \frac{\Sigma X}{N}$$

The Greek letter Sigma (Σ) in the formula means "sum all the observed values of the variable." N is the total frequency, the total number of cases, and $\overline{X}$ is the symbol for the mean of the X distribution.

Every case's value must be included in the sum. Another way of saying this is that each value of the variable has to be weighted by its frequency when we compute the sum.

> Algorithm for the mean— a step-by-step procedure:
>
> **1. Sum:** Add up all the values, one value for every case in the distribution, making a grand pool of all the goodies.
>
> **2. Division:** Divide this grand sum by the number of cases in the distribution (the total frequency) to find out how much of the pool would go to each case if the pool were divided equally.

- Not a single case's value can be left out of the calculation of the sum in the top, or numerator, of the fraction.

- Not a single case can be left out of the bottom or denominator of the fraction. We have to divide by the number of cases, not the number of categories.

One way of thinking about the mean is that the mean expresses how much of the total amount of the variable each case would get if the total quantity were divided equally.

You can think of the mean as a little imp who would like to divide everything up equally—height, income, number of cars owned, weight—so that each case has exactly the same amount as every other case. The mean is a number in the mind of the imp and not in the real world. It is a construction or abstraction, not an empirical reality (see Cuzzort and Vrettos, 1996, p. 93).

Computing the mean can get a little confusing if the data are numerical-discrete and a small number of values appear over and over again. Often this will be the case when the data are presented in a frequency distribution.

Table 5: Variable—Truck ownership among Greasy Bob's customers

Values of the variable: Number of trucks owned	Number of cases ($N = 30$): Frequency
0	2
1	10
2	10
3	3
4	5

What is the mean of this distribution? The mean is the answer to this question: what is the average number of trucks owned by Bob's customers? And it is the answer to this question: if the customers decided to share their trucks equally, how many would each person get?

A good first step is to estimate the mean before we calculate it. Just by eyeballing the distribution, we can see that 20 out of 30 people own either one or two trucks, so the answer might well be in this range. But the answer might be a little more towards the high end because there are 8 folks who own 3 or 4 trucks, which will "pull up" the average. We also see that no one owns more than 4 trucks, so the mean could not possibly be higher than 4.

(Say, could the mean ever be a negative number? Yeah, you bet; think about averaging people's debts, represented by negative numbers. The mean would be negative.)

We begin by finding out how many trucks are in the big pool of all the trucks owned by every customer of Bob's. This big pool is the numerator of the division that represents the mean.

Let's do our sum: Remember a value has to be included for every case (the cases are the customers at Bob's). This sum is going to be the grand total of trucks owned by all these folks.

Two people own 0 trucks: $2 \times 0 = 0$ trucks.
Ten people own 1 truck each: $10 \times 1 = 10$ trucks.
Ten people own 2 trucks each: $10 \times 2 = 20$ trucks.
Three people own 3 trucks each: $3 \times 3 = 9$ trucks.
Five people own 4 trucks each: $5 \times 4 = 20$ trucks.

Now we are ready for the sum, the total number of trucks owned for all the customers (cases), the grand pool of available trucks.

$0 + 10 + 20 + 9 + 20 = 59$

This is the number of trucks that would go into the pool if trucks were shared out equally.

How many trucks would each individual get? $\dfrac{59}{30} = 1.9666$

Notice in our computation we had to include every person and every truck. Nobody (no case) and nothing (no value) gets left out in computing the mean.

The mean is represented by *mu* or Greek letter μ for a population and by $\overline{X}$ for a sample.

It is always preferable to compute a mean from raw data, where the values (or scores) for each case are available. If the raw data are not available, and neither are grouped data as in the truck example, the mean can be computed from data arranged into intervals. The midpoint of each interval is taken as the value and multiplied by the frequency (count or number of cases) in that interval; the products for each interval are summed for all the intervals, and then the sum is divided by the number of cases. If some of the intervals are open ended, like "age 60 and over" the mean cannot be computed very accurately.

THE MEDIAN

The median is very different than the mean and is found in a completely different way. The median is the value that belongs to the middle case in the distribution after all the cases are lined up in ascending (or descending) order of their values. The cases must be lined up in order before we can find the median!

We've got to think about the median differently from how we think of the mean. (Remember that the mean was an imp who wanted to make a big pool by summing all the values for all the cases and then dividing that total sum out in equal amounts to each case?)

Here's how to think about the median. You are sitting on a reviewing stand watching a parade. Everybody—all the cases—have

---

Algorithm for the median:
a step-by-step procedure:

1. Line up the cases in order of their values from lowest to highest or highest to lowest, making sure that you include the values for all cases even when two or more values are the same.

2. Find the middle case for an odd number of cases, or the middle two if there is an even number of cases.

3. Look at the value of the middle case or, if there are two middle cases, find the arithmetic mean of their two values. This value is the median. It is the value that corresponds to the 50th percentile of the frequency distribution.

been lined up in order of their value (or score) on the variable in question. They each have a placard around their neck showing their value. For example, the shortest person goes first, wearing a placard that says "5 feet," and the tallest goes last, wearing a placard that says "six feet six inches."

The whole parade marches by you in either ascending order or descending order. You don't bother to look at the values on the placards. Instead, you are keeping count of how many cases are filing by. When you get to the middle case of the total number of cases, you shout "stop!" and then you read the number on that case's placard. That number is the median. If the total number of cases is even, you find the two middle cases and compute the mean of the numbers on their placards. The median is a value of the variable, not a frequency or percentile. As the following "parade" of values shows, the median number of trucks owned by Greasy Bob's customers would be 2 because the mean of the two middle numbers is 2 or $(2 + 2) \div 2$.

$$0\ 0\ 1\ 1\ 1\ 1\ 1\ 1\ 1\ 1\ 1\ 1\ 2\ 2\ \boxed{2\ 2}\ 2\ 2\ 2\ 2\ 2\ 2\ 3\ 3\ 3\ 4\ 4\ 4\ 4\ 4$$

The median can be obtained for ordinal-level data. We line up the observations in blocks corresponding to the ordinal categories and determine into which of these categories the middle observation falls.

THE MODE

The mode is a measure of central tendency that works for categoric data, and is the only measure of central tendency that can be used for nominal-level data. The mode is the value (number or category) with the highest frequency, the most number of cases associated with it. For example, in our eye-colour example, "Brown" was the mode. In our truck example there were two modes, 1 and 2 (both had a modal frequency of 10 people).

The modal frequency is the number of cases for the mode. **Do not confuse the mode and the modal frequency.** The modal frequency must be a number; it is the number of cases associated with the mode. The mode is a category for categoric data and a number in the list of possible values for interval-ratio data.

WHEN TO USE WHICH?

These measures of central tendency can be quite different for the same distribution:

Here are some rules regarding which measure to use when:

1. A mean can only be found for interval-ratio data. The mode is the only measure of central tendency that works with nominal-categoric data. A median can be found for ordinal level data, although typically it is used mainly for interval-ratio data.

2. If the data are quite skewed—if the frequency distribution has a long "tail" in one direction—it is better to use the median. The mean gets "pulled" in the direction of the tail because we have to include every value in the computation. The practical consequence of this mathematical fact is that for income and wealth distributions, which tend to be skewed, the median is often a better measure of central tendency. A small number of rich people "pull up" the mean, making it higher than the median and a somewhat misleading representation of the distribution. Note that "skew" is a long tail in one direction; if the distribution has two long symmetrical tails, it is not skewed, and it is OK to use the mean.

MONKEY BUSINESS WITH MEASURES OF CENTRAL TENDENCY

The following example shows how means, medians, and modes tell different stories about distributions and can be used to manipulate our impression of them. (The example is based on a true story; Béla Kun was a real person and he did order the seizure and redistribution of shoes in Hungary in 1919.)

Count Esterhazy owns a vast estate worked by 999 peasants who live in miserable serf-like conditions. The Count has 1000 shoes, riding boots, slippers, and other pairs of footwear, but all his peasants go barefoot.

Consider the distribution of the variable PAIRS OF FOOTWEAR OWNED ON THE ESTERHAZY ESTATE.

1. Make a frequency table for the values. Hint: In this distribution there are only two values, and they have completely different frequencies.

2. Find the mean, median, mode, and modal frequency.

3. Which of these measures would the Count be most likely to use to convince us that his peasants live decently? Why?

4. Which do you think is the best representation of the distribution?

It's 1919; winds of war and revolution sweep Central Europe. Inspired by the Bolshevik Revolution in Russia, Comrade Béla Kun comes to power and sets out to transform society. He has all shoes confiscated and redistributed to peasants and workers. Count Esterhazy's peasants seize the Count's shoes, leaving him only one pair, and redistribute the others equally among themselves.

5. Now what is the Mean? Median? Mode? Modal frequency?

6. Can you think of examples in which the mean, median, and mode are different and can be used to put different "spins" on the interpretation of a distribution?

Measures of Dispersion

Measures of dispersion tell us about variability, variation, difference, spread, inequality, and possible surprises in a distribution.

Measures of dispersion should always be reported together with measures of central tendency.

Measures of dispersion are essential for analysing the relationship among variables because we define "being related" (correlated or associated) as a situation in which we can predict variation in one variable from variation in the other variable.

RANGE

This is a simple measure of dispersion, found by subtracting the smallest value in the distribution from the largest.

VARIANCE AND STANDARD DEVIATION (SD)

We will now focus on the **variance** and the **standard deviation** (SD). These are closely related measures of dispersion that refer to deviation from the mean of a distribution. We will trace the steps in finding the SD, computing the variance as a step in this process.

Algorithm for the variance and standard deviation:

1. Calculate the mean of the distribution. (We can't find deviation from the mean unless we know what the mean is.)

2. Subtract the mean from every score in the distribution. Some differences will be positive (if the score is above the mean) and some will be negative (if the score is below the mean). (If we added them all up right now we would always get 0, which wouldn't be so useful.) There should be N differences at this step, one for each case. These are called the "deviations from the mean."

3. Square each of the differences you found in step 2. This gets rid of the negatives. We now have the squared deviations. There should be N squares at this step. These are called "squared deviations from the mean."

4. Add up all the squares. This sum is a big pool of all the squared distances from the mean. There is only one sum at this step. We'll call this sum an SS, sum of squares, or more precisely, "the sum of the squared deviations."

5. Divide by N, the number of cases. This division gives us a single number, which is the average (mean) of the squared deviations. This number is called the variance of the distribution. We divide by $N - 1$ for a sample because, once we know what the mean and sample size are, only $N - 1$ of these observations can vary freely. The Nth deviation has to "fit" the given data and be a certain amount, so that all the deviations from the mean add up to 0. So for sample data, we have only $N - 1$ "degrees of freedom." Computer software assumes that the data are always sample data and always divides by $N - 1$, rather than N. Notice that dividing by $N - 1$ gives a slightly higher estimate of variability.

6. Find the positive square root of the variance. This number is the standard deviation.

Notice that whatever units the original measurements are in, the SD is in the same units—pounds, feet, inches, kilometres, dollars, and so on.

The standard deviation refers to deviation from the mean of a distribution. The SD is the most common and powerful measure of dispersion. Like a mean, it can only be computed for interval-ratio data (not categoric data) and should always be reported together with a mean. For a population parameter, it is represented by a Greek letter, a lower-case sigma, σ. The letter s is used to represent it as a sample statistic, the standard deviation for sample data.

The SD can be thought of as "sort of" the average distance or difference of values/scores from the mean of the distribution. We say "sort of"' because it isn't really computed as the arithmetic mean. The computation is a little tricky and lengthy, but it makes good sense if you follow it step-by-step.

Formula:

$$S = \sqrt{\frac{\Sigma\,(X - \overline{X})^2}{N}}$$

In the formula, we have to follow the order of operations. First, complete the operation in the parentheses: subtract the mean from each observation. Then, we square each difference. After that, we sum the squared differences. Next, we divide the sum by N. If we think of these data as sample data, we would divide by $N - 1$. Finally, we carry out the last operation: we find the square root ($\sqrt{}$) of all the stuff we computed in the preceding steps.

Remember!
Like the mean, the SD is a characteristic of a distribution. An individual case does not have an SD of its own. However, we can figure out how many SDs a case's value is from the mean of the distribution.

If every score is exactly at the mean of a distribution, the SD of the distribution is 0. For example, a synchronized swim team in which every member is exactly the same height would have SD = 0 for the height distribution. There is no variation, no variability, no difference.

If everybody in a country has exactly the same income, the SD of the income distribution is 0.

The variance for grouped data: Finding the variance for grouped data involves computing the sum of squared deviations for each group, weighting the result by the frequency of cases in the group, summing the weighted sums of squares for all the groups, and dividing the sum by $N - 1$.

Lab work suggestion: If you have access to a computer and stats software, you can put some data into the computer and play around with finding the mean and SD for your data, to get a feel for the SD.

The variance and SD as measures of inequalities: The SD is more honest about inequality than the measures of central tendency. Go back to Count Esterhazy's estate and compute the SDs for before and after the shoe redistribution. (Hint: begin with the SD for the distribution after the shoes were divided equally, because it's easy to compute.) What does that tell you? (See answer number 7 at the end of this chapter.)

> The variance and standard deviation are powerful measures of inequality in a distribution.

The variance of a proportion: A final important idea is defining the variance of a proportion. Remember that when we have a dichotomous variable we can define its mean as the proportion of cases in the category that was coded 1. The variance of this type of distribution is defined by $v = p(1 - p)$, where p is the proportion of cases in one of the two categories. Notice that the variance has its maximum possible value when $p = .5$. This is the most variability possible. This makes good intuitive sense. For example, if we are in a community that is split right down the middle in its support for two political parties, we would perceive it as the most "varied" or "divided" situation possible and be most likely to come across people of opposed opinions. The SD of the proportion is the positive square root of the variance. Notice that the SD in this case will be greater than the variance, unless the proportion is 0 or 1. For example, if the proportion is .5, the variance is .25 (that is, .5 × .5), and the SD is .5, which is the square root of .25.

Categoric Variables:
Index of Diversity and Index of Qualitative Variation

We are often interested in variability in categoric data. For example, we might want to explore religious or language diversity in a country or racial/ethnic or gender diversity in a university or company. We might have a vague sense, for instance, that the United States and Canada are more ethnically diverse than Japan. We would say that Brown University, with pretty close to a 50/50 gender split, has more gender diversity than the Citadel, a military college where only a very small proportion of women attend. Can we measure diversity more precisely?

Two measures can be used to make these comparisons for categoric data more precise: the **index of diversity** and the **index of qualitative variation**.

Algorithm for the index of diversity:

1. Find the proportion of the cases in each category, expressed as a fraction or a decimal fraction. This value is *p* in the formula, and there will be *k* of these values, one for each of the *k* categories.

2. Square each proportion (i.e., one square for each category).

3. Add all the squares for all the categories (obtain the sum).

4. Subtract the sum of the squared proportions from 1.

The index of diversity, *D*, represents the likelihood that two cases selected randomly fall into different categories. The higher the value of *D*, the greater the dispersion or diversity of the variable. If *D* = 0, it means all cases fall into the same category.

$$D = 1 - \Sigma(p_k)^2$$

Notice that if every citizen of a country were of the same ethnic background (i.e., if all were in the same category), the proportion for that category would be 100% and the index of diversity would be 0. The more evenly cases are spread through the categories, the higher the index.

Here is a very simple imaginary example. There are four religious groups (or categories) at Manchester High: Methodists, Mennonites, Mormons, and Muslims. Each group constitutes a quarter of the student body, so $p = \dfrac{1}{4}$ for each one of the four categories, and $\dfrac{1}{4}$ squared is $\dfrac{1}{16}$.

$$D = 1 - \left[\frac{1}{16} + \frac{1}{16} + \frac{1}{16} + \frac{1}{16} \right] = 1 - \frac{1}{4} = \frac{3}{4} \text{ or } .75$$

This is a relatively high level of diversity.

Notice that the more categories there are, the larger the maximum value that *D* can possibly attain. With two categories, the maximum for *D* is .50; with four categories, it is .75; and with 10 categories, it is .90. *D* encompasses diversity both in the number of different categories and in the proportional distribution of cases into those categories.

The index of qualitative variation standardizes the index of diversity for the number of categories by dividing D by $\frac{k-1}{k}$ where k is the number of categories. In other words, using the "invert and multiply" rule for division by fractions, we multiply D by $\frac{k}{k-1}$. This index has the value 1 when the cases are equally spread out over all k categories, that is, $p = \frac{1}{k}$ for all the proportions.

With these two indexes, we can measure and compare the claims of universities and companies that they are "diverse." You can experiment with a few simple examples, such as computing D for gender diversity for courses you are taking.

PERCENTILE DISTRIBUTIONS

In a percentile distribution we identify the values that correspond to percentiles of the frequency distribution: for example, to quintiles (intervals of 20% that divide the distribution into fifths), deciles (10% intervals), the interquartile range (between the 25th and the 75th percentile), and so on. The median is the value that corresponds to the 50th percentile. For instance, we might hear, "you have to score in the 98th percentile or better to get into the magnet program." Or we might read about the quintile distribution of income or wealth in the United States. In other words, what proportion of the total wealth (or income) goes to the wealthiest fifth of families, what proportion goes to the second fifth, and so on, down to the proportion that goes to the fifth that receives the least?

Part III: Graphing and Visual Displays of Distributions

There is a lot to be said about this subject and many books that say it, so here are just a few basics.

Decide if the data are categoric or continuous.

If they are **categoric,** the most common visual displays are the following:

1. **The Pie Chart:** Each wedge represents the proportion of cases in a category. Use it for variables with 2–6 categories, not more.

2. **The Bar Chart:** A separate bar represents each category of the variable. The height or length of the bar displays the frequency for the category. A bar chart is much like a visual display of the information in a frequency table. Usually the bars are vertical, with height representing frequency. (Bar charts can also be used to display the relationship of two variables. For instance, in a bivariate bar chart, men and women are each represented by two bars that show the proportions of smokers and non-smokers for that gender. Don't confuse the univariate and bivariate bar charts.)

In the next three figures, we see a pie chart, a univariate bar chart, and a bivariate bar chart.

Figure 1: Pie Chart—Respondents' highest degree (GSS data)

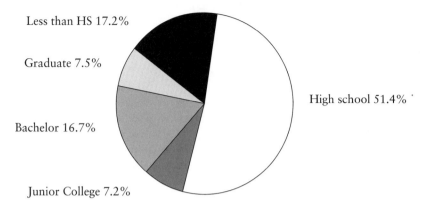

Statistics: Respondents' highest degree

N	Valid	1411
	Missing	8

		Frequency	Percent	Valid Percent	Cumulative Percent
Valid	Less than HS	243	17.1	17.2	17.2
	High School	725	51.1	51.4	68.6
	Junior college	101	7.1	7.2	75.8
	Bachelor	236	16.6	16.7	92.5
	Graduate	106	7.5	7.5	100.0
	Total	*1411*	*99.4*	*100.0*	
Missing	DK	1	.1		
	NA	7	.5		
	Total	*8*	*.6*		
Total		*1419*	*100.0*		

Here we see a pie chart that displays a categoric variable from the General Social Survey, a survey of a large representative sample of adult residents of the United States. The variable displayed is "respondents' highest degree." There are five categories, and the chart has been set up to display percentages rather than total counts. The frequencies table displayed with the chart allows us to see the counts. Missing cases are not shown on this chart. Slightly more than half the respondents have completed high school, but have not completed a degree beyond high school; this is the modal category.

Figure 2: Bar chart—Respondents' highest degree by count (GSS data)

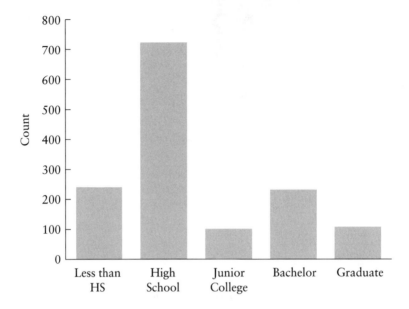

Figure 3: Bar chart—Respondents' highest degree by percentage (GSS data)

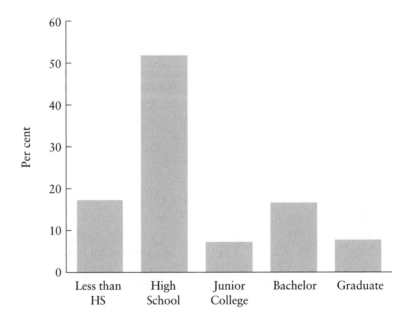

Here we see exactly the same information for the same variable displayed in two bar graphs. The first displays the number (count) of people with each type of degree and the second shows the percentages. In both of these, we see again that "high school" is the modal category, that "bachelors" and "less than high school" have about the same count and percentage and that graduate degrees and junior college completion have the lowest frequencies.

Figure 4: Bar chart displaying two variables—Respondents' degree and use of e-mail

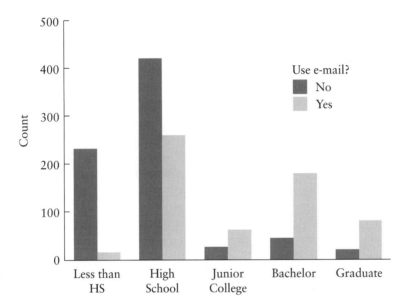

Finally, we see a more complicated bar chart. It displays two variables. Each of the five-degree categories is broken down into respondents who say they use e-mail and those who say they do not. As we can see from the height of the bars, a majority of people in all of the post-high school categories say they use e-mail, a majority of high-school graduates say they do not, and a large majority of respondents with less than high school say they do not. In this table we are looking at the counts, not at percentages. (In a later chapter, we will discuss how to compute percentages for distributions of two variables.)

If the data are **continuous**, the variable is usually displayed in a **histogram**. A histogram looks just like bar chart, except that the bars are all right up against each other, not separated. Each bar represents an interval of the continuous variable, with the height of the bar showing the frequency of cases with values that fall in the interval. If we find the midpoint of the top of each bar and connect all these points for our whole chart, we end up with a **frequency polygon.**

Figure 5: Histogram for a continuous variable—Respondents' age (GSS data)

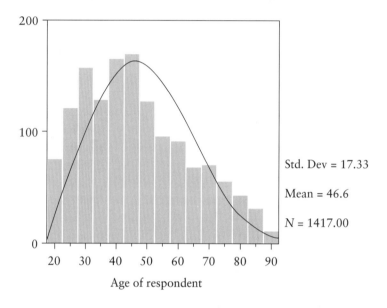

In Figure 5 we see a histogram. It displays the ages of GSS respondents. Age is being treated as a continuous variable. The data have been grouped into intervals of width five years, with the midpoints set at ages ending in 0 or 5. A "bell-curve" has been superimposed on the histogram, and it shows an approximately normal distribution, with more cases around the middle than at the younger and older ages. There is a mild amount of skew in the data, with a tail tapering off towards the older ages, in part because no respondent under 18 was included. The histogram also informs us of the sample size (1417), the mean (46.6 years), and the standard deviation (17.33 years).

The next table (Table 6), stem and leaf diagram (Figure 6), and boxplot (Figure 7) are different ways of exploring the distribution of a continuous variable. The table of descriptives provides not only the mean, median, variance, and standard deviation, but also a "5% trimmed mean" based on the data remaining after the values of the top 5% and bottom 5% of cases have been removed. It computes a confidence interval for the mean, and 95% of the intervals constructed with this procedure will "catch" the population mean, so there is a very good chance that the population mean does indeed lie between 45.66 and 47.47 years, though we cannot be completely sure about this claim. Constructing a confidence interval is a procedure we will discuss in the next chapter. We see the range, Max – Min, and the interquartile range (the value for the 75th percentile minus the value for the 25th percentile), which is 27 years. Skew measures the extent to which a distribution is "lopsided" with a long tail in one direction.

To approximate skew: $\text{Skew} = \dfrac{3(\text{mean} - \text{median})}{\text{standard deviation}}$.

Here we see a moderate amount of positive skew. If the mean is equal to the median, the skew is 0. Kurtosis measures the "peakedness" of a distribution, whether it has a noticeable peak in the middle or is flattened out, with fat tails.

Table 6: Displaying a continuous variable—Descriptives

Age of respondent		Statistic	Std. Error
Mean		46.56	.460
95% Confidence Interval for Mean	Lower Bound	45.66	
	Upper Bound	47.47	
5% Trimmed Mean		45.97	
Median		44.00	
Variance		300.341	
Std. Deviation		17.330	
Minimum		18	
Maximum		89	
Range		71	
Interquartile Range		27.00	
Skewness		.486	.065
Kurtosis		–.589	.130

Figure 6: Displaying a continuous variable—
Stem and leaf plot of age of respondents

Frequency	Stem &	Leaf
30.00	1 .	8999999
91.00	2 .	0001111122233333344444
130.00	2 .	5555555666666677777888889999999
147.00	3 .	000000001111111222222222223333444444
164.00	3 .	55555566666666777777778888888888899999999
164.00	4 .	000000001111122222222233333333333344444444
142.00	4 .	55555555566666666777777788888889999
133.00	5 .	00000000111112222222233333344444444
79.00	5 .	5555666677888899999
82.00	6 .	00000111111222233333444
70.00	6 .	556666677778888999
67.00	7 .	0001122222333444
52.00	7 .	556677788999
39.00	8 .	001123344
27.00	8 .	567899

Stem width:	10
Each leaf:	4 cases

The stem and leaf diagram looks like a histogram lying on its side. Unlike the histogram, it preserves more of the original information or "raw data." The stems represent the tens digits or "leading digits" in people's ages, ranging from 1 for the 18 and 19 year olds in the survey to 8 for the respondents in their 80s. Notice that they are broken down into intervals of five years, so that each decade of age is broken down into the first five years and the second five years. The "leaves" represent the ones-digit in everybody's age for all the cases in the stem, and each of these "leaf" numbers stands for about 4 respondents. For example, if we look at the second 2 stem, representing people from 25 to 29 years, we see there are seven fives. Each one of these fives represents about 4 cases, so there are a total of 28 people (4 × 7) people who are 25 years old. The leftmost column, labelled frequency, shows the exact total number of people in that age group. Notice that the stem and leaf plot preserves all the original information and shows us the shape of the distribution; it combines the virtues of the histogram and the original data file, the complete listing of all the observed "raw" data.

Figure 7: Displaying a continuous variable—Boxplot and percentiles for age of respondents

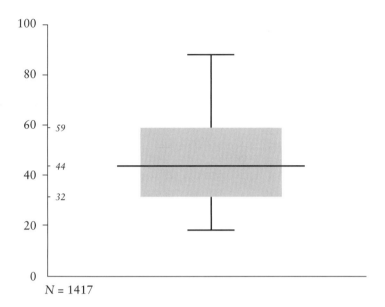

N = 1417

| | Percentiles | | | | | Percentiles | |
Age of Respondent	5	10	25	50	75	90	95
Weighted Average (Definition 1)	22.00	25.00	32.00	44.00	59.00	73.00	79.00
Tukey's Hinges			32.00	44.00	59.00		

Finally we see a boxplot for the age data (Figure 7). The vertical scale here is very different from the vertical scale of the histogram. The histogram's vertical scale represents frequencies (counts or percentages). The boxplot's vertical scale represents the range of values of the variable that appears in the distribution. The width of the boxplot (the horizontal dimension) has no particular meaning. The top and bottom of the box represent the interquartile range (IQR). Here we can see the top is about at 60 years and the bottom of the box is about at 30 years; indeed, when we check this reading against the box that contains the exact information, we see the IQR runs from 32 to 59 years. The line running through the box represents the median; we know from the descriptives table that it is 44 years of age (the age of the respondent at the 50th percentile of the distribution). Notice the median value is not exactly in the middle of the box. The folks between the 50th and the 75th percentile have a slightly more spread-out range of ages (from 44 to 59 = 15 years) than do the folks between the 25th and the 50th percentile (from 32 to 44 = 12 years). That is why there is more room above than below the median. The hinges and whiskers represent the more extreme values; notice the bottom of the range is artificially cut off at 18 because younger people were not included in the sample.

Percentile distributions of interval-ratio variables are represented by boxplots. The boxplot uses the vertical dimension for the values of the variable. A box is formed by the interquartile range, the values that correspond to the 25th and 75th percentiles of the cumulative frequency distribution; a line in the box represents the value corresponding to the 50th percentile, the median. The whiskers, outliers, and extreme values represent values outside of the interquartile box, but they are not always handled the same way in texts and statistical software packages. Often the whiskers represent values that correspond to plus-or-minus 1.5 times the box length, the outliers are values beyond that range but less than 3 box-lengths from the upper or lower edge of the box, and extreme values are beyond the outliers. Note that the median often does not fall exactly in the middle of the box. (We can also make two-variable boxplots when one variable is categoric and the other is interval-ratio; each category of the first variable gets its own boxplot displaying the distribution of the interval-ratio/continuous variable—for example, showing the distributions of achievement test scores for cities, suburbs, and rural areas.)

Don't confuse histograms and boxplots. In the histogram, the intervals across the horizontal dimension each represent a fixed range of values of the variable, while the heights of the bars represent the **frequency** of cases with values in that interval. In the boxplot (or any percentile distribution) the cumulative frequencies are fixed (at deciles, quintiles, 25th, 50th, and 75th percentile, or whatever), while the vertical dimension shows **variable values** that are associated with the percentile range of the distribution. They are almost "opposites" of each other in the logic of the display.

Guidelines for good graphs and charts:

1. **Keep them simple and clean. Avoid clutter and junk.**

2. **Label them clearly, providing all necessary information:** provide a good title and label the axes, the variables displayed, and other key elements.

3. **Avoid cutesy-ness!** Bars should be bars not clever little pictures. (For example, if a bar chart displays the number of immigrants from different countries, do not make the bars little folk with suitcases and ethnic hats!) Bars must be easily comparable, with their size proportional to the frequency or percentage of cases in the category/interval in the total distribution.

4. **Keep them honest!** Charts are prime suspects for "monkey business." Visual displays are easily manipulated to convey misleading impressions. See Darrell Huff, *How to Lie with Statistics* (1954/1993).

Check out the work of Edward Tufte (1997), *Visual and Statistical Thinking: Displays of Evidence for Making Decisions*, for a fascinating look at how good visual displays were used to pinpoint and halt a cholera epidemic and how bad ones contributed to the space shuttle Challenger crash.

Part IV: Standardized Scores or Z-scores

This is one of my all-time favourite topics. It is a brilliant concept and once we "get it," it's an "open sesame!" to a lot of other stuff in stats. Z-scores are a precise way of expressing a completely common-sense idea: **Comparisons.**

> Where does this value stand within its distribution?
> "Janie is tall for her age."
> "The exam scores were so terrible that her miserable 50 points set the curve!"
> "The exam scores were so great that her 95 points was the lowest grade in the class."
> "Last night's game was Michael Jordan' s career high."
> "Welcome to Chicago's funnest neighborhood!" (sign in Lakeview Chamber of Commerce window).

In all these cases, we are saying something about a value or score within a set of scores; we are comparing a score to the other cases' scores in the distribution. We are more interested in the comparison with the other cases in the distribution than in the actual score itself.

Z-scores are a precise way of comparing a score to all the other scores in the distribution.

A Z-score expresses a score in terms of how many standard deviations it is above or below the mean of a distribution. It expresses how different or discrepant an observation is from the mean of the distribution.

> If a score is exactly at the mean, its Z-score is 0.
> If it is above the mean, it has a positive Z-score.
> If it is below the mean, it has a negative Z-score.

A Z-score only makes sense for a specific distribution. For example, among North American women, my height is average at 5'4". My Z-score for height is 0. But if I lived among the Mbuti "pygmies" where women's heights average 4'6", I would be considered a tall person; my

The Mathematical Imagination: The Magic of Z-scores

1. They are entirely sociable: They only exist in a certain distribution. They can only live with other scores in a distribution; take away the distribution and the Z-scores disappear.

2. They are clean: The transformation strips away all those messy units—feet, inches, dollars, milligrams all disappear. Z-scores are expressed only in standard deviation units.

3. They live in a special Z-score heaven, an abstract place, far removed from real life. We can think of Z-scores as a way of transporting our data to a very pure place, a scale with 0 as its mean and 1 as its SD. All data are moved and accordioned onto this scale. (Subtracting the mean moves the score over; dividing by the SD scrunches or stretches it into place.)

4. They make it possible to compare everything, not just apples and oranges, but anything that lives in any distribution. Z-scores make it possible to compare grapes and watermelons: Is this grape bigger in the grape distribution than that watermelon in the watermelon distribution? But even more amazingly, we can compare any scores-within-their-distribution to any other scores-within-their-distribution! We can compare the sizes of watermelons with prices of jewellery or income in dollars or value of homes. We can now give perfectly precise and serious answers to these (and similar) questions:

- Does this very big grape have a bigger grape-size Z-score than Bill Gates's mansion has a mansion-price Z-score? In other words, is this grape bigger than Bill's mansion is expensive?

- Gary W., the CEO of Global Crossing, a company that recently went bankrupt, had received enough compensation to build himself the most expensive mansion in the United States—it was estimated to cost $67 million. If we found a grape the size of a medicine ball, would its grape-size Z-score be greater or less than Gary's mansion-cost Z-score?

Thanks to the concept of the Z-score, these kinds of questions now have very precise and serious answers!

Algorithm for converting an unstandardized score into a standardized score (Z-score):

1. Find the mean and SD of the distribution.

2. Subtract the mean from the score. Notice that this difference is positive if the score is above the mean; it is negative if the score is below the mean; it is 0 if the score is right at the mean.

3. Divide the difference found in Step 2 by the SD.

Z-score for height would be a positive number, probably over +2, showing I am two standard deviations above the mean of women's heights. In Sweden or Senegal, I would be a rather short person in the women's height distribution and have a negative height Z-score.

Z-scores are easy to compute. Here are the steps for computing the Z-score for a case in a distribution.

Formula for converting an observation, or "raw score" into a Z-score or "standardized score":

$$Z = \frac{X - \overline{X}}{S}$$

The Z-score equals the difference between X and the mean of the X-distribution ($\overline{X}$), then divided by the standard deviation of the distribution.

Usually we compute the Z-scores for all the cases in the distribution.

Most software packages allow us to do this very easily and quickly.

Notice you can't compute your Z-score for height (or any other continuous variable) by yourself! You have to be in a group, a class, or bunch of friends. Your height only has a Z-score within a distribution, a set of cases. It doesn't have a Z-score by itself. So first you have to get everyone else's height, compute the mean and the SD for the whole set of cases, and only then can you compute your height's Z-score for this particular distribution of heights.

Z-scores will be important in answering two questions that come up in data analysis.

First, is this observation significantly different or discrepant from a specified condition? For example, is the survival rate of patients who took an experimental drug significantly different from the survival rate of those who received a placebo? Z-scores are a way of expressing difference, and so they will be used to examine these kinds of questions (Chapter Three).

Second, is the distribution of one variable that describes a set of cases similar or proportionate to the distribution of another variable that describes the same set of cases? For example, to what extent are people's weights proportionate to their heights? To what extent is vehicles' gas mileage proportionate to their weight? To what extent are people's salaries proportionate to their years of education? In all of these questions, we can look at the extent to which all cases' Z-scores for the first variable "line up" or "match up" with their Z-scores for the second variable. (Z-scores will be used to compute the correlation coefficient in Chapter Four.)

Most software packages have a way of computing and saving Z-scores so you don't have to go through all the steps of the formula for transforming each score into a Z-score. If you are working with a computer, enter some data sets and for each variable, run the Z-score transformation. Notice the typical range of Z-scores. You will probably observe that they usually fall between −3 and +3, with many of them (probably around 2/3) between −1 and +1. Z-scores more extreme than −3 or +3 are fairly rare in the distribution of most common variables.

Math Interlude: Chebycheff's Inequality

Having encountered two powerful concepts—the standard deviation and the Z-scores—we conclude with a "believe it or not" theorem that connects the two concepts in a remarkable conclusion.

Chebycheff's Inequality is a theorem first proved by a nineteenth century Russian mathematician, Pafnuty Chebycheff. It states that the further an observation is from the mean of the distribution, the less likely or probable it is. In all finite distributions, observations many SDs from the mean occur less often than those close to the mean.

The precise statement is as follows: The probability that the absolute value of an observation's Z-score is k or more standard deviations from the mean is less than or equal to 1 divided by the square of k.

(Probability is always expressed as a number from 0, which means it's impossible, to 1, which means it's absolutely certain.)

$$\text{Prob}\left(|Z| \geq k\right) \leq \frac{1}{k^2}$$

So if $k = 2$, the statement reads this way.

$$\text{Prob}\left(|Z| \geq 2\right) \leq \frac{1}{4}$$

If $k = 10$, the statement reads this way.

$$\text{Prob}\left(|Z| \geq 10\right) \leq \frac{1}{100}$$

Observations that are 10 or more standard deviations from the mean are not very likely in any distribution!

Two things to note about Chebycheff's Inequality:

- It is a statement about probability. It just says that observations far from the mean are less likely, not that they are impossible. Observations "thin out" with distance from the mean. The more distant an observation is from the mean, the lower the probability of encountering it.

- It is true regardless of the shape of the distribution. No matter how skewed or oddly shaped! No matter what we try to draw or imagine—like an extremely long two-humped camel of a distribution—the statement holds true.

Chebycheff's Theorem seems amazing—it makes you want to get out pencil and paper and try to draw a distribution that disproves it, or at least challenges it. Just go ahead and try to sneak a lot of observations into the far reaches of the distribution. Remember, however, that when you add a lot of observations way out there, you are going to increase the standard deviation.

(For a more formal statement and proof, see Seymour Lipschutz and Marc Lipson, *Probability*, 2nd ed., Schaum's Outline Series, New York: McGraw-Hill, 2000, pp.140-141 and 169-170.)

An alternative statement of the theorem is that for every positive number k,

$$p\left[(\mu - k\sigma) \leq x \leq (\mu + k\sigma)\right] \geq 1 - \frac{1}{k^2}$$

The probability that the observation lies between the mean and plus or minus k standard deviation units is equal to or greater than $1 - \left(\frac{1}{k^2}\right)$.

For instance, if $k = 5$, the statement reads:

$$p\left[(\mu - 5\sigma) \le x \le (\mu + 5\sigma)\right] \ge \frac{24}{25}$$

Conclusion

This chapter presented many different ways to summarize and display a distribution of a variable. Distributions are a fundamental concept of statistics. Ways of describing a distribution include frequency tables, graphs, and summary measures of central tendency (mean, median, and mode) and variability (also known as spread or dispersion). Variability is a key concept for all distributions. When the data are interval-ratio or continuous data, the variance and the standard deviation are the most important and common measures of variability. The variance (and/or standard deviation) should always be reported together with the mean. Z-scores express scores/observations in terms of their distance from the mean in standard deviation units, and Chebycheff's Inequality states mathematically the theorem that, in all finite distributions, observations many SDs from the mean are less likely than those close to the mean.

Key Terms

frequency distribution
intervals and grouped data
measures of central tendency:
   mean, median, mode
measures of dispersion
   (variability, spread):
     range
     variance
     standard deviation
     index of diversity and
       index of qualitative
       variation

percentile distribution
boxplot
stem and leaf chart
histogram (continuous variables)
pie chart and bar chart
   (categoric variables)
standardized scores (Z-scores)
Chebycheff's Inequality

Chapter Two: Answers

1. Pairs of Footwear on Esterhazy Estate; N: 1000

Value	Frequency
0	999
1000	1

2. The mean is 1, the median is 0, the mode is 0, and the modal frequency is 999.

3. The mean would be used to convince people that peasants are well off on the Esterhazy Estate because it suggests that each person has one pair of shoes instead of that one person has all the shoes, which is the case.

4. In this case, either the median or the mode gives the best information about distribution.

5. Pairs of Footwear on Esterhazy Estate after 1919; N: 1000

Value	Frequency
0	0
1	1000

The mean is 1, the median is 1, the mode is 1, and the modal frequency is 1000.

6. In determining income distribution, the mean could be very misleading, especially in cases where considerable wealth is in the hands of very few. The mode could mislead if there are almost the same number of cases at very different ends of the distribution. For example, imagine we are trying to analyse a population by age, and we find the mode to be 60 years, but there are two fewer cases of people who are 6.

7. The standard deviation for the shoe data before 1919 is 31.6. It is 0 after the shoe distribution. This shows that 31.6 standard deviation indicates a great disparity.

Chapter Three: Statistical Inference

In this chapter, we will return to statistical inference, the process of generalizing from a sample to a population. We will meet one of the most amazing concepts in introductory statistics, the **sampling distribution**. We will think about ways to cope with the **uncertainty** of sampling, because sample outcomes are neither all identical to each other nor to the situation in the population. We explore two methods for statistical inference. One ingenious way of coping with variability is to use our observed sample data to test a "null hypothesis," a conjecture about the population. The second method of statistical inference is constructing confidence intervals.

Part I: Thinking about Statistical Inference

Statistical Inference: What Are We Trying To Do?

The characteristics of the population are unknown, and these are what we want to know. The sample data, which we know, are used to reach a conclusion about the unknown population characteristic. The sample data are used to estimate a value in the population. Inference means that the conclusion we reach about the population might not be true, but it is probable that it is true given what we know about the sample. Inference means that there is a probability—a risk—that the conclusion is false, but, given what we know about the sample and sampling, the risk is fairly low.

In the following pages, we will put together five main ideas that form the basis of statistical inference:

1. **Variability:** Sample outcomes are not all the same.

2. **The sampling distribution:** The sampling distribution is the set of all possible sample outcomes. The sampling distribution has an expected value, the mean, and variability, the standard deviation.

The standard deviation of the sampling distribution has a special name—the standard error—and its own calculational formula.

3. **Probability:** Sample outcomes are not all equally likely; the ones that are closer to the situation or value in the population are more likely.

4. **The normal curve:** As sample size increases, the entire set of sample outcomes—the sampling distribution—is normally distributed, that is, it assumes the shape of a bell curve, which allows us to specify the probability of the sample outcomes.

5. **Coping with variability:** In **hypothesis testing,** one of the main forms of statistical inference, we test a "null hypothesis" about the population against our observed sample data. Alternatively, we can use the sample data to **construct a confidence interval** that has a good likelihood of containing the population value we are trying to estimate.

A preliminary word about notation: The convention is that measures for the population are called **parameters** and are assigned lower-case Greek letters while the corresponding measures for a sample are called **statistics** and are assigned Latin letters. For example,

- the population mean is called *mu*, μ,

- the population standard deviation is called *sigma*, σ, and

- a population proportion is called *pi*, π.

The corresponding measures in a sample are called: $\overline{X}$, the sample mean; s, the sample standard deviation; and p, the sample proportion (which might be expressed as a decimal fraction, percent, or ordinary fraction).

In statistical inference we are trying to figure out the population parameters when all we know are the statistics for the observed sample data. In elementary statistics, the population parameters we are often trying to estimate are a **population mean** or a **population proportion.** For example, we could use sample data to estimate the mean height or the mean years of education of a population. We might use sample data to estimate the proportion of the electorate who will vote for a candidate or the proportion of people who will become sick with a disease after they have been vaccinated against it with a new vaccine. In Chapter Four, we will see that other population parameters we infer are measures that represent the relationship among two or more variables.

A simple example: Let's look at an example of variability in sample outcomes and see where it takes us. Imagine a student survey at a very large university aimed at finding the average number of books owned by students. Imagine taking 1000 **random samples** with 100 students in each sample. For each sample, we ascertain the mean number of books owned by the 100 respondents, noting also the standard deviation from the sample mean. We find the mean by adding up all the books owned by all 100 students in the sample and then dividing by 100. We find the sample means for all 1000 samples. In this case, the sample outcome in which we are interested is the sample mean. We sample "with replacement," putting all the students in each sample "back into the pool" so that they are available to be sampled for another sample.

> It is highly unlikely that all of these 1000 samples would produce identical means.

Mathematical thought
Here you may want to recall **Chebycheff's Inequality**, which sounds similar to this question, and remember how values that are many standard deviations away from the mean are unlikely in any distribution.

Our concern is how much variability is there likely to be in the sample outcomes. How far off could a sample mean be from the mean number of books owned for the whole population?

For the sake of the example, let's pretend we already know the population parameter—the mean number of books owned by students at the university. In real life, we would not know the population parameter—that is precisely what we are trying to estimate from the sample data.

How different can the sample means be from the population mean? Small differences are likely, but large ones are not. If the mean for the population is 75 books, with a standard deviation of 36 books, would we ever draw a random sample of 100 people who own no books at all—for whom the sample mean is 0? If this sample outcome were the only information we had, it would lead to a very bad estimate of the true mean!

With the parameter—the population mean—equal to 75 books and samples of 100 students each, would we ever find a sample with a mean of 100 books?

Intuitively we can see that samples that are very "off" are rather unlikely, though not impossible. Most samples will have means around 75, but they will not all be exactly at 75. Some will be higher, some lower. Very few will be as "off" as 100 and even fewer as "off" as 0. This variability is inherent in the "nature of things" or the "way the world works," and it is OK. In fact, if all the samples had exactly the same mean, we would feel that something was "fishy"—someone tampered with the process or faked the results to make all the sample outcomes identical!

If you don't believe that there will be variability in the sample outcomes, run a similar small experiment for yourself. Ask twenty of your friends a yes/no question and record their answers. This distribution will be considered the population, and its percentage of "yes" answers will be considered the population parameter, in this case a proportion. Next group your friends—on paper!—into a large number of samples of ten people. Use the data in your original survey to identify the percentage of "yes" answers for each of the samples you have created on paper. Record the percentage of "yes" answers for each sample. You will see that the proportions of "yes" answers in the ten-person samples will not be identical to each other and may differ from the overall proportion among the twenty people in the population—unless every single one of your twenty friends answered the same way. If you compare your results in this experiment with those of friends, you may discover that the closer the population percent of "yes" answers was to 50%, the more variability in the sample results. In this case, the population parameter is a proportion, not a mean, but for both means and proportions, there is variability in the sample outcomes.

The variation or variability in sample outcomes is called **sampling error.** This is a rather misleading term because the variability is not the result of an error, a mistake, but inherent in "the way things are." Not all samples will have the same outcome (mean). In all research based on samples, we want to know how much variability we will encounter. We especially want to know how likely we are to encounter a sample outcome that would lead to a really misleading conclusion in our research.

If the population parameter we are trying to estimate is 75 books, and the standard deviation is 36, in what proportion of samples will we find a mean of 0? Of 25? Of 50? Of 80? Of 76? Of 74.5? Of 120? Some of these sample means are really "off," very discrepant from the population mean we are trying to estimate. It would be most unfortunate for our attempt to reach a conclusion about the whole university if we happened to draw a sample with such a discrepant outcome.

Now let's imagine a histogram of the sample outcomes. We systematically compute, record, count, and chart all the sample outcomes. Samples with means that are near the population parameter of 75 books would be more frequent than samples with means that are further away from 75.

The histogram for this frequency distribution looks sort of like this. The figure is only a rough approximation to what a completely precise and detailed histogram would look like.

Figure 8: Histogram for distribution of sample means
Values of sample means: (What is the sample mean?
Sample size = 100, for each sample)

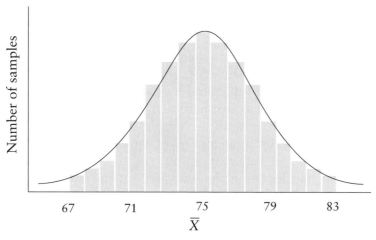

Notes:
- Underlying variable: Number of books owned by each student
- Displayed variable, charted on horizontal axis: Sample means, for samples of 100
- Histogram is a rough approximation, rounded to nearest whole number
- Population mean = 75 books
- Normal curve is superimposed on the histogram

Of our 1000 samples, a lot of samples have sample means near 75, and a few samples have means that are rather different from 75, for instance, 60 or 90. We might even find a few with a mean of 100 or (very few!) with a mean of 0. If we were using data from our sample to infer or estimate the population mean, the samples with sample means at or near 75 books (the population parameter) would give us good estimates of the parameter, while the ones that are more distant from this value would give us bad estimates.

Let's take a closer look at the histogram.

- The horizontal dimension represents possible sample outcomes—the **sample means**. In theory, it could show the full range of values from a mean of 0 books for the sample to much higher values of the mean, like 100 or more. (Like wealth and income, this variable is skewed; it is possible to have a lot of books, but few people do, but it is not possible to have fewer than 0 books.) However, we are only displaying the range from 65 to 85 because so few sample outcomes fall beyond this range.

- The vertical dimension—the height of the bar over a particular value on the horizontal axis—represents the number of cases that have that particular outcome, that particular value for the sample mean.

- The histogram displays a frequency distribution. The cases are samples, and the height of each bar over a value on the horizontal axis represents the number of samples that produced that particular outcome, that particular value for the sample mean. Each bar represents all the samples with the same outcome, namely a specific mean number of books.

- There are a lot of samples—tall bars—at and near 75. The bars at 70 and 80 are distinctly shorter; there are fewer samples with these outcomes. If we could see the bars at 100 and at 0, we would see that they are extremely short, because few samples have outcomes (in this case, means) this far "off" or discrepant from the population parameter of 75.

- Thus, this histogram does not display the distribution of an ordinary variable, like height, weight, or income. It displays a special variable—the distribution of sample outcomes, given a particular value of the population parameter (in this case, the population mean of 75 books).

- Superimposed on the histogram is a smoothed representation of the distribution that we would get if we measured the mean number of books as a truly continuous variable, with infinite subdivision, and an infinite number of samples. This line is an imaginary construct. We could really take 1000 samples of 100 people each, but we can create the "smoothed" histogram, the continuous probability distribution, only in our imagination. For this imaginary construct, we look at the likelihood of an outcome not as the height of the bar, but as the area under the curve between points along the horizontal axis. (To fully explore this imaginary object requires calculus.)

- The histogram represents a **probability distribution**. If we think about all sample outcomes, the outcomes near the population parameter are quite probable—we are likely to encounter them in our sampling—while the others, the outcomes that are distant from the population parameter, are unlikely or improbable. Only a small proportion of the samples will have a sample outcome (a mean) that is very far from the 75 books (the population mean).

- One of the factors that shapes the distribution will be the standard deviation of the population. In this case, we said it was 36 books. If it is relatively large, the curve for the distribution for the sample outcomes will be more spread out, and if it is small, the curve will be more tightly concentrated around the mean. As you look at the curve, you may feel quite surprised at how most of the sample means fall quite close to the population mean: more than two-thirds of the sample means seem to cluster between 71 and 79. Although the population standard deviation was 36, variability in the distribution of sample means (the standard deviation of the distribution of sample means) looks a lot smaller!

- Finally, you may also be surprised that the distribution of sample outcomes looks symmetric, although we suspected that the underlying distribution of number of books owned by students is skewed, with a long positive tail reflecting students with large personal libraries.

At this point, you probably feel that you followed the example pretty well, but you may be puzzled by two questions. How do we know that the sample outcomes will be distributed in that bell-shaped curve? And why do we care that the distribution of sample outcomes looks like a bell curve—so what?

OK, first—why do we care? We care because, in the real world of research, we are constantly collecting data from samples, and we would like to be reassured that the sample data will not be totally "off" from the actual condition we want to know about in the population. Well, more honestly, we want to be reassured that most of the time—with a high degree of probability—the sample data will not be totally "off." Unfortunately, that is the best we can hope for; there is always some degree of uncertainty. We might get one of those infrequent, really "off" sample outcomes.

Fortunately for the real world of empirical research we know a lot—in mathematical terms—about the probability of outcomes. If we know a population parameter, sample size, and sampling error (the variability of the sample outcomes), we can specify exactly what the distribution of sample outcomes will look like. More specifically, we can state the probability that any particular sample outcome will be within a given distance—measured in SD units—from the population parameter. Wait a minute though! In real life, we don't know the population parameter (that is what we are trying to find out!), and we can only estimate the sampling error, so we have to adjust the logic of the process, as we shall see shortly.

This brings us back to our first question, however: How do we know the sample outcomes will be distributed in a bell curve? We cannot give a rigorous answer to this question. We have an inkling that it might be true from Chebycheff's Inequality. We already know, though without proof, that highly discrepant values are unlikely in any distribution. But this takes us only part way to the claim that the sampling distribution will look like a bell curve. To answer the question why the distribution looks like a bell curve requires a lot of math in probability theory and calculus, beyond the scope of this book; so what we will do in the next sections is to explore the question with examples, imagination, and a couple of theorems to take on faith. I want the reader to be absolutely clear that the discussion in the next pages is an exploration, an adventure of the imagination, not a rigorous mathematical argument. In order to carry out our exploration, we will first look in more detail at the list of concepts from the beginning of the chapter.

Variability

Sample outcomes are usually not identical. Each sample outcome is likely to be different from other sample outcomes and from the population parameter. There is variability in the sample outcomes. Variability is a fundamental concept in thinking about samples. For example, if we took samples from a statistics class, the mean heights for the samples would not all be identical to the mean height for the class as a whole, the population. Most sample means would be slightly different from the class mean. We want to know how much variability to expect. Are we likely to get a sample outcome that is way "off" from the population parameter we are trying to estimate?

THE SAMPLING DISTRIBUTION

As I noted in Chapter One, our concern is that a correct random sampling procedure (not a poorly designed, biased sampling procedure) might by random chance—bad luck—produce a sample with very misleading values for the sample statistic. Such a sample statistic would lead us to make an incorrect inference about the population parameter. If we have correctly carried out a random sampling procedure, we know just how probable sample outcomes are, given a hypothetical assumption about the population. Fortunately once we specify a condition for the population (hypothetically, of course), we know exactly what the distribution of all possible sample outcomes for samples of size N will look like and how likely each outcome is.

This very large imaginary object—the distribution of sample outcomes for all samples of size N—is called a sampling distribution.

To understand the sampling distribution we will introduce four related concepts: **Sampling** and the **simple random sample, probability and expected values,** the **normal curve,** and **sampling error.**

Sampling and the simple random sample: "Random" is often used in a negative sense. "My friend's wardrobe seems random—lots of unmatched clothes"; or "the paper was completely random —just opinions thrown together with no organization." But in statistics, random is a very positive term! It means that a sample has been drawn entirely by chance so that the bias of the researcher does not enter the process. It also means that the sample is a probability sample for which we can specify the likelihood of any case being included.

How do we draw a simple random sample? Here is the ideal way: First we decide how large a sample we want and call the number of cases in the sample N. We prepare a sampling frame, a list of all the cases in the population, for example, a list of the names of all students who attend this university if this is our population. Next we assign a number to each case in the sampling frame. Finally, we use a random number generator to identify the cases to include in our sample of N cases drawn from the sampling frame. For example, if the first random number to come up were 1401, we would find case 1401 in our sampling frame and include him/her in the sample. We would continue in this fashion till all N cases are drawn.

There is a lively discussion among mathematicians about how you can tell if a process really produces random numbers. For example, is the decimal expansion of *pi* (ratio of the circumference of a circle to its diameter) really random? Computer-generated random numbers are not really random, but they are close enough to it to be OK for practically all research purposes. See Deborah J. Bennett, *Randomness*, Cambridge MA: Harvard University Press, 1998, for more.

In practice, this procedure is not always followed. It is usually very difficult actually to create the sampling frame. Furthermore, many populations are thought of as "infinite"—they are large and unspecified. For example, when medical researchers test new drugs or vaccines, they would like them to be effective for everyone in the future as well as now. Researchers find other ways to create samples that are close to being simple random samples. In social science research and national opinion polls, they may carry out multilevel sampling, creating a sampling frame of all census tracts, randomly sampling the tracts, and then sampling households within the tracts. Notice that if at this point they randomly sample individuals within households, they will end up oversampling individuals who live in small households. In this book, we will not delve into inference from more complicated multilevel and/or cluster samples, but always use "sampling" to mean a simple random sample.

A simple random sample is drawn using the largest possible element of chance. Paradoxically this makes it a better sample, one from which we can draw more precise conclusions, than a sample formed by the judgment of a researcher (let alone one formed by convenience—"hey, think I'll ask my friends"). The random sample is not biased, and we can specify mathematically exactly how likely sample outcomes are when we consider all possible samples drawn from a population.

In a simple random sample, each case in the population is equally likely to be in the sample. Furthermore, each sample of N cases is equally likely as every other set of N cases. But what is *not* equally likely is the outcome of the statistic (mean, proportion) for the samples. Outcomes (values of the sample statistic) near the population mean are more likely. We will get back to this important fact after a little detour into probability and expected values.

Probability and expected values: Probability, understanding the expected values of outcomes in processes involving chance, is a fascinating area of mathematics. Here we will cover only the basics, enough to provide an intuitive understanding of the probability of a sample outcome among all the possible outcomes from random samples.

You can get some idea of probabilities and expected values by thinking about questions like these: How likely is heads or tails in a flip of the coin? If you flip a coin twice, how likely are two heads? Two tails? One head and one tail? How likely are snake-eyes or a seven in craps? Three boys in a family with three children? A full house in poker? All of these questions can be thought of in terms of drawing tickets from a box or jar that contains a fixed distribution of outcomes. The box is like the population and the sets of draws (rolls of the dice, flips of the coin, etc.) are like the samples.

Simple example: In roulette, as played in US casinos, when you bet on a colour (red, for example) you are betting on a box that looks like this:

18 wins and 20 losses.

There are 18 slots on the wheel that are red and hence wins; and 20 slots that are losses—the 18 black slots and the two green slots numbered 0 and 00.

Let's say all bets are dollar bets; in that case, the expected value for this box is –$2/38. Yes, that's minus 2/38 of a dollar to you, Mr./Ms. Gamester! This is the expected value of the box, computed by finding the sum total of values in the box (+18 – 20 = –2) and dividing it by the number of tickets, corresponding to slots on the roulette wheel (38). Any one spin is unpredictable, but after a large number of spins, the ratio of wins to losses will be close to 18:20. The expected value of the payoff is negative for the gamesters and positive for the casino. No roulette "system" is going to beat this, although after one spin or even at the end of the day, some players may leave the table as winners. The expected value is a loss, but there is variability around this expected value, meaning that there can be (and usually are) some winners.

The same inexorable tendency toward a loss—a negative expected value—is present in all games against the house. For example, a casino may brag that its slots are "loose," meaning that you can expect to lose only 93 cents for every dollar you play. Incidentally, slots are among the worst games in terms of the expected value; craps is probably the closest to a break-even casino game, with the probability of a win for the shooter being a bit over .493. Counting cards in blackjack can be a winning strategy, but if observed or suspected of using it, you will be asked to leave the casino. Until recently, there were a few consistent winners in sports gambling, but they had to work very hard at assembling information that gave them an edge. (See John Trijonis, "Vegas Winners," *Engineering and Science*, number 2, 2001, pp. 35-41.) In Illinois, the average outcome per person per visit to a casino is –$104—a loss of $104. Which is why casinos are moneymaking enterprises.

"The more you play, the more you'll win," say the casino ads; yes, that's right. And the more you'll lose. In the long run, as you continue to play, the ratio of wins to losses will approach more and more closely the expected value for the game, according to a theorem called the Law of Large Numbers. If you win on your first bet, your best strategy is to leave immediately with your winnings.

Let's look at a couple more examples that are less fascinating than casino gambling but closer to the applications we see in elementary statistics when we try to infer a population proportion from sample data.

Imagine a tiny population, which for some mysterious reason has been hidden in a large jar. It contains two men, Brad and Kiljoong, and two women, Yolanda and Aisha. The population parameter—

the proportion of men—is .50 (or 50% or $\frac{1}{2}$, depending on how we choose to write it).

We will now think about all possible different random samples of two people that could be drawn from the jar, rather cruelly replacing them in the jar after we inspect them. We are doing this in order to estimate or infer the population parameter, pi, the proportion of men in the jar, from p, the sample statistic, which is the proportion of men in the sample. (In real life, we would not know what is in the jar, since that is what we are trying to infer.)

Sample 1: Aisha and Brad: $p = .5$
Sample 2: Aisha and Yolanda: $p = 0$
Sample 3: Aisha and Kiljoong: $p = .5$
Sample 4: Brad and Yolanda: $p = .5$
Sample 5: Brad and Kiljoong: $p = 1.00$
Sample 6: Yolanda and Kiljoong: $p = .5$

With replacement, we could keep drawing samples indefinitely, but this is the basic distribution of outcomes. In fact, the longer we repeated the process, the closer the distribution would be to the one we have displayed above. Each sample of two people is equally likely. But a larger proportion of these samples has $p = .5$ than the other possible values of the sample statistic ($p = 0$ and $p = 1.00$). Notice that a majority of samples—in fact, $\frac{4}{6}$ of the samples—would have outcomes that would lead to a correct inference about the proportion of men in the jar, the population parameter that we are trying to estimate. We can specify exactly how likely the correct and the incorrect outcomes are for this very simple model.

In these samples of two, every person has an equal chance of being drawn out of the jar, and in fact, every combination of two people has an equal chance. However, the sample outcomes are disproportionately likely to match the correct population parameter (pi = .5) than to be the other, "wrong" estimates of 0 and 1. A sample that is all male or all female (a "misleading" sample for inferring pi) is less likely to be drawn than samples from which we would infer the correct population proportion.

While we cannot predict the outcome of any one draw, over a large number of draws, we would find that about $\frac{2}{3}$ of the samples would have the proportion men = .5, leading to a correct estimate of the population proportion. Only 1/3 of the samples would not have that proportion male, having instead proportions of 0 or 1.0, therefore leading to an incorrect estimate of the population parameter.

In real life situations, of course, there are many more people in the jar, and our samples would also be much larger. The same logic applies, however: while we cannot specify in advance what any one sample will look like, the values that show up more frequently in the set of all the possible sample outcomes would be values of the sample statistic (in this case, proportion of men in the sample) that are closer to the population parameter (in this case, the proportion of men in the jar).

This example is similar to tossing a coin. On any one toss, we cannot say in advance if it will be a head or a tail. But if it is a fair coin, after a large number of tosses, the results will be very close to the proportion of 50% heads. If we toss a coin twice and keep track of the proportion of heads we get in this "sample" composed of two tosses, we will see that after many such double-tosses (after many samples), we will approach a definite distribution of sample outcomes. By "approach" we mean that it does not always come out exactly the same way, but over many samples of two tosses, it will get very close to the following distribution: In half the samples, the outcome is p = .5 for heads (1 head, 1 tail). In a quarter of the samples, the outcome is p = 0 heads (both tosses are tails), and in a quarter of the samples, it is p = 1.00 for heads (both tosses are heads).

The fair coin toss, like the fair roulette wheel and the simple random sampling process, has no memory. Each sample represents a set of independent events. Each toss is unaffected by the outcome of the previous toss. A string of eight heads (or eight tails) in a row would be unusual, but not impossible. Some folks might think that after eight heads we are "due" for a tail; others might think that the next toss is more likely to be another head. But if it is a fair coin, the probability on the next toss remains exactly 50/50. Long runs of heads (or tails) are never reversed or "balanced"; they are only "diluted" in the overall tendency of the process to approach 50/50, the expected value, as the number of tosses increases. Assuming it is a fair coin and that the tosses are independent of each other, we can calculate exactly how likely it is to get a string of eight heads (or any other number of heads or tails).

The Law of Large Numbers unfortunately leads many gamblers to believe that the roulette wheel will "flip" after a long run of one colour to keep the proportions of black and red close to being equal. This is a fallacy. The spins (or throws of the dice) are independent of each other and have no memory. On each spin, black and red are equally likely, regardless of what happened previously. The averages do get close to the expected value, but we cannot predict the length of runs of one colour.

The likelihood of an event is expressed as a probability, written as a fraction with the range from 0 to 1. A probability of 0 means the event is impossible and will not and cannot occur. A probability of 1 means that it is certain. If I look out the window and see it is raining, the probability of precipitation is 100% or 1. If I am in Death Valley on a sunny day, with not a cloud in the sky, the probability of precipitation is very close to 0.

Let's look at one more example of outcomes in a probabilistic process. This time we are going to roll two dice and add up the numbers on the top faces. Each face is equally likely to show up on top. But when we look at the distribution of **sums,** the outcomes of the rolls are distributed as we see in the table: The top row shows what faces could turn up on the first die, all of them being equally likely, and the left column shows what faces could turn up on the second die, each of these being equally likely as well. The cells of the table show the sum of dots that would be the outcome for each possible roll of the two dice.

		First die					
		1	2	3	4	5	6
	1	2	3	4	5	6	7
	2	3	4	5	6	7	8
Second die	3	4	5	6	7	8	9
	4	5	6	7	8	9	10
	5	6	7	8	9	10	11
	6	7	8	9	10	11	12

There are 36 possible sums. Statisticians refer to this set of all elementary outcomes as a sample space. Although all the faces on each die have an equal probability of turning up, **the sums have different probabilities**. There is only one way of getting a 2 (both dice show a 1) or a 12 (both dice show a 6). On the other hand, there are a lot of ways of getting a 7. A 7 is the most likely outcome; there are 6 ways of getting 7 as the sum. Count 'em up from the table!

We could next make a table of the outcomes, the sums, showing their probability. We can think of this table, which is similar to a frequency table, as a probability distribution. It shows how likely we are to get each sum in the course of many, many tosses of the two dice. Notice that the probabilities add up to 1.

    Y is called a random variable, a variable produced as the outcome of a random process. The Law of Large Numbers states that, as the times we conduct this experiment (the roll of two dice) increases, the distribution of outcomes will approach this probability distribution. If we conduct the experiment a huge number of times, we will see all the possible sums come up in a distribution that is very close to this set of probabilities. The expected value of this distribution is 7. We obtain this result by multiplying each sum (each possible value of Y), by its relative frequency—its probability—and adding up these products, just as we computed a mean for a frequency distribution:

$$\text{Expected value} = \left(2 \times \frac{1}{36}\right) + \left(3 \times \frac{2}{36}\right) + \left(4 \times \frac{3}{36}\right) + \left(5 \times \frac{4}{36}\right)$$

$$+ \left(6 \times \frac{5}{36}\right) + \left(7 \times \frac{6}{36}\right) + \left(8 \times \frac{5}{36}\right) + \left(9 \times \frac{4}{36}\right)$$

$$+ \left(10 \times \frac{3}{36}\right) + \left(11 \times \frac{2}{36}\right) + \left(12 \times \frac{1}{36}\right)$$

$$= 7$$

Y = Sum:	Probability of Y
2	$\dfrac{1}{36}$
3	$\dfrac{2}{36}$
4	$\dfrac{3}{36}$
5	$\dfrac{4}{36}$
6	$\dfrac{5}{36}$
7	$\dfrac{6}{36}$
8	$\dfrac{5}{36}$
9	$\dfrac{4}{36}$
10	$\dfrac{3}{36}$
11	$\dfrac{2}{36}$
12	$\dfrac{1}{36}$

Finally we can make a histogram for the random variable Y that shows the probability distribution of Y, the sum of the upward faces of two dice. If we had to bet on a single outcome, the best bet would be a 7. Snake-eyes or 12 would be a bet that is likely to lose. You might be surprised how many people are confused about this example, thinking that because each face of each die is equally likely to turn up, the sums have equal probabilities as well!

Figure 9: Histogram of the probability distribution of the sum of the upturned faces of two dice

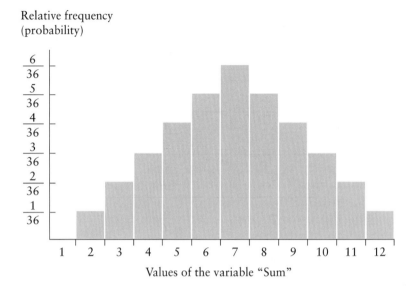

See Freedman et al., *Statistics* for the best non-calculus discussion of probabilities and expected values, using a box model. (The full citation for this text is in the bibliography.)

We have looked at four small experiments in probability: The roulette wheel with dollar bets, the tiny population of men and women in a jar, the tosses of a fair coin, and the sum of the upward faces of two dice. These are simple experiments in the sense that the probabilities of outcomes and the expected values are known in advance and easy to compute. In real life research, the population (the distribution of values in the box or jar) is unknown and the range of possible values is larger, unknown, and possibly more complicated. These small experiments have, however, alerted us to the concept of the **probability distribution of possible outcomes** as we **sample** the population values. So they have prepared us for thinking about the variability of sample outcomes and their distribution.

Especially the example of the two dice alerts us to the way in which a sample outcome (in this case, the sum of the two upward faces) has a probability distribution that can be represented in a histogram peaked around the expected value. Other outcomes are less likely and are represented by shorter bars in the "tails."

The Mathematical Imagination: A World Without Variability

Key concepts of this part of the chapter have been "expected value" and "variability." These two concepts help us understand probabilistic thinking about the world, which is so strikingly illustrated by casino gambling. All casino games have an expected value that is positive for the house and negative for the gamester. When we look at the expected values, we see that the customer is, on average, going to lose money. The key phrase here is "on average"; while the expected value is negative, a loss, there is variability around this average. The outcome is not always a loss, but sometimes a win. No one would go into a casino if the outcome were always exactly the expected value—a loss. The thrill of gambling lies in variability.

Use your imagination to think about a universe without variability. All distributions of quantitative variables are completely and permanently concentrated at their means. All people are the same height and the same weight. Everyone in the country has the same income. Every restaurant meal is a fixed price meal, and there is no a la carte ordering. Every time someone walks into a casino in the state of Illinois, he or she will lose exactly $104. Every slot machine keeps exactly 7 cents of every dollar put into it. Without variability, there would be no point in gambling. Whatever outcome is found in a sample, we know it is identical to the value in the population as a whole, as well as to the outcome of every other sample. In this fixed universe, there are no surprises, no thrills, no uncertainty, and no risk.

We have some idea what this would be like if we have ever flown and found, to our dismay, that every seat on the plane is exactly the same size, regardless of how tall, short, or large we are ... not to mention that all the meals are identical too.

Obviously we do not live in a universe without variability. In the world as we know it, there is variability around the means of practically all distributions. Consequently, sample outcomes can and do vary from each other and are usually different from the population value. Gambling offers thrills, and everyday life is full of risk and surprises.

The thought experiment of "a world without variability" alerts us to the problem of sampling in the real world. In the real world, sample outcomes are not identical to each other nor are they identical to the population value. When we draw a sample, its outcome (mean, proportion, etc.) almost certainly will not be exactly the same as the corresponding value in the population. Our task will be to understand how much variability we are likely to encounter.

We will not go deeply into probabilities, nor are we stating the basic ideas in a rigorous manner with math proofs. Rather the point is to provide an intuitive understanding of how we can infer a conclusion about a population from sample data, seeing that by random chance our sample outcomes will not all be the same and that we run the risk of drawing a sample with a misleading outcome. The point is that we know mathematically how likely these "extreme" samples are. We know from the laws of probability exactly what the distribution of sample means or sample proportions is for all possible samples of a particular size. We can calculate exactly how likely each possible sample outcome (value of the sample statistic) is, once we specify (in our minds, in a "hypothesis") what the population parameter is. We know how much variability to expect, even if the variability itself creates a situation in which we don't know exactly how different any one sample outcome is from the population value.

In other words, we hypothesize or guess "what's in the jar." Once we set up this provisional hypothesis, we can calculate mathematically what the distribution of all possible sample outcomes looks like. If we then draw a real sample, we can determine whether the sample outcome is likely or unlikely under the terms of this hypothesis. If it is not very likely, we use the sample outcome as evidence against our hypothesis—our provisional guess about the jar was probably not true. For example, we might hypothesize that half the tickets in the jar are red. If we then draw a sample of 25 tickets of which only 3 are red, we might think of this sample outcome as evidence against our initial hypothesis. It might be true—we just got a discrepant sample—but we would feel doubtful about it. On the other hand, a sample of 25 tickets in which 13 tickets are red seems more compatible with the initial hypothesis, and we would be less inclined to doubt it.

The Normal Curve

Before we return to the shape and variability of the sampling distribution, I would like to introduce you to a special curve that describes the distribution of many variables, the bell curve or normal curve. It is a continuous probability distribution, that is, it is a "smoothed" version of a histogram that displays frequencies. The horizontal dimension shows the range of values of the variable. The vertical dimension shows the relative frequency of each value. The higher the height of the bar (before we smooth the histogram), the more cases there are for that value of the variable. When this histogram is "smoothed," the width of the bars is shrunk and distribution of frequencies is represented as the area below a single continuous line. This line represents the "frequency polygon" that is smoothed into a curve as the bar width shrinks. The relative frequencies are no longer presented as bars but as probabilities of observing an outcome within an interval between two values of the variable. The total area under the curve is 1, meaning that the probabilities of all the outcomes together is 1 (similar to all the relative frequencies in a frequency distribution adding up to 100%).

There are many such continuous probability distributions possible, but the normal curve is an especially common and important one. It has several characteristics:

- Its mean is equal to its mode and its median. This is the peak or maximum height of the curve.

- It is symmetrical.

- We can standardize a normal curve—convert all the values of the variable to Z-scores. It will then have a mean of 0 and an SD of 1. The total area under the curve is 1.00, representing the sum of all the probabilities for all the cases in the distribution.

- The curve is highest around the mean. In other words, values around the mean of the variable are most probable. It tails off, with lower probabilities for values further away from the mean.

Figure 10: The standardized normal curve

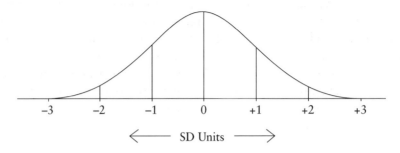

Notes:
- Mean = 0
- Standard deviation = 1
- About 68% of the observations/values/scores are between +1 and −1 standard deviation from the mean
- 95% of the observations/values/scores are between +1.96 and −1.96 standard deviations from the mean (in the diagram, this spread is rounded to +2 and −2)
- 99.7% of the observations/values/scores are between +3 and −3 standard deviations from the mean

The distribution of values for the normal curve has a precise form, in fact:

- 68% of the cases have values between plus or minus one standard deviation from the mean; or to put it more simply, approximately 2/3 of the cases have values within one standard deviation on each side of the mean.

- 95% of the cases have values between plus or minus 1.96 standard deviations from the mean, or approximately two standard deviations on each side of the mean.

- 99% of the cases have values between plus or minus 2.58 standard deviations from the mean.

- 99.7% of the cases have values between plus or minus 3 standard deviations from the mean.

Thinking about the normal curve brings to mind Chebycheff's Inequality. In all distributions, values that are very discrepant from the mean are unlikely. The normal curve is a special type of distribution in which a stronger statement than Chebycheff's Inequality holds true.

Many variables in nature have an approximately normal distribution. For example, people's height and weight are each distributed approximately normally.

But contrary to popular opinion, not everything is distributed normally. For example, income and, even more so, wealth have a skewed distribution with a mode and median that are below the mean, and a long tail at the higher values representing the relatively small numbers of the very rich. Other distributions are also possible, such as bimodal distributions. If well-prepared and poorly prepared students have enrolled for a class, with few "in-between" students, the grade outcomes could form a bimodal distribution. It is essential to realize that, in nature, many variable distributions are possible; not all characteristics are normally distributed for all populations. (I have met professors who believe that all grade distributions must be normal, and cram their classes into this "procrustean bed." Procrustes was a criminal in Greek mythology who forced his victims to sleep on his "average-length" bed, cutting off their feet if they were too tall and stretching them on a rack if they were too short.)

Sampling Distributions and the Normal Curve

A key idea in applied statistics is that the sampling distribution of the mean (and other statistics) **is** very close to a normal distribution when sample size is sufficiently large. We will now look at the concept of sampling distributions in more detail. The sampling distribution is the set of all outcomes—sample statistics, in this case **means**—of simple random samples from a population. Since we replace the cases after drawing a sample, in theory the sampling distribution is infinite. We can picture the histogram of the sampling distribution of the mean. Across the horizontal axis we plot all the possible values for the sample means. The variable plotted horizontally is "values of the sample means." On the vertical axis we plot the relative frequency for that particular sample mean. Since our distribution is infinite, we can smooth it out from a histogram with bars to a continuous probability distribution, a smooth curve. This curve will be a normal curve, **regardless of the distribution of the underlying variable.**

Let's picture ourselves taking all possible random samples of five people from a statistics class, over and over again, and plotting the sample mean height for each of these samples. If we look at this sampling distribution of the mean of heights for samples of size 5, we are just as likely to get a sample of 5 specific tall people as a sample of 5 specific medium height people; but there are fewer ways of getting a tall **mean** height for a sample than of getting a sample mean height that is near the class mean. We can get a tall sample mean only from samples of mostly tall people, whereas there are more ways of getting a sample mean near the class mean. A sample composed of tall and short people whose heights "cancel each other out" would produce a sample mean near the class mean, and so would samples with a lot of medium height people. In many distributions of the underlying variable, there are more cases rather close to the mean to begin with. For example, there are probably more medium height people in the class than there are tall or short people. If the underlying variable (height, in this case) is distributed normally to begin with, then many samples will have a lot of people in them whose heights are near the class mean.

But even if the underlying variable is not normally distributed, the "cancelling out" pattern will insure that the sample mean is "pulled" in towards the population mean. It's like rolling a seven with a pair of dice (lots of combinations add up to seven), compared to rolling snake-eyes or a twelve. Although every face of each die has an equal probability of turning up (as does any batch of N cases in a random sample), there are six combinations that add up to a seven (1 and 6, 2 and 5, 3 and 4, 4 and 3, 5 and 2, 6 and 1) and only one combination that adds up to 2 (1 and 1—snake-eyes) and one combination that adds up to 12 (6 and 6).

We can specify exactly how likely a particular sample outcome is assuming a particular condition in the population, a specified value of the population parameter.

This "intuitive" feeling is what the sampling distribution and the Central Limit Theorem are all about; in the next sections, we will state the main ideas of this important theorem.

The sampling distribution of the proportion, mean, and other statistics is a probability distribution. We cannot say what the outcome of any given sample will be, but we do know exactly what the expected frequencies of these outcomes are in the sampling distribution, the imaginary distribution of all sampling outcomes. We can represent this probability distribution by a bell curve or normal curve.

This curve is a smoothed-out (continuous) histogram of the frequencies expected in the probability distribution.

Please note once again that **this histogram does not represent the distribution of an underlying empirical variable.** It represents the sampling distribution of the mean (for a continuous variable or interval-ratio variable) or proportion (for a 0/1 dichotomous variable).

Sampling Error: Variability of the Sampling Distribution

It is crucial to realize what the histogram means; it is the probability distribution of all sample outcomes in the sampling distribution. The heights represent the frequencies of the outcomes.

The histogram represents the distribution of **sampling error.** "Error" is a confusing term here, since we did not make a mistake in sampling. "Error" is a way of referring to the inherent variability of the sampling process, which does not produce the same result each time. Each sample statistic can be and often is different from the population parameter. When we take random samples from a class and compute sample mean heights to infer the mean height of the class, most of the sample means are a bit "off" from the class (population) mean. They are not "off" because we sampled incorrectly or computed sample means incorrectly. They are "off" because there is inherent variability due to chance effects in the random drawing of the samples. It is these chance effects that constitute "sampling error" and cause concern that we may have, by chance, drawn a sample with a statistic that is quite discrepant from the population mean.

The Central Limit Theorem

The central limit theorem tells us three nice things happen in the probability distribution as sample size increases. They are nice because they help us to understand how much sampling error we are likely to encounter. We state the Central Limit Theorem without proof.

1. **The mean of sample means tends toward the population mean.** The population mean is the expected value of the sampling distribution comprised of all the sample means. For example, if we are looking at a statistics class as a population and drawing samples to infer mean height from it, the mean of the sample means will tend toward the population mean as N gets large. If N is sufficiently large, the mean of the sample means will be very close to the population mean. The mean of the sample means approaches the population mean.

$$\mu_{\overline{X}} \;\rightarrow\; \mu$$

On the left side, $\mu_{\overline{X}}$ represents the mean of all the sample means. As N increases, this value approaches the population mean for the empirical variable (height, weight, etc.). The population mean is represented by μ (*mu*), the symbol on the right side.

2. **The shape of the probability distribution tends toward a normal curve,** with sample outcomes near the population mean being the most frequent—the histogram is highest around the value of the population mean—and outcomes that are different from the population mean being less frequent—the histogram "tails off" towards the two ends. Because we know exactly how the normal curve is distributed, we can specify exactly how probable outcomes are. **The histogram of the sampling distribution of the mean takes on this shape** *even if the distribution of the underlying variable is not normal.*

3. **The least obvious but extremely important part of the Central Limit Theorem is that the SD of the sampling distribution does *not* tend to the SD of the population, but to a *much smaller value.*** Believe it or not, the sampling distribution has a much smaller SD than the SD of the distribution of the variable in the population and the sample. The SD of the sampling distribution of the mean is called the "standard error," and its formula is this: sigma divided by the square root of the sample size. In other words, whatever the SD is for the population divide it by the square root of sample size. As you can see, the bigger the sample, the smaller the standard error. What this implies is that the sampling distribution gets very "tight" around the population mean when sample size is reasonably large. In terms of our histogram, it implies that

sample outcomes that are more than one standard error from the mean are unlikely and that sample outcomes more than two standard errors from the mean are very unlikely.

$$\sigma_{\overline{X}} \quad \rightarrow \quad \frac{\sigma}{\sqrt{N}}$$

The standard deviation of the sampling distribution of the mean is shown on the left side and is represented by $\sigma_{\overline{X}}$. It is the amount of variability in the distribution of all the sample means (for a given sample size, N). As N increases, this value approaches the standard deviation of the empirical variable in the population divided by the sample size. This value is called the standard error of the mean.

Here then is the answer to our question about variability in sampling. We can calculate exactly how much variability to expect in sampling by a mathematical formula, which we presented with an intuitive argument but no formal proof. The variability—the standard deviation—of the sampling distribution can be calculated as sigma divided by the square root of sample size. If we don't know sigma (the population standard deviation) we have to estimate it from the sample standard deviation.

- Standard error = sigma divided by square root of sample size

$$SE = \frac{\sigma}{\sqrt{N}}$$

- Estimated standard error = sample standard deviation divided by square root of sample size.

$$\text{The estimated } SE = \frac{s}{\sqrt{N}}$$

While there is some disagreement about what a "reasonably large" sample is, it's surprisingly small: When $N = 30$, the sampling distribution is already pretty normal and "tight" around the population mean; when $N = 100$ it's really a nice bell curve.

Math Thoughts

You may be wondering why the sampling distribution of the sample means always converges on the normal distribution as N gets large. Why is the Central Limit Theorem true? This question can be answered in several ways.

We can continue to give an intuitive and empirical answer as we did earlier in the chapter. Try a few examples of sampling distributions of sample means (for variables like class height or commuting times) and see how the "big values" tend to "cancel out" the "little values" in most samples, driving the outcome towards the population mean. As the sample size gets bigger, the "outlier" values are ever more likely to be "swamped" by the weight of numbers and the sample outcome is "pulled in" towards the mean. I'm putting a lot of phrases in quotation marks because they are intuitive and not very precise. We could look at a lot of examples and feel comfortable with the repeated results, but many people would not be satisfied with this intuitive and empirical line of thought and would wonder if there is a counter-example lurking somewhere to refute these fuzzy notions.

Alternatively, you may prefer math proofs and you may want to look at mathematically sophisticated and rigorous arguments. In that case, check out the books in the bibliography, giving special attention to proofs of two related theorems: Chebycheff's Inequality, which concerns the probability of values that are discrepant from the mean of a distribution, and the Central Limit Theorem itself, which is about the shape and variability of sampling distributions.

Finally, we might turn to a more philosophical view, contemplating why, "in the nature of things," random processes produce regular patterns that are fixed and predictable. Even though each separate event is random and independent of the others, the overall pattern is stable and predictable. Randomness is fascinating, and these considerations are now increasingly linked to the exciting field of chaos theory (Beltrami, 1999). Mathematicians are looking at how the iteration of determined processes can suddenly produce a "flip" or phase transition into randomness as well as vice versa, when a random process produces a fixed and determined outcome. See the bibliography for books on these subjects.

In any case, a reminder is in order: Here (and in most applied statistics books), the Central Limit Theorem was stated without proof.

The Central Limit Theorem, and especially its third part, about the standard error, tips us off to two important characteristics of sampling.

One is obvious: A bigger sample will give better results in the sense that the standard error will be lower and the sample outcome is more likely to be near the population mean. Note, however, that the standard error decreases as the square root of sample size, not as a linear function of sample size. For instance, if we were to quadruple sample size from 400 to 1600, the standard error would be only halved,

from $\frac{s}{20}$ to $\frac{s}{40}$.

The second is a little trickier, but makes sense both intuitively and by looking at the formula: The less variation there is in the population the better our inference will tend to be. If the original population distribution has values that are tightly clustered around the mean (like heights of a synchronized swim team), the sampling distribution has a lower standard error and our sample outcome is more likely to be significant for a given sample size, or to put it a bit differently, we can make a better estimate than if the standard deviation is large. Similarly for proportions: if the population proportion is around 50% so that the population variance $p(1-p)$ is at a maximum, we need a larger sample for a good estimate. However, if the proportion is near 0% or 100%, it's easier to infer the population proportion. This makes obvious sense when you think about election poll results; an election is most often "too close to call" in hotly contested districts, not safe ones.

Summary: Let me repeat the main ideas in a slightly different way. **Regardless of the distribution of the variable in the population, as the number sampled or sample size (N) gets larger, the sampling distribution rapidly approaches a normal distribution.** A normal curve is symmetrical; its mean, median, and mode are equal, and it has two long tails. The histogram in which we plot the sample outcomes (sample statistics) looks like a bell curve. Sample outcomes (e.g., means or proportions) near the population mean (or proportion) are most likely. **The more "different" a sample outcome is from the population value (which is the expected value of the sampling distribution) the lower its frequency.** In other words, the less likely it will be to come up when we sample. **Extremely discrepant or deviant values of the sample statistic are possible, but *not likely*.**

Statistical inference refers to the probability distribution, the sampling distribution and its variability, represented by the normal curve. We are always asking the question, "How likely is this sample outcome in the distribution of outcomes of all random samples of size N?"

Since the probability distribution approaches a normal curve, we know how to answer this question. About 68% of the sample outcomes will lie between −1 and +1 standard deviations from the population mean; 95% will be between −1.96 and +1.96 standard deviations from the mean, and 99% of the outcomes will be between −2.58 and +2.58 standard deviations from the mean. Notice that we have moved the whole operation over onto the Z-distribution; when we look at the sampling distribution we always construct the histogram in terms of Z-scores (standard deviation units), not the measurement units of the variable in question.

The "variable" that is plotted along the x-axis in the histogram is not a variable like height or weight measured on actual people; the variable represents all the sample means. The cases are not people, but samples. The vertical dimension charts "how many cases" (samples) have a particular value for their sample mean. Many cases (samples) have a sample mean that is near the population mean; few cases (samples) have a sample mean that is very different from the population mean.

Note that the standard deviation of the sampling distribution is the standard error, not the population or sample SD.

A final "believe it or not" note: Population size doesn't matter! If the sample size is more than 10% of the total population, the standard error is indeed slightly reduced, but the exact size of the population doesn't matter and is often either unknown or "infinite" in a vague way—for example, all the people who might ever be exposed to AIDS. From the formula, we can see the standard error is based on two values, the standard deviation and sample size. Population size is not in the formula.

Let's look at some examples of sampling distributions and the Central Limit Theorem at work:

Figure 11: Sampling distributions of means of samples $N = 2$, $N = 4$, and $N = 30$ from three different types of populations

These figures illustrate the Central Limit Theorem by showing how, regardless of the form of the parent population, the sampling distribution of means approaches normality as N increases.

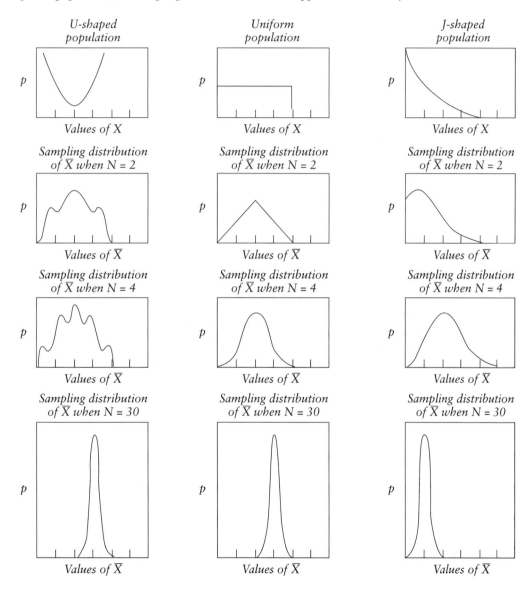

Reproduced by permission of McGraw-Hill from *Fundamentals of Social Statistics* (Elifson et al., 1998, figure 13.2, p. 306).

Underlying Distributions and Sampling Distributions

IMAGINARY HISTOGRAMS

The first page of graphics (Figure 11) shows how rapidly and dramatically the distribution of sample means takes on a normal shape as N increases, regardless of the distribution of the underlying variable. Even very non-normal variable distributions—the U-shape, the uniform distribution, and the ski-jump—produce sampling distributions of the means that are definitely normal when N = 30. Notice the symmetrical bell shape of the sampling distribution histogram for N = 30 and its "tight" compression around the population mean, reflecting its small standard error. Remember that every "case" in this histogram is a sample. The relative frequencies of samples are charted vertically. The variable value is the sample mean, charted horizontally.

A (FICTITIOUS) EMPIRICAL EXAMPLE: YEARS OF SCHOOLING

In the next graphic (Figure 12), we see at the bottom the sampling distribution for N = 400 for the town's mean years of schooling. The mean of the sampling distribution is the same as the mean years of schooling for the real population. The SD of the sampling distribution—the standard error—is, however, only .2, while for the real variable in the real population, it is 4. In the middle of the page, we see the years of education of one simple random sample of 400. The sample statistic is indeed a bit "off" from the population parameter (11.6 years of schooling rather than 12 years). The sample's distribution looks pretty similar to that of the population, as we can see by comparing the two upper histograms; neither looks at all like the distribution of the sample means, which has a normal shape and a much smaller SD.

Figure 12: Educational histograms

The Town

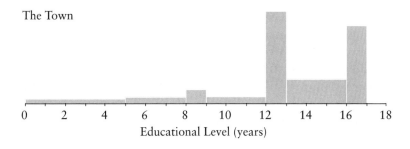

Educational Level (years)

The Sample

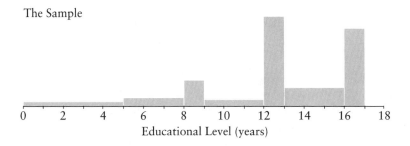

Educational Level (years)

Probability Histogram for the Sample Average

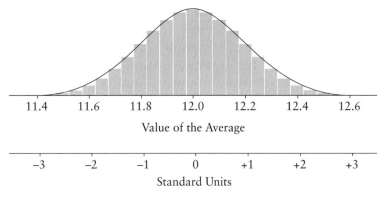

Value of the Average

Standard Units

The top panel shows the distribution of educational level among people age 25 or over in the whole town. The middle panel shows the distribution of educational level in the sample. These are histograms for data. The bottom panel shows the probability histogram for the average of 400 draws from the box; it is close to the normal curve. The endpoint convention for the data histograms: the class interval 12-13, for example, includes all the people who finished 12 years of schooling but not 13—high school graduates who did not finish a year of college. The average in the town is 12.0 years, and the SD is 4.0 years; in the sample, the corresponding figures are 11.6 and 4.1. (From *Statistics*, second edition by David Freedman, Robert Pisani, Roger Purves, and Ani Adhikari. Copyright 1991 by W.W. Norton & Company, Inc. Used by permission of W.W. Norton and Company, Inc.)

REVISITING OUR FIRST EXAMPLE—BOOKS OWNED BY STUDENTS

The Central Limit Theorem helps us understand the example at the beginning of the chapter about the mean number of books owned by students at a university. The sampling distribution of the means for all random samples of 100 students (or 1000 such samples, to be a little more realistic in the empirical world) can be approximated by a normal-shaped histogram. The mean of the sample means is 75 books (equal to the population parameter). The standard error, the standard deviation of the sampling distribution, is $\frac{36}{10}$. In this formula for the standard error, 36 is the population standard deviation, and 10 is the square root of sample size ($N = 100$). Notice the standard error is **considerably less** than the population standard deviation.

From our knowledge of the normal distribution, we now can say that about 68% of our sample means will fall between plus or minus one standard error of the expected value of 75 books. In other words, slightly over two-thirds of the sample means will be between (75 - 3.6) and (75 + 3.6), i.e., between 71.4 books and 78.6 books. Also, 95% of the sample outcomes (the sample means) will be, roughly speaking, within plus or minus two standard errors of the mean—between 68 and 82 books. (For exactness freaks, it is actually the case that 95% of the sample means will be within plus or minus 1.96 standard errors of the mean; in other words between 67.944 and 82.056.) The relatively small value of the standard error is the reason that we were able to draw a histogram that showed most sample means being pretty close to 75.

CLASS EXERCISE: MEAN HEIGHT OF THE CLASS AND SAMPLE MEANS

We could now carry out a class exercise on an empirical approximation of the sampling distribution of a mean, for instance for class height. First, we would chart the distribution for small samples and larger samples and describe what we see. This result is only an "empirical approximation" because we are not going to calculate sample means for an infinite number of samples! You will be surprised how samples of only ten people have means that are within a few centimetres (or an inch or two) of the class mean height. We can carry out a similar exercise for the sampling distribution of a proportion, such as the % of men and women in a class.

The Sampling Distribution of a Proportion

So far we have focused on estimating a population mean from a sample mean. Similar reasoning applies to estimating a population proportion from the proportion in a sample. Here we are concerned with proportions that represent the values of a dichotomous variable. Examples include became ill or did not become ill (if we are testing a vaccine), died or survived (for a clinical test of a medical treatment), and favour or oppose a public policy (in an opinion poll).

Let's think about the results of a survey at a big university to determine the number of smokers on campus. For example, if the population is 40,000 students at the University of Toronto and the proportion of smokers in this population is 20%, we can picture all the random samples of size N that can be drawn. There are a lot of them. With replacement, there is an infinite number. Remember that the sampling distribution of size N for a statistic like a proportion (or a mean) is a huge imaginary object. It exists only in our minds, not in the real world.

Now think about all the possible sample outcomes for the proportion. Some samples will have no smokers in them at all. Some will include a few smokers, but less than 20%. Some will have more than 20% who smoke. A few will have a lot more than 20%, and, unless we make N very large, we will get a sample that is 100% smokers. Notice that if N is bigger than 8000 our sample will always have at least one non-smoker in it.

In real life we can't possibly draw all these samples; we usually only draw one of them.

OK: Think about all these possible samples and the outcome of each for a moment, for a given N. Now think about all the possible samples and their outcomes as N gets bigger.

You can see ("intuitively") that if N is small, there may be quite a lot of samples that have outcomes different from the population parameter of 20%. For example, if our samples had only two people in them, we would find quite a few in which both (100%) were smokers. And we would only come up with the values, 100%, 50%, 50%, and 0%, which are not very good estimates of the population parameter, the true population value of 20%. If we drew a two-person sample to find out how many U of Toronto students smoke, we might end up making a rather incorrect inference. But if our samples are large—let's say 500 or more people—we feel ("intuitively") that we would be less likely to get, just by the bad luck of the draw, a sample composed entirely of smokers, given that there are only 8000 smokers on campus. It's pretty likely that a random sample of 500 people would include some non-smokers, and, in fact, a random sample that large probably has a proportion of smokers that is not too terribly different from the true population proportion of 20%.

When we look at the distribution of the values of proportions, we use the following notation. The proportion for one of the two outcomes—sometimes referred to as the "success" (for example, stayed healthy, survived, favours the policy) is p, and the proportion for the other outcome (got sick, died, does not favour the policy) is q. The sum of p and q is always equal to 1. In other words: $p + q = 1$. So $q = 1 - p$. The probabilities of something happening or something not happening add up to 1, certainty. Something either happens or it doesn't happen.

We can observe p and q for a sample of n cases, and from this observation, we will try to estimate pi, the proportion of successes in the population. A simple example, which we will explore in more detail below, would be using sample data to estimate the proportion of students at a large university who favour a foreign language requirement for graduation.

The sampling distribution for a proportion is somewhat different from that for a mean. It takes a form called the binomial distribution. We saw this distribution when we looked at the number of heads (and tails) expected in n tosses of a coin. All tosses are independent of each other, the probability of a head is p, and the probability of a tail is q.

If the coin is fair, $p = q = \dfrac{1}{2}$. In this case, for 100 tosses (n = 100), the

expected number of heads is 50. But in a set of 100 tosses we would not necessarily get 50 heads. Conceivably, we could get all heads (100 heads) or all tails (100 tails), although these outcomes do not seem very likely. Let's imagine repeating the sets of 100 tosses over and over again, for a huge number of times. For each set of 100, we count how many heads came up, and we keep track of these results; we chart the results in a histogram. The horizontal axis shows values from 0 (no heads came up for the 100 tosses) to 100 (all the 100 tosses were heads). This range of values represents the possible sample outcomes. In the vertical dimension we chart how often—in how many of the samples of 100—we got a particular result. We would see that the histogram peaks around 50 as the expected value for the number of heads in 100 tosses, and that most samples of 100 tosses ended up with values fairly near 50 heads. You and your friends can while away an hour or so doing this experiment, but it is a bit tedious to do a lot of samples with 100 tosses for each sample. Do not confuse the number of tosses in a sample—sample size = 100—with the number of samples whose outcomes you record. You would find very few, if any, samples that had sample outcomes of 0 heads or 100 heads.

As sample size increases, the distribution of sample outcomes (the number of heads in this case, or more generally, the number of "successes") approaches the normal distribution. Even if the proportion is not 50/50, if p and q are not equal to each other as in the toss of a fair coin, but tilted like 90/10, the binomial distribution approaches the normal distribution, as long as both np and nq are at least 5.

Most of the sample outcomes will have a proportion of "successes" that is near the population proportion. Sample proportions that are "off" from this value will be less likely, just as sample means that are very discrepant from the population mean are less likely.

- For the distribution of sample proportions, the expected value, the expected number of "successes" out of the total, is *mu = np*.

- The variance is *npq*.

- The standard deviation is the positive square root of *npq*.

    Here are the same equations in symbols:

    n = sample size

    $\mu = np$

    $s^2 = npq$

    $s = \sqrt{npq}$

Let's return to our example of the foreign language requirement. Let's pretend we know the population parameter is 60% in favour of the requirement. In real research, we wouldn't know that; it is what we are trying to estimate. We are going to take a very large number of samples of 100 students and, for each sample, record how many of the 100 students favour the requirement (the "successes"). We will record all these sample outcomes and then chart them in a histogram. The expected value of the sampling distribution is np = 100 $\times$ .60 = 60. In other words, the expected value is that 60 out of the 100 students will say "yes" to the requirement.

The **variance** is npq = 100 $\times$ .60 $\times$ .40 = 100 $\times$ .24 = 24.
The **standard deviation** is the square root of 24 = 4.8989 (nearly 5).

After we plot a very large number—preferably an infinite number—of sample outcomes, we will see the distribution approach a normal curve. This means that 68% of the sample outcomes will be within plus or minus one standard deviation of the expected value. In other words, about 68% of the sample outcomes will fall, roughly, between 55 and 65 students saying "yes." And 95% of the sample outcomes will be within plus or minus two standard deviations of the expected value of 60 students. In these samples, there will be proportions between 50 and 70 students (roughly) saying "yes." In other words, with samples of 100 students we are not likely to find a lot of samples with outcomes that are very far "off" from 60. This is really rather amazing! We don't even know the size of the entire student body, and yet a single random sample of 100 students would allow us to say with a good deal of confidence whether or not a majority favoured the requirement.

Warning!
Be very careful here.

There are two different proportions in this example. One is the proportion of students who favour the language requirement, either in a sample or in the student body—the population—as a whole. This proportion is the answer to an empirical question: "What proportion of people is in favour of...?" The other proportion in the problem is the proportion of sample outcomes that falls within a certain number of standard deviations of the expected value. We calculate this proportion from the near-normal distribution of sample outcomes. This proportion is the answer to a mathematical question: "What is the probability distribution of sample outcomes? How likely is a discrepant sample outcome that is this many standard deviations "off" from the expected value?" Do NOT confuse these two completely different types of proportions when using statistical inference to estimate a proportion.

From this example, we can see that if we work with samples of 100 we are unlikely to be extremely far "off" in our estimate. But if we go to a higher sample size, say 1600, the standard deviation would be relatively smaller (though larger in absolute terms) and our estimate would be better. Here is the math:

Sample size: $n = 1600$.

Expected value: $np = 1600 \times .60 = 960$. We would expect 960 out of 1600 students to say "yes."

Standard deviation: Square root of npq = square root of $(1600 \times .60 \times .40) = 19.6$

Notice that relative to the range of sample outcomes, this is a smaller standard deviation than the standard deviation for samples of 100. We are now really "closing in" on the expected value. Very few samples would be "off" by a lot, and it is unlikely that we would get a sample that would lead us to estimate a majority opposed to the language requirement, when in reality, there is a 60% majority in favour of it. As an exercise, you can draw the histogram for $n = 1600$, and you will see that 95% of sample outcomes will be (roughly) between 920 and 1000.

Finally, let's see what happens when the population proportion is really tilted—let's say 90% are in favour and only 10% opposed. When we use sample data to try to estimate this value, with samples of 100, we find the following:

The expected value: $np = 100 \times .90 = 90$ students out of 100 in favour.

Standard deviation: Square root of npq = square root of $(100 \times .90 \times .10)$ = square root of $9 = 3$.

Notice that this is a smaller standard deviation, for samples of 100, than when $p = q = \frac{1}{2}$. This makes intuitive sense; there is maximum variability in a situation where there is a 50/50 split. These are the situations that are "hardest to call" in an election poll. It is extremely unlikely that, when a population is split 90/10, we would get a sample that would lead us to make a mistake about which side is going to win. A mistaken estimate is most likely when the split is near 50/50.

At this point, we have looked at sampling distributions of means and proportions. Now we are ready to apply the concept of sampling distribution in our research, with a couple more considerations.

THE *T*-DISTRIBUTION

Notice that to compute the standard error we needed to know sigma, the population SD. In real life, we usually don't know it and have to estimate it from the sample SD. When this is the case, we can't use the *Z*-distribution but have to use a more conservative one called Student's *t* or just "*t*" for short. (It got this name because W. Gossett, the guy who thought it up, worked for Guinness Brewery and wasn't supposed to publish math papers that might have given away trade secrets, so he had to use the alias "Student.") "Conservative" means that it is less peaked at the middle around the mean and fatter in the tails: they drop off less quickly than in the normal *Z*-distribution. The *t*-distribution is almost identical to the *Z*-distribution once sample size is large. Most software packages compute *t* rather than *Z* for data analysis, assuming that we do not know the population SD but only the sample SD. Most research reports *t*-tests.

Other Probability Distributions: Finally, we note that the basic logic of a probability distribution works not only for means and proportions but also for fancier statistics derived from squares of *Z*-scores, the chi-square statistic, and the ratios of chi-squares or the *F*-test. We will use them when we look at the relationship of two or more variables. All of these distributions ultimately are based on the *Z*-distribution of sampling error and the logic of sampling distributions that we have just discussed. The basic question is always this: How likely is this outcome (sample statistic) in the sampling distribution, given a certain value of the parameter in the population?

Part II: Doing Statistical Inference

The Logic of Statistical Inference

This section of the chapter presents a brief overview of how to go from sample data to a conclusion about a population. Imagine that we have identified a population—it might be a very large, vague, "infinite" one, like all people who may ever be exposed to measles, or a more clearly specified one, like all registered voters in the state of Illinois in 2005. We have selected a random sample and collected data from it—observations. How do we decide what conclusion we can draw about the population from the sample observations? There are two ways of doing statistical inference.

1. Confidence intervals: Using our observed sample data, we construct an interval that probably contains the population parameter we are trying to estimate (usually a mean or a proportion). We cannot say with certainty that the interval contains the population parameter. We can only say that a high percentage of intervals constructed in this manner (usually 95% or 99%) contain the population parameter. We use our knowledge of the Central Limit Theorem, the standard error, and the normal curve to construct the interval. For example, in a sample survey of smoking at a large university, we draw a random sample in which 22% of the respondents are smokers. We construct an interval around 22% (a "margin of error" in layman's terms) that probably contains the true population parameter. If we make the width of the interval plus or minus two standard errors, we know that 95% of the random samples we draw in order to construct the interval will produce an interval that contains the population proportion of smokers. Only 5% of the random samples will have outcomes that are so discrepant that the interval we construct around the sample outcome will fail to contain the population value.

2. Hypothesis testing: We make believe that the population parameter has a certain value, and we then decide whether our sample statistic (based on our observations) is or is not compatible with this value. The make-believe statement about the population parameter is called the **null hypothesis**. Using our knowledge of the Central Limit Theorem and the normal curve, we look at the probability that the sample statistic is an outcome in a sample drawn from a population in which the null hypothesis is true. If it is very unlikely that this sample outcome came from a population in which the null hypothesis is true, we reject the null hypothesis. However, we can never rule it out completely because there is a small probability that it is true.

In either case, we can think about the process of statistical inference with the following image. The characteristics of the population are true but unknown to us. Between the population and us, there is a huge wall. We cannot see the population; we can only guess or infer its characteristics from the observed data based on a random sample. Usually time and money permit us to look at only one sample of all the possible simple random samples we could draw.

The sampling distribution for a given sample size N is a series of windowless rooms. Each room corresponds to one possible sample. We are allowed to enter one of these rooms (our sample). We cannot see the population from this room; all we can see is a poster on the wall that displays the sample statistic that corresponds to the population parameter we want to infer (mean, proportion, etc.). If we had entered a different room—drawn a different simple random sample (SRS) in the sampling distribution—the sample statistic on the wall poster would probably have shown a different value.

If we are unlucky, random chance "handed us" a sample outcome that is not very probable in the sampling distribution, one of those outcomes in the tails of the normal curve, and then our conclusions from the sample observations (the sample statistic) will not be very good estimates of what is true about the population parameter. These estimates would lead to the construction of a confidence interval that fails to "catch" the population parameter and to a rejection of a null hypothesis that is really true. However, we already know from the Central Limit Theorem that these misleading "tail" sample outcomes are not very likely. They have a low probability.

Knowing the one sample statistic displayed in our room and the characteristics of probability distributions, what can we do to reach a conclusion about the population parameter?

Let's spend a little more time going over the logic of the two statistical inference procedures and then move on to an actual application called a *t*-test.

Confidence Intervals

We draw a simple random sample and obtain the statistic that we will use to estimate the population parameter, usually a mean or a proportion. We place our sample outcome in the middle of the interval and construct a confidence interval around it, a "margin of error." We identify a confidence level for this interval, usually 95% or 99%, meaning that, in the large number of samples we might use to construct an interval, the true population value will fall into the interval 95% (or 99%) of the time. The procedure, if it were repeated over and over again, would "catch" the population value in 95% (or 99%) of the attempts. We know that 95% of sample outcomes fall within about + or – 2 standard errors from the population parameter, and 99% of them fall within + or – 2.58 standard errors. We decide in advance if we want a 95% confidence level or a 99% confidence level. (Of course, other levels are possible, but these are the two most commonly selected.)

To say that we are constructing an interval means that we have to specify an upper and lower limit for the interval, the two numbers that mark the top and bottom end of the interval.

Here is how we do it.

We pick a Z-score that matches the number of + or – standard errors within which 95% (or 99%) of the sample outcomes will fall. If we pick 95% as our confidence level, we have to pick Z = 1.96 for the Z-score. (We can round off to 2, if we like.) If we pick 99% as our confidence level, our Z-score has to be 2.58. A Z-score of 2.58 means that over a vast number of samples, only 1% of the sample outcomes produce an interval that fails to "catch" the population mean because the sample outcome is too discrepant from the population mean. Only sample outcomes that were in the "tails" will produce intervals that fail to catch the population value, and we know these discrepant sample outcomes are quite unlikely.

Notice that the higher the confidence level, the wider the confidence interval has to be, all other things (variability and sample size) being equal. A 99% confidence level requires a wider confidence interval than a 95% confidence level. There is a trade-off between confidence level and confidence interval width. We would like the interval to be as narrow as possible, but making it narrower lowers the confidence level—like making a smaller bull's eye on a target—making it less likely that our procedure will "catch" the true value.

We use four numbers to construct the interval.

- $\overline{X}$ or p is the sample mean or proportion, the observed data we use to mark the middle of our interval.

- Sigma (σ) is the standard deviation of the population. We usually have to estimate it from our observed sample data. It would be better if we knew the population standard deviation, but usually we do not know it.

- Sigma divided by the square root of N, $\left(\dfrac{\sigma}{\sqrt{N}}\right)$, is the standard error, the standard deviation divided by the square root of sample size. We designate it as SE in the formula. It is estimated by $\dfrac{s}{\sqrt{N}}$ since we usually have to use the sample standard deviation, not knowing the SD for the population.

- Z is the number of standard errors that corresponds to our desired confidence level, usually 95% or 99%.

Using this information we compute the upper and lower confidence limit for an interval centred on the sample statistic that we observed.

$$UCL = \overline{X} + (Z)(SE)$$

$$LCL = \overline{X} - (Z)(SE)$$

We set the sample mean at the centre of the interval.

We pick a Z (number of standard deviation units) to match our confidence level, corresponding to how much we will accept in the tails of the distribution. If we pick $Z = 1.96$, it means that over a large number of repetitions, only 5% of the samples will produce intervals that miss the population value. Only sample outcomes in the tails of the sampling distribution, beyond $Z = +$ or $- 1.96$, will produce intervals that don't "catch" the population mean. If we pick $Z = 2.58$, it means that only 1% of the samples will produce intervals that miss the population value; but note that if $Z = 2.58$, the confidence interval is wider than for $Z = 1.96$. The Z specifies the number of standard deviation units of the sampling distribution that we are using to construct the interval. A standard deviation unit for this distribution is the standard error $\left(\dfrac{\sigma}{\sqrt{N}}\right)$, which is computed by sigma divided by the square root of sample size. Z is a number that specifies a number of standard errors and is associated with the probability of a sample outcome being within that many standard errors of the population parameter that we are trying to "catch" in the interval. As noted above, since we do not generally know the population SD (sigma), we have to estimate it by the sample SD and then use a t-distribution rather than the normal distribution. We also have to do this if our sample size is small, and computer software practically always uses the t-distribution for confidence intervals.

This formula produces an interval centred on the sample value; it has an upper and a lower bound. We are saying that, when we construct an interval this way, using the sample mean, in 95% (or 99%) of such constructions, the population mean will be in this interval. We won't, however, know if it is or isn't in any one case.

Look at the formula and notice how it supports two intuitive conclusions.

- A large N (large sample size) decreases the interval width, for a given confidence level.

- Low variability (a small sigma, population SD, usually estimated by the sample SD) decreases the interval width for a given confidence level. If the population is very varied it is harder to come up with a narrow interval—it will take a larger sample—than if it is very uniform.

Let's look at a couple of very simple examples.

The first example is for estimating a population mean by constructing a confidence interval. How long does it take workers in a widget factory to assemble a widget?

We find that for a random sample of 100 workers, the mean time for widget assembly is 10 minutes. To make the problem a little simpler, let's pretend that we know the population standard deviation and that it is 3 minutes, although typically we would have to estimate it from sample data and then use the *t*-distribution, rather than the *Z*-distribution.

- $\overline{X}$ = 10 minutes.

- Sigma (σ) = 3 minutes.

- $SE = \dfrac{3}{10}$ (standard deviation divided by square root of sample size).

- Z = 1.96 (here we specify the number of standard errors in the sampling distribution that includes 95% of sample outcomes).

- $UCL = 10 + (\dfrac{3}{10})(1.96) = 10 + .588 = 10.588$ minutes

- $LC = 10 - (\dfrac{3}{10})(1.96) = 10 - .588 = 9.412$ minutes

So we are saying that it is very likely that the true mean time for assembling a widget is somewhere between 9.412 and 10.588 minutes. Can we be sure the true mean time (the population parameter) is in this interval? No, but with this method, only 5% of the intervals constructed from data based on random samples will fail to include the population parameter.

If we wanted a 99% confidence level, our constructed interval has to be wider. There is a trade-off between confidence level and width. The more confident we want to be (high % for the confidence level), the wider the interval has to be. We would like the interval to be as narrow as possible, but a narrower interval means a lower probability (confidence level) that it includes the population parameter.

- High confidence level, but a wide interval: I am sure Professor X will be in the office sometime this year.

- Low confidence level, but a narrow interval: I hope Professor X will be in the office between 3:30 and 4:00 today, but I am doubtful.

Let's see what happens in this example when we decide on a 99% confidence level.

- $\overline{X}$ = 10 minutes.

- Sigma (σ) = 3 minutes.

- $SE = \dfrac{3}{10}$.

- Z = 2.58 (This interval is based on the number of standard errors within which 99% of sample outcomes fall).

- $UCL = 10 + (\dfrac{3}{10})(2.58) = 10.774$ minutes

- $LCL = 10 - (\dfrac{3}{10})(2.58) = 9.336$ minutes

Note that we are now more confident that our interval contains the population parameter, but the interval had to be wider, and therefore less precise.

Our third example will be the construction of a confidence interval for a proportion, a very common application in election polls.

Let's say we want a 95% confidence level.

In the simple random sample of 900 voters in a two-candidate election we find that 54% support Candidate Q.

- P = .54 (We convert the percentage into a proportion expressed as a decimal fraction).

- $S = \sqrt{(.54)(.46)} = .498$ (by definition of the standard deviation of a proportion).

- $SE = \dfrac{.498}{\sqrt{900}} = \dfrac{.498}{30} = .0165$

- $UCL = .54 + (.0165)(1.96) = .57234$ or 57.23%

- $LCL = .54 - (.0165)(1.96) = .50766$ or 50.77%

In layman's terms, the margin of error is plus or minus 3.23%. In this case, we would predict a victory for candidate Q. Even the Lower Confidence Limit is over 50%, though not by a lot. If 50% had fallen into the interval, we would have been forced to say, "The race is too close to call."

Notice the following conclusions about this procedure; they should make sense intuitively, and you can also check them by looking at the formula.

- Larger sample size gives a narrower—better!—interval, all other things being equal.

- Low variability—a low standard deviation or a proportion near 0 or 1—gives us a narrower interval.

- Selecting a lower confidence level allows us to construct a narrower interval.

Hypothesis Testing (The Null Hypothesis and *T*-tests)

In this method of statistical inference, we make believe that a certain value prevails in the population. We set the population parameter to a certain value in a statement called the null hypothesis, usually represented by the symbol H_0. We then decide if our sample statistic is or is not compatible with this value. We ask how probable it is that the sample statistic is an outcome in a sample drawn from a population in which the null hypothesis is true. If it is very unlikely, we reject the null hypothesis, but we can never rule it out completely. There is always a small risk that it might be true and that our sample outcome was an "extreme" outcome in the tails of the sampling distribution.

One statistics text puts it this way: "In drawing an inference we first hypothesize that a population has a mean equal to some value, *mu* or μ. If the discrepancy between the observed sample mean and the hypothesized population mean is too large—that is, if it is too 'deviant' to have come from a population with a mean of *mu*—we reject the hypothesis about the value of the population mean, *mu*." (George Bohrnstedt and David Knoke, *Statistics for Social Data Analysis*, Itasca, IL: Peacock Publishers, 1994, p. 81).

The discrepancy between the observed sample data and the hypothesized population parameter is calculated by a **test statistic**. If the value of the test statistic is extreme, it is evidence against the null hypothesis—it is unlikely that such a discrepant sample outcome would happen if the null hypothesis were true about the population. We then feel relatively "safe" in rejecting the null hypothesis. Yet there is a risk that the null hypothesis was true because the discrepant sample outcome was just an "extreme" value in the sampling distribution. In this case our rejection would be a mistake, technically referred to as Type I (or alpha) error. Type I error is rejecting a null hypothesis that is true. Type II (or beta) error is failing to reject a null hypothesis that is, in fact, false.

If the test statistic's value is not extreme or discrepant in the sampling distribution, we interpret the result to mean that there was a high probability of obtaining this sample outcome in the sampling distribution from a population in which the null hypothesis is true. In this case, we cannot reject the null hypothesis.

Here are the steps of hypothesis testing as most researchers go through them.

Our procedure is designed to answer this question: Is the observed situation in the sample a probable sample outcome when samples are drawn from a population in which the null hypothesis is true?

The first step is to set our "alpha" level, the acceptable risk level for Type I error. This level is almost always conventionally set at .05 or $\frac{5}{100}$. Few research journals will publish results with an alpha level of higher than .05. This level of risk is also referred to as the level of significance of the results. We want this risk to be very, very low. Setting acceptable risk of Type I error at a low level keeps us from confusing random sampling variability with a real difference between our observed data and the values specified in the null hypothesis.

For example, if 80% of an unvaccinated control group survived Ebola fever and 81% of the vaccinated group survived, we would be rash to assert that the vaccine makes a real difference in survival. Unless the sample is very large, this small amount of difference in survival rates could well be due to sampling error, to variability in sample outcomes, and not due to a true difference in survival rates between the vaccinated and the unvaccinated. There is a high probability that the vaccine does not really improve survival rates.

The low risk of Type I error required in empirical research is similar to the concept of "guilty beyond reasonable doubt" in jurisprudence. In Anglo-American criminal procedure, we have to accept (or "fail to reject") the null hypothesis of innocence unless we have very powerful evidence against it. The "innocent until proven guilty" null hypothesis is based on the idea that evidence of guilt often has a random character. For instance, eyewitnesses are often confused about the perpetrator's identity, and material evidence may be ambiguous. Someone may look like the perpetrator without being the perpetrator; someone may have been near the scene of the crime without having committed it. A verdict of guilty can be reached only when the evidence is overwhelming and coherent beyond the possibility that eyewitnesses or detectives misinterpreted random events as evidence of guilt. In the same way, statistical significance requires a level "beyond reasonable doubt" to conclude that an observation is not just the product of variability in sample outcomes, the random play of sampling error. Thus, the alpha level is set very low—conventionally at .05. The observed results must be very discrepant from the value specified in the null hypothesis in order for us to be able to reject the null hypothesis. Only in 5% of random samples drawn from a population in which the null hypothesis is true will we get an outcome with **this great** a discrepancy from the value specified in the null hypothesis.

The .05 cut-off level is just a research convention, not a law of nature. See Sweet and Grace-Martin, *Data Analysis with SPSS* (2003) for an insightful discussion of how one might use a different cut-off in situations such as assessing health effects of a nuclear reactor, where "weight of evidence" rather than the stringent "beyond reasonable doubt" might be used to make decisions or set policy. In these situations, it might be better to err on the side of safety and set a higher alpha level, a higher risk of mistakenly concluding that there are effects of the reactor in a situation in which the higher rates observed in the data are just the result of sampling error. Furthermore, statistical significance should not be confused with "social significance" or importance. Remember, it is just a defense against confusing random variability in sample outcomes with real differences.

Type II error is the mistake of failing to reject a null hypothesis that is not true. In other words, the observed result is not just due to sampling variability, but we mistakenly treat it as if it were. To continue the analogy with criminal trials, Type II error is like acquitting a guilty defendant. We have mistakenly interpreted the evidence as being just coincidental. Therefore, we failed to convict a person who is actually guilty, that is, a person about whom the null hypothesis of innocence is not true. As in jurisprudence, in statistical inference, we give priority to avoiding Type I error (mistaken rejection of a true null hypothesis; conviction of an innocent person) over avoiding Type II error (mistaken failure to reject a false null hypothesis; failing to convict a guilty person).

The second step is to specify the null hypothesis. It is a hypothetical statement about the population, a statement that might be true about the population. We will "make believe" that it is true. It specifies a population parameter. As soon as we do this, we "bring into being," in our mathematical imagination, the sampling distribution associated with this value of the parameter. **From the laws of probability, the Central Limit Theorem, the characteristics of the normal distribution, and mathematical calculation, we know exactly how likely any sample outcome is in this distribution.** More specifically, we know exactly the probability of an outcome depending on how discrepant it is from the expected value of the distribution (in this case, the parameter specified in the null hypothesis). We do not have to calculate this probability ourselves; the probabilities are available in printed tables (see Appendix) and are built into statistical software. The probabilities of outcomes in terms of discrepancy from the expected value are referred to as *p*-values ("*p*" for probability). Discrepant outcomes have a low probability, that is, a low *p*-value.

Third, we compute a test-statistic that expresses the difference or discrepancy between the observed sample data (the sample statistic) and the expected value specified for the population parameter in the null hypothesis. If this discrepancy is extreme, usually evident from a high absolute value for the test statistic, we can reject the null hypothesis with a low probability of Type I error. The test-statistic represents a large discrepancy between the sample outcome and the population parameter hypothesized under the null hypothesis. The sample outcome is in the tails of the sampling distribution that we would obtain if the null hypothesis were true. It is improbable that the sample was drawn from a population in which the null hypothesis is true. If the null hypothesis were true, it is unlikely that we would get such a discrepant result. It has a very low probability that we can specify exactly from the sampling distribution and our knowledge of the normal curve that describes the sampling distribution. The discrepant test statistic and its low *p*-value are evidence against the null hypothesis. We can never be 100% certain that the null hypothesis is untrue, however.

The probability of a sampling outcome as extreme as the one we obtained in the sample, *when the null hypothesis is true*, is called the **p-value** of the particular test statistic.

Like all probabilities, the *p*-value is always a number between 0 and 1. A 0 *p*-value means absolute certainty that this outcome could not appear in the sampling distribution, and we will never see a true 0. (For example, in a commonly used software package called SPSS, computer output will print .000, but this means only that p is very small.) A p-value close to 1 means this sample outcome is very likely when the null hypothesis is true about the population; it would be very risky to reject the null hypothesis.

- If the obtained p is $\leq$ alpha, we reject the null hypothesis because p is our risk of Type I error. If p is sufficiently low (less than or equal to .05 as the conventional alpha choice), we say the results are statistically significant. If $p \leq .01$, we can say the results are "highly significant." (Low p, high significance!)

- If the obtained p is $>$ alpha, we fail to reject the null hypothesis. The risk of Type I error is too high. We say the results were "not statistically significant." (High p, not significant!)

If p is small and the result is "statistically significant," we reject the null hypothesis. In this situation, one of two mutually exclusive situations is true. One of them is that the null hypothesis is indeed not true and should have been rejected. This situation is a good outcome for the researcher. The null hypothesis is usually set up to represent a situation that is dull or disappointing, like a vaccine not being effective or two variables being unrelated to each other. The other possible situation is that the null hypothesis is true. We were unlucky in our random sampling and got an improbably "extreme" sample outcome while the null hypothesis really is true. We should not have rejected the null hypothesis and did so only because the sample we had drawn had an extreme and therefore misleading sample statistic. This situation is unfortunate and potentially embarrassing.

Unfortunately, we cannot know which of these situations is true. We can only use our knowledge about the probability distribution of sample outcomes to specify how likely it is to get an "extreme," discrepant sample outcome that would lead to a mistaken rejection of the null hypothesis. That probability is the p-value.

Hypothesis testing as a method of inference takes a little while to get used to. It has a lot of peculiar features, like setting up the null hypothesis, which is entirely imaginary and expressed in the subjunctive ("if it *were* the case …"). The backwards logic of the whole procedure takes a while to get used to. At first, it is confusing to remember that if the test statistic has a high absolute value (big discrepancy from the value specified by the null hypothesis), its p-value is low, and it is significant. If the test statistic has a low absolute value (small discrepancy from the value specified by the null hypothesis), its p-value is high, and it is not significant. As we see more examples of applications, the procedure will become more comfortable. Just a little hint as you begin to look at computer output: most experienced researchers look first at the p-value (which in SPSS is labelled "Sig" for "significance"), and they feel happy when they see a very small decimal fraction there—no more than .05!

It may be useful to memorize the following steps:

Steps in the test process: Column One or Column Two?

Extreme, discrepant test statistic (High absolute value)	Test statistic not discrepant from value expected under the null hypothesis (Low absolute value)
Low p-value ("sig") $p \leq .05$ low risk of Type I error	High p-value $p > .05$ high risk of Type I error
Reject null hypothesis	Fail to reject null hypothesis
Result is significant ($\leq .05$) or highly significant ($\leq .01$)	Result is not statistically significant

Articles in the research literature often simply use asterisks to indicate results that are significant* (.05 level) or highly significant** (.01 level) or significant at the .001 level***. Some articles may report the value of the test-statistic, its degrees of freedom, and the p-value. Very few articles actually specify the null hypothesis, which is usually implicit in the data analysis.

SETTING UP THE NULL HYPOTHESIS

Here are three tips for setting up a good null hypothesis.

- The null hypothesis usually specifies a dull or disappointing outcome. The null hypothesis means that we cannot announce exciting research results, take action, or establish a new finding. If the null hypothesis is true, there is no relationship between two variables; a supplier has not cheated us; a new curriculum does not improve reading scores—in short, we get a boring result. Therefore, the null hypothesis is a statement we would like to be able to reject.

- The null hypothesis is about the **population**, not the sample. Once we set it up, we "bring into being" the sampling distribution associated with this expected value in the population. The probabilities of sample outcomes are known, on the basis of the Central Limit Theorem. The null hypothesis is a hypothesis or imaginary statement about the population, a conjecture that might be true.

- The null hypothesis is a specific numerical statement. It specifies a definite numerical value that can be tested against our observed sample data.

ONE SAMPLE *T*-TESTS

In this section, we will outline the logic of one of the most basic tests, the one-sample, one-variable *t*-test. We use a *t*-test when we want to infer—estimate—a population parameter, typically the mean, from the sample statistic. We use a one-sample *t*-test for means when we are concerned or hopeful that the mean exceeds (or falls short) of a certain value.

The basic idea is that most samples will not have a sample mean that is exactly the value of the population mean, but most samples will have outcomes that are pretty close to the population mean. Only a few will be very different, and we know the probability of the sample mean being extremely discrepant from the population value. How do we know that? Because the Central Limit Theorem tells us so: The sampling distribution of sample means has a normal distribution for which we can specify the probability of outcomes. If the sample mean is very discrepant from the population value specified in the null hypothesis, this discrepancy can be used safely as evidence against the null hypothesis being true for the population.

For example, let's say we have introduced a new reading curriculum, and we hope that now the mean performance on a reading test exceeds the old mean score of 100.

We test a group of 400 randomly selected kids from schools using the new reading curriculum, and we find the mean score for this sample is 102, with an SD of 16. Can we conclude that the reading curriculum has boosted mean performance over 100, or was the high sample result just a reflection of sampling variability, of chance or random error? Did we just happen to draw a sample with a high mean score, when for the population the mean really remains at 100?

In other words, how likely is a mean score of 102 for a sample of 400 when the population mean score is only 100?

Notice a couple of things about this set-up:

- The null hypothesis is *mu* = 100. We write μ_{H_0} = 100. It is "given" by the logic of the problem, which sets the baseline we would like the new curriculum to exceed. Notice that the null hypothesis always refers to the population parameter. Once we have hypothesized this imaginary value for the population parameter, we bring into (imaginary) being the whole sampling distribution of the mean for samples of 400. The expected value for this distribution is 100.

- We are going to perform a one-tailed test, because we are only interested in whether the performance exceeds the hypothesized value. A two-tailed test checks for difference or discrepancy from the null hypothesis value. A one-tailed test checks for discrepancy in a certain direction—either higher OR lower, but not both—from the value specified in the null hypothesis.

Now we compute t, our test statistic. It expresses the discrepancy between the observed sample statistic and the hypothesized population parameter specified in the null hypothesis. If this discrepancy is large, it is evidence against the null hypothesis and we can risk rejecting the null hypothesis. If the discrepancy is small, we cannot reject the null hypothesis; it is too likely that the sample data came from a sample drawn from a population in which the null hypothesis is true.

Algorithm for testing the null hypothesis:

1. Find the observed mean from the sample data, $\bar{X}$.

2. Estimate the standard error (SE) by dividing the sample standard deviation by the square root of sample size.

3. Specify the expected value, *mu*, under the null hypothesis, as a numerical value for the population that represents a situation in which "nothing happens."

Subtract mu from $\bar{X}$ (observed sample value minus null-hypothesis population value), and divide this difference by the *SE*.

Formula:

$$t = \frac{\bar{X} - \mu_{H_0}}{SE} \quad \text{or} \quad t = \frac{\bar{X} - \mu_{H_0}}{\frac{S}{\sqrt{N}}}$$

Notice that this formula is exactly like our old friend, the formula for Z scores, used for converting a score into a standardized score. The only difference is that we are looking at the *t*-distribution because we have to estimate the standard deviation from our sample data, rather than knowing the population standard deviation. What we are doing is asking how discrepant is this sample value for *t* in the distribution of sample outcomes relative to the variability of the sample outcomes (the standard error)? The *t*- or Z-distribution expresses the distribution of sample outcomes in terms of their discrepancy from the mean (which is the population parameter and the expected value of the distribution). This discrepancy is expressed in standard error units (the standard deviation of the sampling distribution) instead of in values representing units of the empirical world (such as heights or weights).

a) The general formula:

$$t = \frac{(\text{observed value} - \text{expected value of null hypothesis})}{SE}$$

b) The formula for means:

$$t = \frac{\bar{X} - \mu_{H_0}}{\frac{S}{\sqrt{N}}}$$

Now we substitute the values from our actual problem:

$$t = \frac{102 - 100}{\frac{16}{\sqrt{400}}} = \frac{2}{16 / 20} = \frac{2(20)}{16} = 2.5$$

Notice a few of things about the formula (the one labelled "b"):

- We subtract the hypothesized population mean from the observed sample mean. This difference is the first step in obtaining the discrepancy.

- We divide by the standard error of the sampling distribution, the *SD* divided by the square root of sample size. For the *SD*, we have to use the sample *SD*, *s*, since we don't know the population *SD*, σ or sigma. Therefore we have to use the more conservative *t*-test, instead of the normal distribution and Z-scores.

- Dividing by the standard error completes the test for discrepancy, since we are looking at the difference in means relative to the standard error (the variability) of the sampling distribution. "Are these means far apart, relative to the spread of the distribution?" (The difference is "big" or "small" only relative to the spread; for example, a pound difference in weights is a big deal for newborns, but really insignificant for adults.)

- This computation does NOT refer to either the population distribution of reading scores or the distribution of reading scores for the sample of kids. It refers to the sampling distribution of the means. We are asking how "far out" or discrepant from the expected value (in this case the mean score of 100 specified in the null hypothesis) is this value among all the possible sample outcomes (means).

Our computed *t*-statistic, $t = 2.5$, indicates that our observed value in the sample is 2.5 standard errors distant from the value specified in the null hypothesis. It is 2.5 standard deviations of the sampling distribution (i.e., 2.5 standard errors) above the expected value, μ or *mu*. How likely is this sample outcome? Is it likely to get this discrepant a sample outcome among all the possible sample outcomes?

Now we compare our result, $t = 2.5$, to the t-distribution. We do this by looking it up in the table (see Appendix) following these steps:

- Compute degrees of freedom by the formula $df = N - 1$. The bigger N is, the closer the t-distribution is to the normal distribution. Here $df = 399$.

- We look down the left column and see that 399 is greater than 100. If we have 400 cases in the sample, the t-distribution is pretty close to the normal curve. We "interpolate" between 100 and infinity (sometimes indicated by symbol ∞).

- We decide to do a one-tailed test because we are only interested if the results exceeded the baseline, not if they were different from it in either direction.

- Moving our eyes rightward along the interpolated row, we see that a t-value of 2.5 would fall between the .01 and .005 level of significance in a one-tailed test if the distribution table were continued. This very low fractional level means that a sample outcome this discrepant from the hypothesized population parameter is very unlikely in the sampling distribution. Yes, it is possible, but unlikely, by random chance to get a sample result that is this discrepant when the null hypothesis is true for the population. Such a result would cause a Type I error, a rejection of a null hypothesis that is true! However, this result has considerably less than a .05 chance of occurring, which is the conventionally acceptable level of Type I error in hypothesis testing.

In this example, less than .01 (in other words, $\frac{1}{100}$ or 1%)

of the samples drawn from the population in which the null hypothesis is true would have an outcome this discrepant. Yes, it is possible to get a 400-case sample with a mean of 102 (and an SD of 16) on a test when the population mean is only 100, but it's very unlikely, happening in less than 1% of the samples. Remember, the lower the probability, the p-value that expresses significance, the more confident we can be in rejecting the null hypothesis.

Chapter Three: Statistical Inference

So in this example, we can reject the null hypothesis that the population mean is only 100. We can feel safe in saying in plain English that the reading curriculum raised the mean score above the baseline level. There is only a small risk (less than 1 in 100) that we were misled by difference that was due only to sampling variability rather than to a real difference in performance.

Now try the following exercises using the *t*-test formula:

1. What conclusion would you draw if the sample mean were 100.5, only a half-point above the test baseline of 100, with an *SD* of 16?

2. What conclusion would you draw if the sample mean is 102, the *SD* is 16, but the sample size had been only 64?

3. What conclusion would you draw if the sample size is 400, the sample mean is 102, and the sample *SD* is 25—i.e., if sample variability (the basis of our estimate of population variability) had been higher?

See the end of this chapter for answers to these questions.

This series of computations shows how the results and conclusions of hypothesis tests vary with the size of the sample and variability, as well as the discrepancy between sample data and the null hypothesis parameter. All other things being equal,

- a large discrepancy makes it more likely that we can conclude the results are significant,

- a large sample makes it more likely that we can conclude the results are significant, and

- low variability makes it more likely that we can conclude the results are significant.

You can convince yourself of this both intuitively, thinking about some real life examples, and by inspecting the formula.

T-tests like this one are also used to test whether a supplier is providing a defective product (for example, light bulbs that fall short of the advertised hours of life) or short weighting us (for example, putting less broccoli into packages than specified by the contract).

TWO INDEPENDENT SAMPLES *T*-TEST

A very commonly seen variation of the one-sample *t*-test is the two independent-samples *t*-test. In this test, we examine a *t*-test statistic that expresses the discrepancy between the means from two independent samples. "Independent" refers to the fact that the samples were drawn by random sampling and are not before-and-after results from the same cases or results from cases that were matched or paired. For example, we might compare grades of random samples of men and women from our university to test whether their GPAs are different. The two samples would not only have different means, but they might also be different in size and in their *SD*s. The *t*-test is a test of the null hypothesis that the discrepancy between the population means is 0, in other words, that there is no difference.

The *t*-test measures by how many standard errors the sample data—the difference between the two sample means—are discrepant from the hypothesized value of 0. The null hypothesis specifies that the difference between the means for the two groups is 0, that there is no difference in means.

The conceptual formula is this:

$$t = \frac{\text{difference in sample means} - 0}{\text{standard error of the difference}}$$

- The numerator specifies how discrepant the difference in means is from 0 (the null hypothesis value).

- The denominator is the standard error of the sampling distribution of the mean difference.

- The formula as a whole compares the discrepancy from 0 to the spread of the sampling distribution of the difference.

It is computed by the following formula:

$$t_{(N_1 + N_2 - 2)} = \frac{(\bar{y}_1 - \bar{y}_2) - (\mu_1 - \mu_2)}{S_{(\bar{y}_1 - \bar{y}_2)}}$$

$$= \frac{(\bar{y}_1 - \bar{y}_2) - 0}{\sqrt{\left(\dfrac{s_1^2}{n_1} + \dfrac{s_2^2}{n_2}\right)}}$$

Let's work through a simple example with some fictitious data:

At Lake Placid University, grades are computed on a scale of 0 to 4.

For a sample of 100 sophomores, the GPA is 3.0, with an *SD* of .5. For a sample of 110 seniors, the GPA is 3.2 with an *SD* of .5.

Can we conclude that at Lake Placid University there is a difference in sophomore and senior GPAs?

Is the discrepancy we see in the sample data big enough to conclude that this difference is **not** just a chance difference that results from sampling error?

$$t = \frac{3.2 - 3.0}{\sqrt{\left(\dfrac{(.5)^2}{110} + \dfrac{(.5)^2}{100}\right)}}$$

$$= \frac{.2}{.069}$$

$$= 2.89$$

We look up this value in the table of the *t*-distribution. We can look it up for a two-tailed test since we are interested in difference, regardless of direction. The degrees of freedom are $N_1 + N_2 - 2 = 208$. We see that the value of *t* is significant at the .01 level—highly significant! With these sample data, we can conclude with only a small risk of Type I error that there is a difference in sophomore and senior GPAs.

We have worked through a simple example in which, on the basis of sample data, we can assume equal population variances. The computations become more complicated if we find *SD*s in the samples that are so different from each other that we cannot assume the populations have the same variances. We determine this using computer software (such as the Levene test for equal variances).

Now that you understand the basic logic and steps for a *t*-test, you can consult a comprehensive text for the more complicated applications:

- *t*-tests for proportions as well as means.

- *t*-tests where the population variances cannot be assumed to be equal (which also require a small adjustment in the formula for degrees of freedom).

- *t*-tests for paired samples, such as before and after tests for the same cases, and *t*-tests for other situations where the samples are not independent.

T-tests are very commonly used in educational testing and biomedical research. Notice that they only work for two groups. In the next chapter, we will learn a data analysis technique called ANOVA that can be used for two or more groups. You may have noticed that the two *t*-test samples are almost like groups defined by a two-category independent variable (e.g., men and women, people who got a vaccine and people who didn't, seniors and sophomores). Indeed, ANOVA is usually thought of as a technique for analysing two or more variables, for examining whether groups corresponding to the categories of the independent variables can predict differences in the means computed for the continuous dependent variable.

Conclusion

In this chapter, we thought about statistical inference and learned two methods for doing it. We began by focusing on the variability of sample outcomes, the main challenge in using sample data to reach a conclusion about a population. The chapter took us through consideration of variability, probability, and the distribution of sampling error. We saw how sampling distributions approximate the normal distribution, allowing us to calculate the probability of sample outcomes once we specify a hypothetical population value. The Central Limit Theorem tells us the expected value, shape, and standard deviation (standard error) of the distribution of sample outcomes. Sample outcomes that are highly discrepant from the expected value (the population parameter) are possible but not very probable.

This mathematical knowledge allows us to reach conclusions based on empirical data from samples. We use our observed sample value either to construct a confidence interval or to test a null hypothesis, a conjecture about the population parameter. We ended the chapter by doing t-tests, tests for the discrepancy of an observed sample value from a null-hypothesis value that we would like to reject.

The chapter, as a whole, is about uncertainty and variability. The sample data vary from the population parameter, and we can never be sure exactly how discrepant a sample outcome is—but the probability of it being very discrepant is low.

Key Terms

sample statistics
population parameters
sampling distribution
simple random sample
expected value
variability, uncertainty
normal curve
binomial distribution
sampling error
central limit theorem
standard error
Chebycheff's Inequality

confidence interval, confidence level
hypothesis testing
null hypothesis
critical value
type I and type II error
alpha level
level of significance
p-value
one-sample t-test, independent samples t-test
t-distribution
degrees of freedom

Chapter Three: Answers

1. $df = (400 - 1) = 399$ and

$$t = \frac{100.5 - 100}{\frac{16}{\sqrt{400}}} = \frac{.5}{16/20} = \frac{.5(20)}{16} = \frac{10}{16} = .625$$

Because .625 is less than 1.282, it yields a greater than .10 value for a one-tailed t-test. Therefore, we fail to reject the null hypothesis because we have a greater than 10% chance of getting a sample result that is this discrepant.

2. $df = (64 - 1) = 63$ and

$$t = \frac{102 - 100}{\frac{16}{\sqrt{64}}} = \frac{2}{16/8} = \frac{2(8)}{16} = 1$$

Because the $df = 63$, which is between 60 and 65 on the t-distribution chart, the t-score of 1 would result in failing to reject the null hypothesis. Why? The t-score of 1 is less than either 1.295 or 1.296, which yield a .10 value for a one-tailed test for df values of 65 and 60 respectively.

3. $df = (400 - 1) = 399$ and

$$t = \frac{102 - 100}{\frac{25}{\sqrt{400}}} = \frac{2}{25/20} = \frac{2(20)}{25} = 1.6$$

Interpolating in the T-table for $df=399$, we find that this result is significant at the .10 level but not the .05 level.

Chapter Four: Relationships Among Variables

Part I: An Overview—Thinking About Variable Relationships

Usually we are doing intro statistics not for the fun of imaginary constructs like the sampling distribution, but because we want to answer real-life ("empirical") questions about relationships among variables, especially with an eye towards understanding cause and effect. Does smoking cause cancer? Does air pollution contribute to the prevalence of asthma? Will a new reading curriculum improve reading outcomes? Does religion make a difference in attitudes towards the death penalty? Does social inequality in a country have an impact on life expectancy?

There are many data analysis techniques designed for exploring the relationships among two or more variables. These techniques look quite different, but they are all "sisters under the skin" that share a basic logic. All of them focus on the question of whether variability in a dependent variable (DV) is related to and predictable from variability in one or more independent variables (IV). Here are the steps in the logic:

First, we decide on a DV and an IV (or several IVs, but to start with, we will just do "bivariate analysis," with one DV and one IV).

Second, we look at the distribution of the DV and variation in this distribution. Does knowing something about the IV help us to improve our prediction for the DV—does it allow us to predict where cases fall in the DV distribution? **The concept of a "relationship among** variables" is defined to mean that knowing variation in the IV allows us to predict variation in the DV. Remember that, if we don't know much about the DV, our best prediction for its value is the mean (for an interval-ratio variable) and the mode (for a categoric value). Does knowing something about the IV help us to improve our prediction for the DV, to do better than just guessing the mean or mode? For example, let's say we are trying to estimate the weight of students in a statistics class. If I know that you are 5 feet tall, will that information help me guess your weight? In this example, height is the IV; weight is the DV. If you are 5 feet tall you probably weigh less than the mean weight of the class, and so knowing your height, I could guess your weight a little more precisely than just guessing the mean. Overall, knowing everybody's height would probably lead to a better set of predictions for everybody's weights than just guessing the mean weight over and over again as the predicted value for each person's weight. Similarly for categoric variables and proportions: Voters in the United States split about 50% Democrat and 50% Republican overall, but knowing a person's race allows me to make a better guess about their voting in the past election.

Third, we have to decide whether the difference in the DV that is associated with the IV is strong enough to be considered meaningful. Once again, we are thinking about this question: "Is the difference really different?" If we find a little bit of difference in the DV for different values of the IV, at what point can we conclude that the variables are really related? For example, if the mean weight of tall people in the statistics class is 160 pounds and the mean weight of short people is 159.8 pounds, we might feel that this is not a meaningful difference and that knowing height does not improve our estimate of weight. If 50% of people who were vaccinated stay healthy and only 49.8% of the unvaccinated do, we might wonder if the vaccine "really makes a difference." We will be looking for a precise way of deciding the answer to this type of question. We can ask two closely related questions, one about the strength of the relationship and one about its significance.

- Is this relationship strong?

- If we are looking at sample data, is the relationship strong enough that we can reject the null hypothesis that there is no relationship between the variables? Can we conclude that the variables are probably related in the population—that the variation we found in the DV is indeed related to IV variation and not just due to chance in the sampling? Answering this question involves deciding that the differences we found are large enough not to be merely sampling error.

For example, we might find in a survey that 21% of men smoke and 19% of women smoke. Different, but not very different! If this is sample data from a small sample, we probably will have to accept the null hypothesis: we cannot conclude that men and women smoke in different proportions. The differences were very likely just the result of sampling error. If the sample is very large, or if the data represent a population, we might conclude that there is a relationship between GENDER and SMOKING, but it is certainly not a strong one.

When we find a relationship among the variables (association or correlation), we cannot jump to the conclusion that it is causal. All we can say is that the variables are related and not independent of each other. We can use the IV as a predictor of the DV (or outcome variable), but we cannot assert that they are causally related until we have looked at their time sequence and analysed the data further to rule out confounding variables.

OK: That's it—that's the basic logic of all multivariate analysis. It is all about using IV variability to estimate or predict variability in the DV. Now all that's left are the details of checking out these relationships in slightly different ways, depending on the variables' levels of measurement. How much better is our prediction of variation in the DV when we have information about the IV? If the prediction is definitely better, we can conclude that these variables are related. If the IV information does not improve our DV prediction at a statistically significant level, we fail to conclude that they are related. Now we just need to find procedures to make this intuitive idea more precise. These techniques are usually referred to as data analysis techniques. Most of the techniques for doing this were invented in the late nineteenth and early twentieth century, often in association with applied research in agronomy (e.g., which fertilizers work best to increase yield per acre?), biology, and industrial processes.

Four Types of Data Analysis Techniques

In this section, we will present a brief overview of four major types of data analysis technique, depending on the variables' levels of measurement.

Correlation/regression or regression analysis: In this case, both the IV and the DV are interval-ratio data that we can treat as continuous data, so we can compute a mean and an *SD* for each variable. We look at the **correlation** of the two variables and develop a **linear regression analysis.** We ask whether the distributions of the IV and the DV are lined up in such a way that knowing the Z-scores of the IV allows me to predict the Z-scores of the DV.

- Usually, we first inspect the "line up" visually, in a **scatterplot** that graphs the two variables in the *x-y* plane. If the two variables appear to have a linear relationship, we can proceed with the linear regression analysis. (Example: if we plot people's heights and weights as ordered pairs (x = height, y = weight), does the plot look something like a straight line?)

- Then we make the conclusion precise by computing a formula for their correlation that tests how closely the Z-distributions match each other. This formula computes the **Pearson correlation coefficient**, expressing the strength of the relationship. For example, does knowing where a person falls in the height distribution allow me to predict where she falls in the weight distribution? Most people would say, yeah, knowing height improves the weight prediction, but doesn't make it perfect. The variables are correlated, but not strongly so. The correlation coefficient makes that intuitive notion precise.

- After computing the correlation coefficient, we create a linear model by writing another formula: the equation for the **ordinary least squares regression line.** This formula allows us to calculate, estimate, or predict the DV values from the IV values. (Example: we could write an equation that allows us to plug in people's heights and get the corresponding estimated weight for each person.)

- In a **multiple regression**, the procedure is very similar, but there is one DV and more than one IV. (Example: we could write an equation for estimating people's weights, given two pieces of information for each person: height and average daily calorie intake.)

Crosstabs/contingency tables: In this case, both variables are categoric. Our question is whether knowing about the distribution of the IV allows us to predict into which category of the DV the cases will fall. For example, is age related to music preferences? Does knowing a person's age category allow us to predict the individual's music preferences? The two categoric variables here are age (young, middle aged, old) and music preference (hip hop, rock, blues, jazz, country, and classical). Without any additional information, my "best bet" for where a case falls in the DV distribution is to guess that she or he falls in the DV modal category. If the variables are related, knowing a person's age category would improve my prediction of which of the six music preference categories the person falls into. If the variables are related, the DV distributions are different for different IV categories (the age groups). In a crosstabs analysis, we lay out the distribution of the two variables jointly in a table called a "crosstab" or contingency table and examine this joint distribution.

Analysis of variance (ANOVA): The IV is a categoric variable that defines "groups," and the DV is an interval-ratio variable for which we can compute a mean, SD, and variance (i.e., treat it as if it were continuous). Here our question is whether knowing which of the IV "groups" a case falls into tells us anything about where its DV value is likely to fall in the distribution of DV values. The variance of the DV could be related to group membership ("between groups variance"), or it could be related to other factors that we don't know about, which cause a lot of variation within the group. ANOVA computes the ratio of between-groups variance (predictable from the IV, so it's "good" variance in our research) to within-groups variance (not predictable from the IV, so it's "residual" or "error" variation, "bad" variation in terms of our interest in finding a relationship among the variables).

For example, let's say we think that racial-ethnic groups in the United States have different mean incomes. Our ANOVA question would be how much variation in individual incomes can be predicted from race/ethnicity and how much of the variation in individual incomes is due to other reasons, ones that operate **within** the racial/ethnic categories? For example, it is true that whites in the United States have a higher mean income than African Americans. However, some African Americans (e.g., Oprah Winfrey, Michael Jordan) are very wealthy, a substantial number are middle income, and a substantial number of whites are poor. Knowing someone's race/ethnicity might improve my guess about his or her income, but it might well be a bad guess because of the variation within each racial/ethnic group. There is variation within racial categories, not only between them.

ANOVA can be used to analyse results from an experimental design. The means of a continuous variable that represents the outcome of the experiment are computed for two groups formed by random selection, the experimental group subjected to an experimental condition and the control group that is not. For example, the mean music competence test scores could be calculated and compared for two groups, one that took a new music curriculum and one that did not.

In ANOVA, we compare means by comparing two types of variance, the between-groups variance associated with the IV and the within-group variance associated with residual, unknown variables. The basic idea is to see whether knowing the IV (group) improves prediction of the DV, specifically, whether the DV means of the groups are different.

ANOVA is a precise procedure that corresponds to the common sense term "on the average." "On the average, men are taller than women." This expression suggests that the statement is not true in every case, but asserts that there is a difference between the means of the two groups.

The astute reader will have noticed that the comparison of the means of two groups sounds a lot like a *t*-test for the difference between two independent-sample means. Yes, indeed! The conclusion for an ANOVA with two IV groups will be identical to that for the independent-samples *t*-test. The big difference is that the ANOVA can be used with more than two groups. In some software packages, ANOVA is placed together in the menu with *t*-tests under the more general heading "compare means."

Logistic regression: Here the IVs (there are usually more than one) are continuous or 0/1 variables, and the DV is a dichotomous or binary variable—a 0/1 variable. The DV is often referred to as the outcome variable. The DV can be expressed as an "odds ratio"—the odds of voting Liberal in the Canadian federal election (or not); of having a baby out of wedlock (or not); of dying of AIDS (or not); of catching a communicable disease (or not); or of being sentenced to life imprisonment for manslaughter (or not). In other words, an "odds ratio" can express any kind of situation that can be represented by a 0/1 variable. The logistic regression then explores whether a given IV (or bunch of IVs) changes the odds ratio of the outcome, compared to what the odds ratio is when no IV is used. Does a defendant's being from a racial/ethnic minority increase the odds of receiving the life imprisonment sentence? Does being a wealthy white male change the odds of voting Liberal? Does taking a new AIDS medication reduce the odds of dying of AIDS? Does a new vaccine change the odds of catching a disease? The logic is pretty simple but the math is a little tricky.

The underlying logic of all these techniques is the same: We ask whether information about the IV distribution improves our knowledge of variation in the DV distribution, whether this knowledge improves our ability to predict where cases will fall in the DV distribution. If it does, we conclude that the variables are associated or correlated. Once again, an empirical question is transformed into a procedure that focuses on variability, in this case, the joint variation of two or more variables.

Beyond Bivariate Analysis: Adding Variables and Staying Alert

Before looking at these data analysis techniques in more detail, we need to emphasize that bivariate analysis is only a first step in applied statistics. It is rare that variation in a dependent variable is completely explained by variation in only one independent variable. Most situations in the real world are more complicated and require multivariate analysis, the analysis of several independent variables that may be related to the dependent variable.

As we explore the role of additional variables, we often find one of the following situations.

The third (fourth, fifth, etc.) variable shows that the initial bivariate relationship—called the 0-order relationship—was **spurious**. The two initially selected variables are not related, except through their relationship to a third variable. For instance, in looking at districts in northern Europe, we find that those with many storks have a high birth rate. Can we conclude that the presence of storks is related to high birth rates, maybe even that that there is a causal relationship and that storks bring babies? Not really. There is an underlying third variable, the degree to which a district is rural, that is related to both the presence of storks and a high birth rate. Similarly, the apparent relationship between the number of fire-fighters at a fire and the amount of property damage caused by the fire should not lead us to conclude that fire-fighters cause property damage; the size of the fire is the underlying third variable that causes many fire-fighters to be present *as well as* a high level of property damage, creating the spurious bivariate relationship between the number of fire-fighters and the level of property damage.

In other cases, the third variable is best considered an **intervening** variable, one that helps to explain or elaborate the bivariate relationship but does not completely dispel it. The third variable "lies between" or links the initial two variables. To use a hypothetical example, men may be more avid sports fans than women. The relationship between gender and sports interest may be explained by the intervening variable of childhood sports participation; men are more likely to have participated in team sports, and they are therefore more likely to be interested in viewing sports as adults. Playing experience is an intervening variable between gender and adult sports interest. But unlike in the spurious situation, we still find a link between gender and sports interest, mediated by the variable of playing experience. We are left with the question of why men were more likely to have participated in sports as youngsters. Notice that I have concocted an example in which the time order is very simple (gender identification precedes childhood sports participation which precedes adult sports interest). In real empirical examples of intervening variables, the time order is not always so simple, and the third intervening variable can operate simultaneously with the others.

A third situation in which multivariate analysis elaborates the 0-order bivariate relationship is usually called an **interaction effect**. In this situation, the bivariate relationships are different for each condition or category of the third variable. The great sociologist Emile Durkheim spotted one of these situations in his analysis of suicide in Europe at the end of the nineteenth century. Durkheim believed that the institution of marriage offered protection against suicide. He found that married people had lower suicide rates than the unmarried. However, this relationship between marital status and suicide rate varied depending on a third variable, the strength of the marital bond in a society. Among people who lived in countries in which divorce was difficult or impossible, married people had markedly lower suicide rates than the unmarried. Among people who lived in these countries, there was a strong relationship between marital status and suicide rates. In contrast, among people in countries in which divorces were easy to obtain, married people's suicide rates were similar to those of unmarried people. The relationship between marital status and suicide rate was weak. Here we see an example of an interaction effect or contingency effect of the third variable: The two categories of the third variable (strong or weak marital bonds in the society) were associated with different relationships between marital status and suicide rate, respectively a strong bivariate relationship and a weak bivariate relationship.

A similar logic can be illustrated by data that a colleague and I have collected about variables associated with good grades among high school students. We examined the bivariate relationship between family structure and reported grades. When we included a third variable, racial/ethnic identity, we found an interesting difference. For Euro-American respondents, there was an association between living in a nuclear family and good grades, but for the other racial/ethnic groups in the study (African Americans, Asian Americans, and Hispanics), the relationship between family structure and grades was not significant. Youngsters living in non-nuclear types of families were no less likely to get good grades than those living in nuclear families, among all groups except the Euro-American group.

The logic of these three types of third variable situations is summed up in Figure 13.

Figure 13: Third variables and 0-order relationships

Spurious relationships: the third variable eliminates the
0-order relationship between variable 1 and variable 2

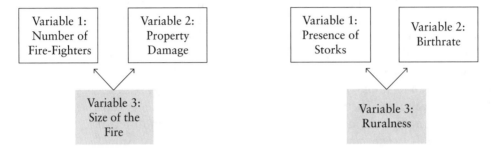

Intervening variable: the third variable helps to explain the 0-order relationship

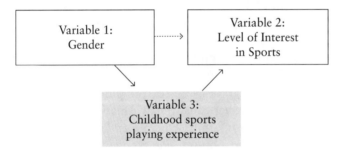

Interaction effect: different values of the third variable are
associated with different strengths of the 0-order relationship

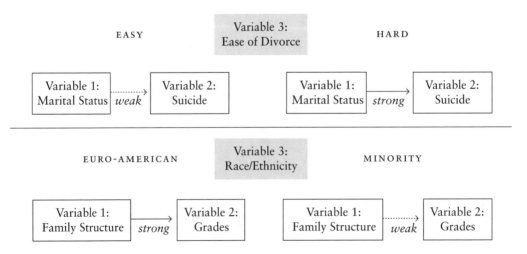

In the intervening variable example in Figure 13, the third variable explains the 0-order relationship. It "lies between" the two variables in the 0-order relationship, but does not eliminate it. Gender is related to playing experience, and playing experience is related to an interest in sports. The relationship between gender and sports interest is not spurious, and it is not eliminated by the third variable (childhood experience playing sports), but only (in part) explained by it. Men and women who have participated in sports (sports experience) have an identical level of interest in it, but women are less likely than men to have participated. We have shifted the question about gender and sports from "why are women less interested than men?" to "why were women less likely to have experience playing sports?"

As we can see from the examples charted in Figure 13, a statistician's work is never done. Introducing even one new variable means that we end up quite surprised to see our bivariate analysis shift and change. Relationships that appeared strong at the 0-order may turn out to be weak or spurious as we add new variables. Our ingenuity and our understanding of empirical situations are constantly being tested, and we are always challenged to improve our models and question our own conclusions.

An example will show how there is no substitute for alertness and that an apparently simple conclusion with strong policy implications may become more nuanced when a third variable is added to an analysis. It is based on a true story but simplified to highlight the logic. The acceptance rates among men and women applicants to Happy Valley University's graduate school appear to be very different, suggesting a strong sex bias. Of 100 male applicants, 70 were accepted and 30 were rejected, an acceptance rate of 70%. Of 134 female applicants, 52 were accepted and 82 rejected, an acceptance rate of only 38.8%. Clear evidence of gender bias and of a strong relationship between the variables GENDER and GRAD SCHOOL ADMISSION? Not so fast! Happy Valley U. has two graduate departments: Communications, which is hard to get into, with a 33% acceptance rate, and Astrophysics, which is easy to get into, with an 85.7% acceptance rate. Table 7 shows that men and women, in fact, have identical acceptance rates in each department, but applied to different departments. Women applied in greater numbers to the department that was harder to get into and thus appear to have a lower acceptance rate.

Our analysis has not eliminated gender as an issue in graduate school admission, but we realize that we are not looking at a simple case of discrimination against women. The issues are revealed to be

Table 7: Acceptance by gender and department

	Men			Women		
	Communications	Astrophysics	Total	Communications	Astrophysics	Total
Accepted	10	60	70	40	12	52
Rejected	20	10	30	80	2	82
Total	30	70	100	120	14	134

more complicated: Why are women applying to different programs than men? How are decisions made about the rigor of admission standards for different departments and the numbers of admissions to different programs? Is gender a factor in these types of decisions? A more careful statistical analysis leads to a better understanding of the complexity of gender bias. It would be unfortunate if our second take on Happy Valley University's admission statistics led to a smug crowing about "no sex bias here!" On the contrary, it suggests that gender inequalities in society are reproduced in apparently gender-neutral institutional decisions as well as in socialization experiences that lead to different choices of majors and careers. Gender inequalities are not only and simply a product of individual bias. (This example is a greatly simplified version of a real study of sex bias in admissions in the Graduate Division of the University of California, Berkeley. The real data—which involve twelve departments, not just two—are reported and discussed by David Freeman, Robert Pisani, Roger Purves, and Ani Adhikari in *Statistics*, 2nd ed., W.W. Norton and Company, 1991, pp. 16-19. The original report was written by Eugene Hammel, P. Bickel, and J.W. O'Connell, "Is there a sex bias in graduate admissions?" *Science*, 187 (1975), pp. 398-404.)

A similar need for attention to "lurking" variables appears in the statistical analysis of institutional performance, such as hospital mortality rates and school testing outcomes. Sometimes it turns out that hospitals with high mortality rates or schools with bad testing outcomes are not failing institutions. In the case of hospitals, a hospital with high mortality rates may be serving sicker populations; or it may be offering more services with high mortality rates, like a large ER, a burn unit, or a high-risk neo-natal unit. In the case of schools, a school with low test outcomes may be serving a disadvantaged population. It is always necessary to match the outcomes with other variables, such as the characteristics of the students when they enter the school, and to consider the "value-added" outcome—how well the school has performed in improving outcomes from the initial baseline.

These examples suggest that data analysis should never be a mechanical process, just plugging numbers into formulas. Data analysis requires constant alertness and reflection on the complexity of the real world. Good research means thinking about variable relationships, looking for new "lurking" variables, and even questioning the basic assumptions of our own research design, such as variable definitions.

Part II: Data Analysis Techniques

Now let's look at the data analysis techniques in a little more detail.

At this point, we face the question of what is the best order for learning about these techniques. If you glance at a sample of introductory statistics texts, you will see that the order is not consistent. Books that are oriented toward psychological applications begin with ANOVA because it is a commonly used technique in psychology and works well with experimental design. Many sociology texts (and books that are oriented toward math aversive students) begin with crosstabs or contingency tables because these apply to categoric variables, use simpler math, and are commonly used to analyse qualitative data, which is more common in fields like sociology, anthropology, and political science. Statistics texts with a general orientation often begin with correlation/regression precisely because it is the most mathematically sophisticated technique. The most precise results come about when both variables are continuous or, at least, when interval-ratio variables can be treated as continuous variables. Even though the math is a little more difficult, starting with regression analysis will be worth the extra effort at the beginning because it represents the most developed procedure for the most precisely measured data—the "gold standard" of data analysis and the technique that can best be adapted to multivariate analysis (more than one independent variable). Increasingly, virtually all advanced statistical work in all disciplines builds on regression analysis, especially in situations where controlled experiments cannot be carried out.

SECTION ONE: REGRESSION ANALYSIS

Here both variables are interval-ratio variables that can be treated as continuous. A good first step is to plot them in the x-y plane with the IV on the horizontal x-axis and the DV on the vertical y-axis. Each case is then represented as a point, with its x-coordinate as the IV and its y-coordinate as the DV. For example, my height and weight (if those are our two variables) would be represented by the ordered pair (64", 118 lbs).

This graph is called a **scatterplot,** and it builds on the idea that the DV (graphed on the y-axis) can be thought of as a "function of x" (the IV, graphed on the x-axis); the DV values are thought of as predictable from the IV values.

If we plot all the points (cases), and the result does not look at all as though a line could be drawn through it, we probably should not proceed with a linear regression. For instance, the points might fall in a U-shape or a "hump" shape; these distributions are not good candidates for linear regression.

Math Interlude: The Natural Log Transformation

All is not lost however! Sometimes one of the variables in a "bad-looking" relationship, one whose plot looks like a "hump" or a "U," can be transformed, usually using a natural logarithm transformation (*ln*) to create a new and linear relationship. To take a simple example, if the values of X are 0, 1, 2, 3, and the corresponding values of Y are 1, 10, 100, 1000, the relationship does not look linear at all. Try graphing it and you will see. Presto, magic, if we write the Y sequence as powers of 10, namely 0, 1, 2, 3, the exponents themselves are in a perfect linear relationship with the values of X. In most cases, instead of using the exponent base-10, we use the natural log, the exponent base e ($e = 2.718...$). For example, the per-capita gross domestic product of countries ("capgdp"), a good measure of national wealth, has a skewed distribution. A few countries have high per capita gdps, but many countries have low per capita gdps. But if we transform this variable into *ln*{capgdp}, the new variable can be used in linear regressions. Most statistics software will carry out the natural log transformation, so each observation in a data set can be transformed.

If the scatterplot looks as though a line could be drawn through it, we can try a linear regression and proceed to do three things: 1) find the correlation coefficient, 2) compute the regression line, and 3) find the coefficient of determination.

One: Finding the Correlation Coefficient

To obtain the correlation coefficient, we use a formula that expresses how closely the Z-scores of the IV distribution match the Z-scores of the DV distribution. The correlation coefficient (r) can take on all the values between −1 and +1.

A correlation coefficient of +1 means that the Z-scores of the two distributions are perfectly matched. Whatever a person's Z-score for height, that is exactly his or her Z-score for weight, and so it is for all the cases in the data set. As the personal ads say, "Height and weight proportionate"—for everybody! So +1 is a perfect correlation. It is as strongly positive as it could be. A strong positive correlation will show up in the scatterplot as a cigar shaped cluster of points tilted from the lower left to the upper right, with points tightly bunched along a line with positive slope, sloping from the lower left to the upper right.

Figure 14: A strong positive correlation

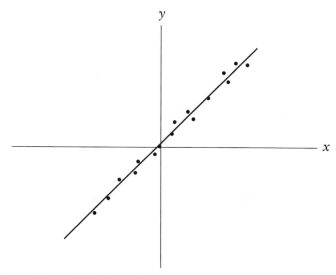

The values of the variables for each case are represented as an ordered pair. The ordered pairs are formed by the standardized scores (Z-scores) for both the x and y component. The points are close to the 45-degree line with positive slope. For each case, the Z-score for one variable is nearly equal to the Z-score on the other variable.

Figure 15: A weak positive correlation

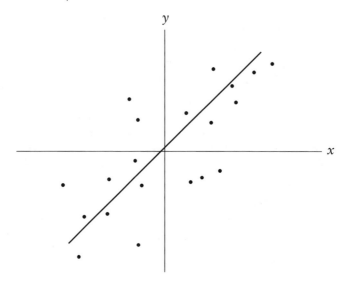

The cloud of points has a positive tilt, but the points are not close to the best-fit line.

A correlation coefficient of –1 means a perfect inverse correlation. Countries that have high female literacy have low infant mortality and vice versa. The heavier a vehicle is, the lower the gas mileage it gets. The higher the values on one variable, the lower they are on the other. Our prediction is perfect again if the value of r is –1. Thus, –1 is the most strongly negative correlation possible. You will see three terms used to describe this type of relationship: negative, inverse, and "indirect." "Indirect" is a bit misleading or confusing. A strong negative correlation will show up in the scatterplot as a skinny cigar shaped group of points tilted from the upper-left to the lower right, with a tight fit along a line with negative slope, sloping from the upper left to the lower right.

Figure 16: A strong negative correlation

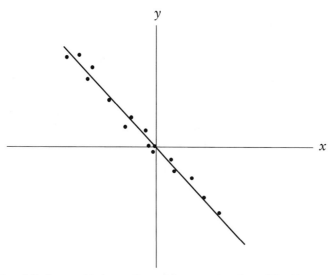

The points fall along a 45-degree line with a negative slope. The Z-score for one variable is matched for each case with a Z-score of an almost equal absolute value and opposite sign on the other variable. Increase in one variable is associated with decrease in the other variable.

Figure 17: A weak negative correlation

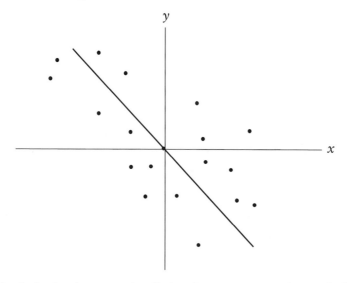

The cloud of points has a negative tilt, but the points are not close to the best-fit line.

A correlation coefficient of 0 means that the two variables' distributions are neither matched nor aligned in any way. Knowing the IV does not help us predict the DV. The points of the scatterplot fall in a big fluffy cloud that has no tilt to it at all. If we tried to draw a line through these points, the line would be horizontal, which represents the fact that the mean of the DV distribution (the mean of the variable mapped as the *y*-coordinate) remains the best guess for every case's DV value. Knowing an adult's shoe size is a very poor guide to predicting her or his IQ; with shoe size as our only information, our "best bet" for anybody's IQ remains the expected value of the IQ distribution, its mean.

Figure 18: A 0-correlation

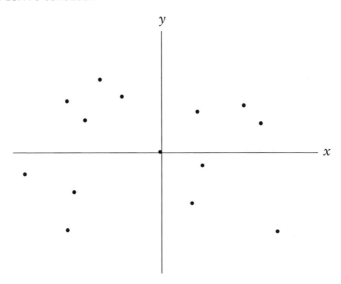

The best estimate or guess we can make for any *y*-component is the mean of the *y*-distribution. There is no relationship between the independent and dependent variables.

Here is the conceptual formula for the correlation coefficient. It expresses how well the Z-scores for one variable are matched to the Z-scores for the other variable.

Algorithm for the correlation coefficient:

1. Compute all the Z-scores for the IV; then compute all the Z-scores for the DV.

2. Multiply the IV Z-score and the DV Z-score for each case. You will have the Z-score product for every case (N cases, N products).

3. Add up all of these products.

4. Divide by N, so that you get an average of the products.

Formula:

$$y = \frac{\Sigma(Z_x Z_y)}{N}$$

The correlation coefficient r is calculated as the average product-moment, where the "product-moments" are the products of the two Z-scores for each case.

This "average product moment" is at a maximum of +1 if the Z-scores for the two variables are perfectly lined up, if $Z_x = Z_y$ for all the cases. It reaches the minimum of −1 if the Z-scores are perfectly inversely lined up, so that $Z_x = -Z_y$ for all the cases. It is 0 when the match is bad and there is no way of predicting Z_y from Z_x. (Proof of all this requires calculus, but is not difficult.)

If $r = 1$, the points representing the Z-scores for the two variables for each case fall exactly on the 45-degree line with positive slope.
If $r = -1$, the points representing the Z-scores for the two variables for each case fall exactly on the 45-degree line with negative slope.

The formula expresses the concept behind the correlation coefficient: How well are the Z-scores on the two variables aligned with each other? Most texts do not show this formula but convert it into other formulas such as the one that divides the covariance of x and y by the product of their standard deviations.

$$r = \frac{\left[\Sigma(X - \overline{X})(Y - \overline{Y})\right] / (N - 1)}{S_x S_y}$$

Here is the algorithm for this formula:

Algorithm for the correlation
coefficient in terms of the covariance:

1. Compute the covariance.
   1.1 For each ordered pair, (X, Y):
       1.1.2 Subtract the mean of the X distribution from X.
       1.1.3 Subtract the mean of the Y distribution from Y.
       1.1.4 Multiply these differences together (product).
   1.2 Sum the products for all the cases.
   1.3 Divide by (N – 1). At this point we have computed the covariance
       of X and Y. Notice that it could be a negative number, unlike the
       variance of a single distribution.

2. Divide the covariance by the product of the standard deviations of the X
   and the Y distribution.

We can think of the denominator of this expression as a "fixed" quantity. The two standard deviations are fixed, and so is their product, regardless of how the two variables are related to each other. On the other hand, the size and sign of the numerator reflects the match of the variable distributions.

• It is large and positive if X and Y are strongly, positively related.

• It is large and negative if X and Y are inversely related.

• It is relatively small in absolute value, if X and Y are weakly related.

This formula for the correlation coefficient in terms of the covariance divided by the product of the standard deviations is a little harder to understand than the average product-moment formula. A small amount of algebraic manipulation will show that they are the same. There is also a calculational formula that you can find in a comprehensive text, in case you have to carry out a regression analysis by hand. Unfortunately, some textbooks show only this formula, which makes thinking about the correlation coefficient very mysterious. The calculational formula was important in the "bad old days" when r had to be calculated by hand, but nowadays it is much better to think about the correlation coefficient in terms of the average product-moments, the line-up of the Z-scores, which makes good sense.

The rule for interpreting the correlation coefficient is that from –.2 to +.2 is considered no relationship: .2 to .4 and –.2 to –.4 are considered weak, .4 to .6 as well as –.4 to –.6 are considered moderate, .6 to .8 and –.6 to –.8 are considered strong, and .8 to 1 and –.8 to –1 are considered very strong. Not all texts agree exactly on this rule of interpretation, but it's an OK starting point for interpreting r.

Remember that in interpreting r we need to consider both its **strength** (values near +1 and –1 are strong) and its **sign**, whether it is positive or negative.

> **Important Warning!**
> The correlation coefficient is not a percentage (nor a probability).

Two: Computing the Regression Line

Now we want to write the equation of a line that allows us to stick an X (the IV value) into the equation and "get out a Y," which represents our best estimate for the DV corresponding to that IV value given the data we have. This involves using all our data and computing the "ordinary least squares" (OLS) regression line. We could draw a lot of lines through our data but the OLS line is the best one in the sense that it minimizes the squares of the deviations between where the equation of the line **estimates** or predicts the Y-value will fall and where the observed Y-value really falls.

It is important to understand that this line is only a model. It is simply the best fitting line that we can draw using the data we have. Not all of our data points will be on the line. Nor is it the case that, in the real world and for the whole population, all the data points are on this line.

$$\hat{Y} = a + bX$$

The little hat on the Y means that it is an estimated Y. In our data (and in the real world), it is not usually the case that the observed Y

(representing the observed value of the DV for a particular case) is exactly where we estimate it to be using the model.

The Y-intercept or constant term for the point where $X = 0$ and the line crosses the Y-axis is *a* in the equation of the regression line. Be warned that, in real life, this point may not make any sense or be in the data set. For example, in correlating vehicle weight and gas mileage, it would be silly to include a vehicle with 0 weight.

The slope of the line is *b*. It is "rise over run" expressing the change in the Y component for every unit increase in the X component. We are particularly interested in computing *b*, because it represents how much we predict the DV will change for each unit change in the IV. For example, it expresses how much we can expect a person to be heavier for every inch of added height.

Slope is calculated as the covariance of X and Y divided by the variance of X. (See the "How To?" section.)

Unlike the constant term, which is often meaningless in the real world, the slope can be interpreted in an empirically meaningful way.

- A positive slope of the line means that the correlation between the variables is positive and that an increase in the IV is related to an increase in the DV. If r is positive, b will be positive, and the line tilts from the lower left to the upper right. Taller people tend to be heavier.

- A negative slope of the line means that the correlation between the variables is negative (or inverse). If r is negative, b will be negative and the line tilts from the upper left to the lower right. An increase in the IV is related to a decrease in the DV. A heavier car gets lower gas mileage; if we put a lot of weight in the trunk, our gas mileage drops.

If we are doing a multiple regression with more than one IV, we get a *b* for each IV.

$$\hat{Y} = a + b_1 X_1 + b_2 X_2 + b_3 X_3 \ldots$$

We obtain a coefficient for each independent variable. We will discuss multiple regression in more detail in Five.

Beta weight or standardized regression coefficient:

- The term "beta" or "the beta weight" refers to the regression coefficient for the standardized scores. It is the slope of the regression line when both variables have been converted to Z-scores. There is no constant term because the regression line for the standardized variables always passes through (0,0), the means of both distributions.

- If we are doing a bivariate regression (two variables, an IV and a DV), beta = r, the correlation coefficient. In the multiple regression, this is not the case.

- Regression output from a computer almost always shows both the unstandardized and the standardized coefficients.

- The un-standardized coefficients make more sense in the real world, answering this question: "How much change is there in the DV for each unit of difference in the IV?" For example, how much does gas mileage drop for each additional pound of vehicle weight?

- The standardized coefficients make it easier to compare the relative effects of all the variables in the regression equation. When we see all the standardized coefficients for the independent variables in a multiple regression, we can immediately see that the ones with larger absolute values are better predictors of the DV.

How exactly do we come up with the regression coefficients, especially with the slope? Calculus is required to compute the formula that provides the "ordinary least squares" linear coefficients, in other words, to show that these are the best coefficients for minimizing the sum of the squared deviations of the real, observed Y-component from the estimated Y-component for the regression line.

If you look at a scatterplot, you can try to draw in the line for yourself, trying to draw a straight line through the cloud of points in a way that minimizes the total deviance between the line and the actual points. You can think of finding this line as stuffing an over-packed suitcase: when we push something in, something else falls out—if we make the line close to one data point it will be further away from another one. The formula for the "best fit line" minimizes the sum of the squared deviations in the Y components for all the cases. The formula for the slope is displayed in the "How To?" section of the book. You can see it is the ratio of the covariance of X and Y to the variance of X.

If we "flip" a bivariate analysis, making the IV the DV and vice versa, the correlation coefficient remains the same, as you can easily see from its formula. However, the un-standardized regression coefficients are not the same. If we flip the IV and DV, the new regression coefficient would be ratio of the covariance of X and Y to the variance of Y. The scatterplot would look different, but the line would have the same sign for its slope, positive remaining positive, and negative remaining negative. Remember that there are many empirical situations, especially with place-level data, where such a "flip" is perfectly meaningful. For example, if we are doing a regression analysis for countries' male and female life expectancy, we could use either one of these social indicator variables as our IV.

Important
Remember that the correlation coefficient is NOT a percentage.

Three: Finding the Coefficient of Determination

The coefficient of determination expresses how much of the variation in Y can be predicted from X. It can read as a proportion or even a percentage (if you move the decimal point over).

The simple way of finding the coefficient of determination is to square r. In fact, we refer to it as R-squared.

Here is how to think about it. Look at Figure 19.

The DV (Y-component) varies. Not every case has a Y that is at the mean of the Y distribution. There are two components of that variation in Y.

- One is a good component, the variation in Y that we predicted from X (the IV). This variation is based on the difference between the mean of the Y-distribution and the value of Y that we predicted in our regression equation—our estimated Y that lies on our regression line. This difference is $(\hat{Y} - \overline{Y})$.

- There is also a bad component of variation of Y from its mean; the bad component is variation that we did not predict from the regression—residual variation. It is based on the distance

Figure 19: Thinking about R-squared

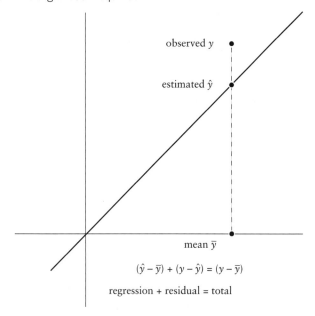

$$(\hat{y} - \bar{y}) + (y - \hat{y}) = (y - \bar{y})$$

regression + residual = total

R-squared is calculated as the ratio of the regression variance to the total variance. The total variance is based on the difference between the observed y value and the mean of the y-distribution. The regression variance is based on the difference between the estimated y on the regression line and the mean of the y-distribution. It is "good variance" using information about the independent variable (x) to estimate variation in the dependent variable (y). There is also "bad variance"—an error or residual term about which we have no information—which is based on the difference between the estimated y and the observed y, in other words, the distance that the y-component is off the regression line.

that the real, observed Y falls from the regression line, that is, from the estimated value of Y that we obtained from our regression model. This is an "error" component; something we were unable to predict. This is based on the difference between the estimated Y and the observed Y, $(Y - \hat{Y})$.

- Finally, we can define total variation, composed of both "good" regression variation and "bad" residual or error variation, based on the difference between the real, observed Y and the mean of the Y-distribution, $(Y - \bar{Y})$.

For the formula, we square these deviations and add them up for all the cases, as we do for the calculation of the standard deviation and the variance. The coefficient of determination is the ratio of good variation to total variation. (See the "How To?" section for the calculational formula.) It answers this question: What proportion of total variation in Y (i.e., total variation of the observed Ys from the mean of the Ys) was predicted by the regression equation (i.e., from information about the distribution of X)?

As you can see, R-squared can range from 0 (whoops, our regression equation failed to predict any variation in Y) to 1 (Yippee! We predicted all of the variation in Y from the regression equation!).

- Notice that if $r = 0$, then R-squared $= 0$.

- If r is $+1$, then R-squared is $+1$.

- If r is -1, then R-squared is 1. In other words, a perfect positive or negative correlation means that all variation in Y was predicted from X and all observed Ys fell exactly on the regression line.

R-squared is a very powerful number. It tells us a lot about how well we can use the independent variable to predict variation in the dependent variable. It is one of a family of measures called proportional reduction in error (PRE) measures because they express the proportion or percentage that we reduce error in our prediction of the DV when we use information about the distribution of the IV instead of just using the DV mean as the best predictor (or for categoric data, the mode of the DV). R-squared tells us exactly how much our knowledge of the IV improved our DV estimates.

The steps in the calculation of R-squared are outlined in the "How To?" section.

R, R-squared, and the regression coefficients (slope and constant) can all be tested for significance. Even a rather weak correlation coefficient can be significant.

A Couple of Empirical Examples

Let's look at a couple of simple empirical examples of regression analysis. In the first example, twenty-three Chicagoans provided the distance that they live from campus in miles and the time it takes them to get to campus.

Figure 20: Regression analysis—Distance and commuting time to campus

	DISTANCE	TIME	TRANS	z-DISTANCE	z-TIME	z-PRODUCT
1	.80	5.00	1.00	−.90578	−1.03514	.94
2	4.21	15.00	1.00	−.58217	−.66998	.39
3	16.20	50.00	1.00	.55999	.60807	.34
4	8.00	20.00	1.00	−.22049	−.48741	.11
5	19.00	60.00	2.00	.82649	.97322	.80
6	23.00	33.00	1.00	1.20722	−.01270	−.02
7	4.50	12.00	1.00	−.55362	−.77953	.43
8	6.10	30.00	1.00	−.40133	−.12225	.05
9	4.50	20.00	1.00	−.55362	−.48741	.27
10	.75	20.00	3.00	−.91054	−.48741	.44
11	7.00	25.00	1.00	−.31567	−.30483	.10
12	12.50	30.00	2.00	.20782	−.12225	−.03
13	2.00	40.00	3.00	−.79157	.24291	−.19
14	4.13	12.00	1.00	−.58883	−.77953	.46
15	25.00	75.00	2.00	1.39758	1.52096	2.13
16	25.00	75.00	2.00	1.39758	1.52096	2.13
17	8.00	20.00	2.00	−.22049	−.48741	.11
18	15.00	45.00	1.00	.44577	.42549	.19
19	.50	10.00	3.00	−.93434	−.85256	.80
20	4.00	10.00	2.00	−.60121	−.85256	.51
21	42.00	120.00	1.00	3.01564	3.16417	9.54
22	1.00	15.00	2.00	−.88675	−.66998	.59
23	4.10	25.00	2.00	−.59169	−.30483	.18

Descriptives

	N	Minimum	Maximum	Mean	Std. Deviation
DISTANCE	23	.50	42.00	10.3165	10.50639
TIME	23	5.00	120.00	33.3478	27.38548
Valid N (listwise)	23				

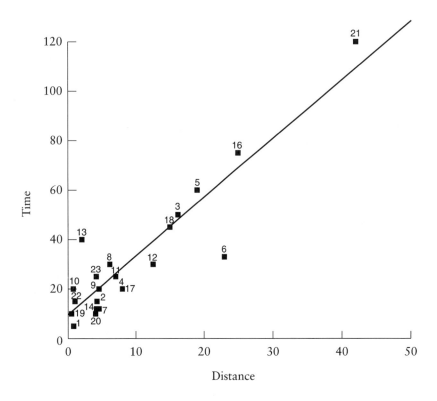

Correlations

		DISTANCE	TIME
DISTANCE	Pearson Correlation	1	.921**
	Sig. (2-tailed)	.	.000
	N	23	23
TIME	Pearson Correlation	921**	1
	Sig. (2-tailed)	.000	.
	N	23	23

** Correlation is significant at the 0.01 level (2-tailed).

REGRESSION TABLES

Variables Entered/Removed[b]

Model	Variables Entered	Variables Removed	Method
1	DISTANCE[a]	.	Enter

a. All requested variables entered
b. Dependent Variable: TIME

Model Summary

Model	R	R Square	Adjusted R Square	Std. Error of the Estimate
1	.921[a]	.849	.842	10.89371

a. Predictors: (Constant) DISTANCE

ANOVA[b]

Model		Sum of Squares	df	Mean Square	F	Sig.
1	Regression	14007.087	1	14007.87	118.031	.000[a]
	Residual	2492.131	21	118.673		
	Total	16499.217	22			

a. Predictors: (Constant) DISTANCE
b. Dependent Variable: TIME

Coefficients[a]

Model		Unstandardized Coefficients		Standardized Coefficients	t	Sig.
		B	Std. Error	Beta		
1	Constant	8.571	3.219		2.663	.015
	DISTANCE	2.402	.221	.921	10.864	.000

a. Dependent Variable: TIME

The information regarding distance and commuting time to campus is displayed in a printout of the data file. In the descriptives table, we see that the mean distance is 10.31 miles and the mean time is 33.3478 minutes. Our question is whether distance and time are related to each other. We decide to use distance as the IV and time as the DV.

In the correlations table, we see each variable correlated with itself in the diagonal where the correlation is always 1, and then in the other cells of the table, with the other variable. Here we can see that the correlation coefficient is symmetric. Distance correlated with time is identical to time correlated with distance. The correlation coefficient, not surprisingly, is strong (.921) and positive. The further we live from campus, the longer it takes to get there. Even though this is a very small data set, the correlation coefficient is significant. It is unlikely that we would find such a strong relationship just by random chance, that is, through sampling error when sampling from a population in which $r = 0$.

In the first part of the regression analysis, we see that the value of R-squared is .849. Almost 85% of the variation in commuting times can be predicted from distance from campus. The table headed "ANOVA" tests R-squared for significance; it is highly significant with a p-value of less than .000, as we can see in the furthest right compartment of this table.

Finally, the output shows us the coefficients of the regression line, both un-standardized and standardized (labelled "Beta"). Both the constant term and the slope are tested for significance and are indeed significant. The equation we write to express the relationship of time to distance is as follows: Estimated Time = 8.571 + 2.402 (Distance). Based on this little data set, we have developed a model that predicts that commuting time in minutes can be found by first multiplying distance from campus in miles by 2.402 and then adding a constant term of 8.571. Try it out for yourself! Does this model predict how long you take to get to campus? Maybe this model only works in Chicago!

As you can see from the scatterplot, the observed data points fall pretty close to a line with positive slope. The original data file includes a categoric variable called "trans," which identifies three modes of transportation and assigns them code numbers: private car (1), mass transit (2), and walking or biking (3). You can see that at least one of the cases is a bad fit for the model—case 13. This case is a walker who takes forty minutes to cover a couple of miles (that's me).

A second small empirical example further clarifies regression analysis. Here is a small table with social indicator data for six Central American countries.

Table 8: Adult literacy and infant mortality rates

Country	ADULT LITERACY RATE	INFANT MORTALITY RATE
1. Costa Rica	95%	14
2. Panama	91%	18
3. El Salvador	78%	30
4. Honduras	73%	33
5. Nicaragua	68%	39
6. Guatemala	67%	41

Note: INFANT MORTALITY RATE is defined as deaths during the first year of life per 1000 live births.

Looking at this table, we can see that there is an inverse relationship between these two variables; as one increases, the other decreases. They are probably not causally related in a simple way ("people who can read can take better care of their kids") but correlated through more complex third, fourth, and fifth variables, such as the wealth of the country, the quality of educational and medical services, and equality (or lack thereof) in the population in terms of access to income and services. At the extremes, Costa Rica has good health services and basic education, while Guatemala is a country with a history of poverty, political repression, and marginalization and oppression of the indigenous majority.

The small table at the top of Figure 21 shows us this data again, as well as the computation of Z-scores for each variable and the product-moments (pair-wise Z-score products), so we can follow the computation of the correlation coefficient.

Figure 21: Regression analysis—Literacy and infant mortality in six Central American countries

	LITERACY	IMR	z-LITERACY	z-IMR	PRODUCT
1	95.00	14.00	1.37911	−1.37670	−1.90
2	91.00	18.00	1.04137	−1.01362	−1.06
3	78.00	30.00	−.05629	.07564	.00
4	73.00	33.00	−.47847	.34796	−.17
5	68.00	39.00	−.90064	.89259	−.80
6	67.00	41.00	−.98508	1.07413	−1.06

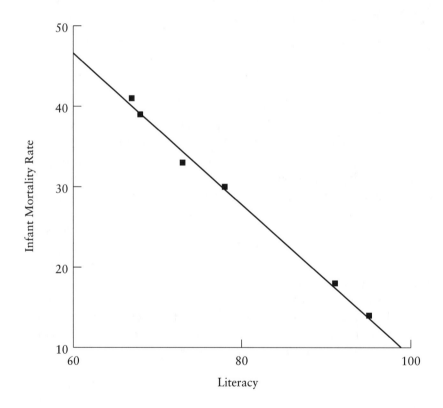

Correlations

		LITERACY	IMR
LITERACY	Pearson Correlation	1	−.997**
	Sig. (2-tailed)	.	.000
	N	6	6
IMR	Pearson Correlation	−.997**	1
	Sig. (2-tailed)	.000	.
	N	6	6

** Correlation is significant at the 0.01 level (2-tailed).

REGRESSION TABLES

Variables Entered/Removed[b]

Model	Variables Entered	Variables Removed	Method
1	LITERACY[a]	.	Enter

a. All requested variables entered
b. Dependent Variable: IMR

Model Summary

Model	R	R Square	Adjusted R Square	Std. Error of the Estimate
1	−.997[a]	.995	.993	.89065

a. Predictors: (Constant) LITERACY

ANOVA[b]

Model	Sum of Squares	df	Mean Square	F	Sig.
1 Regression	603.660	1	603.660	760.995	.000[a]
Residual	3.173	4	.793		
Total	606.833	5			

a. Predictors: (Constant) LITERACY
b. Dependent Variable: IMR

Coefficients[a]

		Unstandardized Coefficients		Standardized Coefficients		
Model		B	Std. Error	Beta	t	Sig.
1 Constant		102.150	2.671		38.251	.000
	DISTANCE	−.928	.034	−.997	−27.586	.000

a. Dependent Variable: IMR

In the correlations table, we see the extremely strong negative correlation coefficient.

The scatterplot shows a very tight clustering of the observed data along the OLS regression line, visually confirming the almost perfect negative relationship.

Even though literacy may not be directly and causally connected to infant mortality, it is a very strong predictor of the infant mortality rates; we see in the display and significance testing of R-squared that the model using literacy as the predictor variable predicts 99% of the variation in infant mortality and is highly significant.

Using the regression coefficients table, we can write the regression equation for the model:

Estimated Infant Mortality Rate = 102.150 − .928 (Literacy Rate).

Do you think this model will work for a larger set of countries, including those that are not in Central America?

Five: Multiple Linear Regression

Multiple regression has a similar logic, but it is more complicated because it involves more than one independent variable. Here are a few things to note:

1. There is more than one IV, but still only one DV. (Advanced models go beyond this logic, but that's beyond the scope of this text.)

2. In a multiple regression, we are trying to identify the relationship of each IV to the DV, controlling for the relationships among the IVs.

3. Each IV is tested as to whether its relationship to the DV is strong and significant; more precisely, the coefficient for that variable in the regression equation is tested for significance with a t-test in which the null hypothesis is usually that the coefficient is 0 in the population.

4. An IV that has a significant and even strong correlation with a DV in a bivariate analysis may turn out to be weakly and insignificantly related to the DV in the multiple regression because it does not have a strong relationship to the DV "in its own right"—independently of its relationship to the other IVs. To see this process, let's look at an empirical example. (See Figure 22.)

Figure 22: Multiple regression—A model using doctors and hospital beds to predict male life expectancy.

Correlations

		MALE LIFE EXPECTANCY 1992	Natural log of DOCTORS PER 10,000	Natural log of HOSPITAL BEDS PER 10,000
MALE LIFE EXPECTANCY 1992	Pearson Correlation	1	.870**	.678**
	Sig. (2-tailed)	.	.000	.000
	N	122	121	116
Natural log of DOCTORS PER 10000	Pearson Correlation	.870**	1	.711**
	Sig. (2-tailed)	.000	.	.000
	N	121	121	116
Natural log of HOSPITAL BEDS PER 10000	Pearson Correlation	.678**	.711**	1
	Sig. (2-tailed)	.000	.000	.
	N	116	116	116

** Correlation is significant at the 0.01 level (2-tailed).

REGRESSION TABLES

Variables Entered/Removed[b]

Model	Variables Entered	Variables Removed	Method
1	Natural log HOSPITAL BEDS PER 10,000 Natural log of DOCTORS PER 10000[a]	.	Enter

a. All requested variables entered
b. Dependent Variable: MALE LIFE EXPECTANCY 1992

Model Summary

Model	R	R Square	Adjusted R Square	Std. Error of the Estimate
1	.877[a]	.769	.764	4.749

a. Predictors: (Constant) Natural log HOSPITAL BEDS PER 10,000, Natural log of DOCTORS PER 10000

ANOVA[b]

Model		Sum of Squares	df	Mean Square	F	Sig.
1	Regression	8463.118	2	4231.559	187.659	.000[a]
	Residual	2548.054	113	22.549		
	Total	11011.172	115			

a. Predictors: (Constant) Natural log Natural log HOSPITAL BEDS PER 10,000, Natural log of DOCTORS PER 10000
b. Dependent Variable: MALE LIFE EXPECTANCY 1992

Coefficients[a]

Model	Unstandardized Coefficients		Standardized Coefficients		
	B	Std. Error	Beta	t	Sig.
1 Constant	50.965	1.815		28.088	.000
Natural log of DOCTORS PER 10000	4.954	.403	.791	12.292	.000
Natural log of HOSPITAL BEDS PER 10,000	1.224	.679	.116	1.802	.074

a. Dependent Variable: MALE LIFE EXPECTANCY 1992

In Figure 22, we are looking at social indicator data for a data set of 122 countries and trying to develop a model to predict male life expectancy as the DV. We begin by looking at two possible IVs, doctors per 10,000 people and hospital beds per 10,000 people. For the variables we enter into the regression equation, we actually use the natural logarithms of these rates, an easy transformation with most statistics software. We find that in three separate bivariate correlations, the number of DOCTORS was strongly correlated with LIFE EXPECTANCY ($r = .870$), the number of HOSPITAL BEDS was strongly correlated with LIFE EXPECTANCY ($r = .678$), and the number of HOSPITAL BEDS and the number of DOCTORS were strongly correlated with each other ($r = .711$). But in the multiple regression, only the number of DOCTORS turns out to be a significant predictor of life expectancy in the regression equation. The number of DOCTORS is significant with a p-value of less than .000, while the number of HOSPITAL BEDS falls short of significance with a p-value of .074. What happened? The number of HOSPITAL BEDS is not significantly related to LIFE EXPECTANCY, apart from its own relationship to the number of DOCTORS. Usually these two characteristics—numbers of beds and doctors—"go together." When they are operating separately from each other, the number of HOSPITAL BEDS makes relatively little difference in life expectancy outcomes. Think about this intuitively and empirically: Where would you rather get sick—in a country with lots of doctors but few hospital beds or in a country with lots of hospital beds but few doctors? Having numerous HOSPITAL BEDS by itself is not a significant predictor of life expectancy, but having many DOCTORS is a significant predictor.

Which variables are identified as significant predictors depends on which variables we choose for the model. We usually select variables that have a strong bivariate correlation with the DV and then see which ones turn out to good predictors when we control for the inter-relationships among the IVs. The model is not magic. It only shows results based on the observed data for those variables we select.

5. In a multiple regression, we look at the adjusted multiple R-squared as the PRE value that tells us how much of the variation in the DV is predicted by the model.

6. Often the betas (standardized regression coefficients) are more useful in a multiple regression than the un-standardized regression coefficients, which may be difficult to interpret in simple empirical terms (as "how much more Y do we get for every additional unit of X?"). The sizes of the betas relative to each other tell us about the relative importance of each variable in the model. The sign of each beta (positive or negative) tells us whether this variable is positively or negatively related to the DV. As noted above, we are usually only interested in the betas that are significant.

7. We can use "dummy variables" to transform a categoric variable into several 0/1 dichotomous variables that can be entered as IVs into the multiple regression. (See a more advanced text for details.) Multiple regressions often include variables that are categoric, such as gender or race/ethnicity—do not be surprised to see this!

8. Multiple regression requires a careful analysis of each variable in a model. Very skewed distributions and other difficulties must be considered, and variables should not be "just thrown into" a multiple regression. A more advanced text needs to be consulted for how to examine variables to decide if they are suitable for use in a multiple regression.

Our coverage of multiple regression is just a start and may help you decipher multiple regressions that you encounter in research articles. Actually doing them yourself will require further study at an inter-mediate level.

SECTION TWO: CROSSTABS

When we have two categoric variables, we cannot compute means and SDs, so we can't do a regression analysis. Instead, we make a table that shows the joint frequency distribution of two variables. This table is called a crosstab, for "cross-tabulation."

We should have at least thirty cases before we do things like compute percentages for the data and obtain the test-statistic called chi-square; so proceed with the rest of the analysis only if there are sufficient data.

First Step: Table Layout with Counts to Reflect the Research Question

Typically, the IV is placed in the table's columns and the DV in its rows. This placement is a convention, not a logical necessity, so we need to look carefully at tables to see if the convention was followed. The table should always be titled "DV by IV"—for example, "Attitude on Same-sex Marriage by Religious Affiliation." The correct wording of the title tells us which variable is the DV, which the IV; it lets us know whether the DV is in the rows and the IV in the columns (the usual arrangement) or the other way around.

Be aware that some software programs will automatically title the table assuming that the IV is in the columns and the DV is in the rows, the conventional layout. If you have decided to reverse the locations (perhaps because it would fit better on the page), you will need to be careful with the table title.

The organization of the table reflects the research question we are trying to answer. In abstract terms, our research question is this: Does knowing which IV categories the cases fall into improve our estimate or prediction of which DV category they fall into?

Let's take a very simple example. Is gender related to enjoying reading? We have two variables, GENDER, with the values "men" and "women" and ENJOY READING, with the values "yes" and "no". Our research hypothesis might be the stereotyped notion that women are more likely than men to say that they enjoy reading, or maybe we just have a research question—are the two variables related?—without a definite hypothesis one way or the other. Let's look at an actual table based on data two students collected in a small survey.

Table 9: Reading enjoyment by gender (counts)

Reading	Gender		
	Men	Women	Total
Yes, enjoy	56	60	116
No, don't enjoy	20	20	40
Total	*76*	*80*	*156*

Here is the table with the observed counts. GENDER, the IV, was placed in the columns ("look down"). READING ATTITUDE, the DV, was placed in the rows ("look across").

The far right column is the "row totals" or "row marginals." It shows how the whole sample, men and women together, split on this question.

The bottom row is called the "column totals" or "column marginals." It shows how many men and women were in the sample. There were more women than men in the survey. Do **not** let this bother you. There do **not** have to be equal numbers of cases in the IV categories. We are interested in comparing the proportion of each gender that enjoys reading, not the absolute numbers. It is very often the case that the IV-categories will have different numbers in a study, and this discrepancy is not a problem unless one of the categories is very small compared to the other or so small in absolute terms that the counts in the cells of the table—the breakdown into DV categories—are tiny.

Second Step: Percentaging the Table

Now we percentage the table. Percentaging allows us to go from the counts to the proportions. Most people do this almost instinctively when they look at a table; they estimate the percentages to come to a conclusion.

Table 10: Reading enjoyment by gender (percents)

Reading	Gender		
	Men	Women	Total
Yes, enjoy	56 (73.6%)	60 (75%)	116 (74.36%)
No, don't enjoy	20 (26.3%)	20 (25%)	40 (25.64%)
Total	*76 (100%)*	*80 (100%)*	*156 (100%)*

> **The percentages must be run in the direction of the independent variable. Run them only in the direction of the independent variable, not any other way.** (See "How To?" for an explanation of this rule. It is very important and must be followed.)

The table in the example has been correctly percentaged, down the columns in the direction of the IV (gender). The column percentages add up to 100%. This is the correct way to compute percentages. It helps us to see at a glance that women were very slightly more likely to say yes: 73% of men, 75% of women, and 74.36% overall (both genders) said yes.

This table shows only a very small difference between men and women in their reading enjoyment. Most people seeing these data would say that this is just "chance"—in our terms, just a result of sampling variability—and that there is no real difference or no big difference or not much of relationship between gender and reading enjoyment.

We might also look at whether the IV categories have the same DV mode; for example, if the mode for men's responses is "yes," is the mode also "yes" for women's responses? In this case the DV modes are the same for both categories of the IV (both "yes, enjoy"). This fact about the modes also suggests that there may not be any great differences here. We need to be careful about using the mode though, as the following examples show: Men might split 51/49 in favour of "yes" and women split 51/49 in favour of "no"; they would have different modal responses but really very similar distributions. On the other hand, men might split 51/49 in favour of "yes" and women 95/5 in favour of "yes." In this case, the modes are the same, but the distributions are really quite different. **So comparing percentages is better than looking at the modes.**

Third Step: The Chi-Square Test of Significance

After carefully comparing the percentage distributions in our example, we already have a pretty good idea of whether men and women are alike or different in their responses. In general terms, after comparing the percentage distributions into DV categories for all the IV categories, we get a sense of whether IV categories make a difference in DV distributions. We will now use a data analysis technique with a test of significance called a "chi-square" to test whether there is a significant relationship here. (*Chi* is a Greek letter and is pronounced "ky.")

CHI-SQUARE TEST: SETTING UP THE NULL HYPOTHESIS

What we are actually testing is a null hypothesis that says these two variables are independent, that they are unrelated to each other, and that knowing someone's gender tells us nothing about whether that person enjoys reading.

This null hypothesis is equivalent to saying that the proportion (percent) of people who say "yes" is the same for men as for women. The null hypothesis for our example says that whatever the percent that enjoys reading is for one sex, it is identical for the other, and for the sample as a whole. Notice that we are talking only about **proportions**, not numbers of people. So it doesn't even matter if we have different numbers of men and women in the sample. This fact is important and convenient, since in most social science research our sample will not include exactly equal numbers for all the IV categories of variables such as sex/gender, race/ethnicity, or majors at a university. Only in a controlled experiment can we make the IV categories have the same counts.

We set up a table of **expected values under the null hypothesis** that shows what the joint distribution for our sample would look like if men and women enjoyed reading in exactly the same proportions, matching the DV proportions for the overall sample. (So if 90% of women say they do, 90% of men say they do; or if the result is 34% for women, it is 34% for men—whatever the overall proportion is.) In real life, we don't make this table, we just have it in the back of minds, or, more accurately, we let the computer keep it in the back of its mind. But it's important to know what it looks like so we can understand the logic of crosstabs analysis.

The null hypothesis states that men and women enjoy reading in the same proportions. The proportion of men who say yes is the same as the proportion of women who say yes, and both are identical to the proportion of the whole sample (men and women together) who say yes. Therefore we use the percentage distribution in the column called "row marginals" or "row totals" (the right most column of the table) to create the expected values table. It represents the overall proportions for the DV (reading enjoyment), regardless of the IV (gender). Whatever percentages we see in this column, we will use in **every** column, namely, for every category of the IV.

The actual formula for the expected value in any one cell is:

$$(\text{Column total}) \times \left(\frac{\text{row total}}{N} \right)$$

We look at the column total for the column in which the cell lies. The column total is at the bottom of the column. It represents all the cases in that particular IV category. Then we find the row total for the cell, the total in the far right column, and divide it by the total sample size. That division gives us the proportion of the cases in the whole sample that falls into this particular category of the dependent variable. It is the proportion we expect if the proportions in the DV category are the same for all the IV categories, if there is no difference between men and women in the proportion that enjoys reading. When we multiply

the column total by the $\left(\frac{\text{row total}}{N} \right)$, we are applying that overall

proportion to the cases in the IV category.

So the **hypothetical**, expected value table is set up by dividing the row total by the total number of cases and then multiplying that proportion by the column total, and doing this for every cell of the table. This operation creates a hypothetical table in which the proportional breakdown of the DV (percentages in the DV categories) is identical for all the IV categories and identical to the overall DV breakdown that we found for the whole sample. In our example, we have four cells: women who like reading, women who don't like reading, men who like reading, and men who don't like reading. We compute how many cases would fall into each cell if there were no difference in the proportions of men and women who say they enjoy reading.

Here is our new, hypothetical table of expected values (counts). It is an imaginary distribution, not the real observed distribution from our sample data.

Table 11: Expected values (counts) under the null hypothesis

	Men	Women	Total
Yes	56.51	59.48	116
No	19.49	20.52	40
Total	*76*	*80*	*156*

Note a few things about this table.

- The marginals are identical to the real table, the observed data table. The distribution of each variable separately is a given; we cannot change it. We can only play with the joint distribution in the cells. We use the "given" overall DV breakdown to create the hypothetical table. (See the "How To?" section for more examples.)

- Notice that we have fractional counts in the cells. This is an imaginary table, not a table of real people.

- Notice that the distributions in the row totals remain identical to the observed count because, in fact, the null hypothesis uses the row totals to establish the expected distribution according to the formula "what is true for all, is true for each IV category."

- The expected count table shows an imaginary distribution in which men and women have exactly identical distributions of yes and no answers based on the observed overall DV distribution.

CHI-SQUARE TEST: COMPUTING THE TEST STATISTIC

If our observed data are very similar to this imaginary table, we would have to conclude that men and women are not very different in their responses to the question. We have a formula that allows us to say precisely whether the observed and expected count tables are similar or not.

We use the formula to check whether the observed cell frequencies (the actual sample data) are close to these expected cell frequencies. If they are close, it's likely that the sample was drawn from a population in which the null hypothesis is true: gender is not related to reading enjoyment. If the observed and expected frequencies are very different, then we can reject the null hypothesis: gender appears to be related to reading enjoyment, with men and women reporting different proportions of "yes, enjoy."

In a box on the next page is the algorithm for chi-square, a test statistic for expressing how different the expected (null hypothesis) values or counts are from the observed values or counts.

The chi-square formula is a precise way of expressing the discrepancy between the observed counts from the sample data and the expected counts under the null hypothesis that the variables are independent of each other.

Chi-square is large when there is a big difference between what we observed in the real data and what we computed as the expected frequencies under the null hypothesis that the two variables are unrelated.

$$\chi^2 = \text{Sum} \left(\frac{(\text{Observed} - \text{Expected})^2}{\text{Expected}} \right)$$

for all cells of the table. Here is the formula:

$$\chi^2 = \Sigma \left(\frac{(O - E)^2}{E} \right)$$

Chi-square test statistic algorithm:

1. For each cell, subtract the expected frequency or count from the observed frequency or count.

2. Square the difference (in each cell).

3. Divide the square by the expected frequency for that cell.

4. Sum these quotients for all the cells of the table. This sum is the value of the chi-square test statistic for the data displayed in the crosstab.

In our example of reading enjoyment by gender, when we substitute the values for our data into the formula, we obtain a value for chi-square that is less than 1, a very low value for chi-square.

$$\text{Chi-square} = \frac{(.51)(.51)}{56.51} + \frac{(.52)(.52)}{59.48} + \frac{(.51)(.51)}{19.49} + \frac{(.52)(.52)}{21.52}$$

$$= .035$$

(There is a little bit of rounding error here.) This is a very small number, corresponding perfectly to our common sense notion that men and women have pretty much the same reading-enjoyment distribution in our observed sample data and that the expected and observed tables look mighty similar.

CHI-SQUARE: IS IT SIGNIFICANT?

The value of our computed chi-square is then checked for significance in a table of the chi-square distribution. We see whether our computed chi-square exceeds or fails to exceed the critical value in the table.

Before we can check this, we have to compute the degrees of freedom, which is (rows minus one) times (columns minus one). The degrees of freedom in chi-square is easy to understand. Notice that when we are making our tables, the marginals are "given" or "fixed." The cells of the table could have a lot of different values or counts in them, as long as they add up to the marginals. Once we fill most of the cells, however, then all the remaining cells have to have certain numbers in them, or they won't add up correctly. If we are looking at a 2 × 2 table, with only four cells, as soon as we fill in one of those four, all the rest—the other three—are forced, so that they will add up to the marginals across and down. In a 2 × 2 table, therefore, we have only one "degree of freedom"—we can "freely" select only one entry for the cells, and then all the rest are forced. You can check the formula out for yourself with a larger table.

Now look at the chi-square distribution chart in the Appendix. The chi-square table is pretty easy to read, since chi-square values are always positive (check the formula—you can see the squaring produces only positive values) and the test is usually considered to be two-sided in the sense that we are checking only for difference, not difference in one direction alone.

A computed chi-square is small or big relative to degrees of freedom. If this chi-square is big enough to exceed the critical value shown in the table, it is said to be significant, so we can reject the null hypothesis with only a small risk of Type I error. Rejecting the null hypothesis is like saying that it is pretty likely that these two variables are related in the population; knowing gender does give us additional information about whether people enjoy reading.

If the chi-square is small relative to degrees of freedom—more precisely, if the computed value does not exceed the critical value—we fail to reject the null hypothesis. In this situation, we fail to be convinced that the two variables are related. Differences between the observed and expected distributions are probably the result of sampling error and are not associated with the IV categories. There is too much risk of Type I error; it is likely that our data came from a population in which the null hypothesis is true and the variables are unrelated.

Let's take a look at our computed chi-square. For the gender and reading enjoyment data, our computed value was very, very small—less than 1. It certainly did not exceed the critical values listed for the .10, .05, and .01 levels of significance, at $df = 1$, in the table. We cannot reject the null hypothesis. Our observed data were very similar to the expected values under the null hypothesis. There was no large discrepancy between the observed data in the survey and the null hypothesis. Men and women in the survey were extremely similar in their proportions that enjoy reading. We fail to conclude that gender and reading enjoyment are significantly related; the variables can be said to be independent of each other. Knowing a person's gender does not improve our estimate of whether he or she enjoys reading.

Of course, we may encounter more complex tables, with more categories for the IV and the DV. The logic is the same, however.

The use of chi-square assumes that we are looking at sample data and want to infer something about the relationship of the variables in the population. If the set of cases is not a sample, but a population, such as all students in a school, we can still compute chi-square, treating the results "as if" we had sample data. Statistically significant results can then be interpreted as reinforcing the conclusion that the percentage differences are strong.

At this point, a warning is in order. Chi-square is very sensitive to sample size. By selecting a large enough sample, we can "pump up" small, unimportant percentage differences into statistically significant ones. This is not a good practice!

Fourth Step: Measures of Association

There are other ways of checking whether two categoric variables displayed in a cross-tabulation are related; these tests are called "measures of association" and can be used whether the data are sample data or considered to represent a population. There are a lot of measures of association and when to use which depends on level of measurement (nominal or ordinal) as well as table dimensions. Some of these measures underestimate the relationship. For example, lambda only checks if the DV modes are different for the IV categories. Because there can be a considerable difference for IV categories without the modes being different, lambda often finds a "no, no relationship" when there really is one. Gamma, on the other hand, tends to overestimate the strength of a relationship. It is best to consult a comprehensive statistics text for all the available measures, when to use them depending on table size and on whether the variables are ordinal or nominal, and how to interpret the measure. Texts often offer a flow-chart or table to help with the choice of an appropriate measure of association and how to interpret the output.

A short discussion and simple table to get you started on selecting and interpreting measures of association are included in the "How To?" section.

Empirical Example

Let's look at one more empirical example of a crosstab, based on General Social Survey data, a large survey of a representative sample of US adults. In the crosstab, two variables are displayed, COLLEGE DEGREE (whether or not the respondent has a college degree) and quartile in which TOTAL FAMILY INCOME falls. By constructing this table, we are asking a research question: Is a person's current family income related to whether she or he has a college degree? Does knowing about whether a person has a college degree or not improve our prediction about which quartile of family income that person is in? Are education and income related or independent of each other? Do people with college degrees fall into higher income quartiles than those without? (These are different ways of asking the same question—in your reading of research articles, be on the lookout for different ways of wording the research question.)

Figure 23: Crosstabs—Total family income in quartiles by college degree, with chi-square and gamma (GSS data)

Case processing summary

	Cases					
	Valid		Missing		Total	
	N	Percent	N	Percent	N	Percent
TOTAL FAMILY INCOME in quartiles by COLLEGE DEGREE	1364	90.9%	136	9.1%	1500	100.0%

Total family income in quartiles by College degree crosstabulation

			COLLEGE DEGREE		
			No College degree	College degree	Total
TOTAL FAMILY INCOME in quartile	1 lowest	Count	323	25	348
		Expected Count	265.3	82.7	348.0
		% within COLLEGE DEGREE	31.1%	7.7%	25.5%
	2	Count	280	46	326
		Expected Count	248.6	77.4	326.0
		% within COLLEGE DEGREE	26.9%	14.2%	23.9%
	3	Count	250	82	332
		Expected Count	253.1	78.9	332.0
		% within COLLEGE DEGREE	24.0%	25.3%	24.3%
	4 highest	Count	187	171	358
		Expected Count	273.0	85.0	358.0
		% within COLLEGE DEGREE	18.0%	52.8%	26.2%
Total		Count	1040	324	1364
		Expected Count	1040.0	324.0	1364.0
		% within COLLEGE DEGREE	100.0%	100.0%	100.0%

Chi-square tests

	Value	df	Asymp. Sig. (2-sided)
Pearson Chi-Square	183.624[a]	3	.000
Likelihood Ratio	183.634	3	.000
Linear-by-Linear Association	170.487	1	.000
N of Valid Cases	1364		

a. 0 cells (.0%) have expected count less than 5. The minimum expected count is 77.44

Symmetric Measures

	Value	Asymp. Std Error[a]	Approx. T[b]	Approx. Sig.
Ordinal by Ordinal Gamma	.595	.035	13.739	.000
N of Valid Cases	1364			

a. Not assuming the null hypothesis
b. Using the asymptotic standard error assuming the null hypothesis

We see very clear percentage differences in the table. People with college degrees, in the 1364 valid cases of the sample, are more likely to be in the higher quartiles than those without such degrees. More than half (52.8%) of the people with college degrees have family incomes in the highest quartile. People with college degrees are unlikely to be in the lower quartiles. On the other hand, people without college degrees are more likely to be in the lower three quartiles, and relatively few of them (18.0%) fall into the top quartile. In short, the percentage distributions are quite different. The DV modes are also different. For people with college degrees, the DV mode is the "highest quartile." For people without college degrees, the DV mode is the "lowest quartile."

This interpretation is strongly reinforced by the computation of chi-square and its test of significance. The results are highly significant, with $p < .001$, as we can see if we look in the rightmost part of the "Chi-Square Tests" box. The $df = 3$ because there are three categories of one variable, and four for the other: $(2 - 1)(4 - 1) = 3$.

Finally, gamma has been computed, as an example of a measure of association appropriate for ordinal data, and it is quite high, showing a moderate to strong positive association between college degree and income quartile—.595.

As is often the case, the bivariate analysis only whets our appetite to learn more. Exactly why are these two variables related? Does having a college degree improve individual labour market opportunities and enable individuals to earn more? In other words, is college degree a direct cause of higher income? Or are college degree and higher income both associated with other variables, such as an enterprising and ambitious spirit, so that the education-income relationship is more spurious than real? Or is higher family income actually the IV, enabling individuals to obtain a college degree (the DV)? In this case, the time sequence of past education and current income quartile suggests that we cannot so easily flip IV and DV, but certainly we could explore this idea in another study. The bivariate data analysis answers one question and immediately opens up others.

In summary, for crosstabs, follow these steps:

1. Create a table with the IV in the columns and the DV in the rows (unless there is a pressing reason to do otherwise).

2. Percentage the table, running percentages only in the direction of the IV. For your conclusion, think about whether the DV percentage distributions are different for the IV categories. This is the most important part of the analysis. Also check if the DV modes are the same or different for the IV categories. This is less important than the percentages.

3. Compute the chi-square test statistic to see if the differences in the DV distributions are statistically significant. Your conclusion here should match and confirm your conclusion based on the percentages. If the chi-square result is not significant, we fail to reject the null hypothesis; the null hypothesis is that the variables are independent of each other.

4. Compute an appropriate measure of association to express the strength of the relationship.

SECTION THREE: ANOVA

In this part of the chapter, we will return to the relationship of a categoric ("group") IV and an interval-ratio DV. ANOVA is a big favourite for psychologists and others who use experimental designs because a good experimental design has two IV groups formed by random assignment to an experimental group, which is subjected to an experimental intervention and a control group, which is not. These two groups are then tested and compared on the outcome for an interval-ratio DV, such as how well they did on a maze running test after the experimental group ate cheese or what their attitudes are about date-rape measured on a 50-point scale after the experimental group saw a violent movie.

For ANOVA, we look at how much variation in the DV can be predicted from the groups (the between-groups variance) and how much seems to be due to other "residual" or "error" factors (the within-groups variance).

At one extreme, the IV-groups could account for all the variance. For example, eating cheese might "make all the difference" in maze-running time. Cheese eaters all have the same great running time, and non-eaters all have the same miserable running time. In this example, between-groups variance is the total variation in maze running time, and we can conclude that cheese-eating and maze running are powerfully related. This would be good because then we have an IV that predicts the DV very well.

At the other extreme, the performance of the cheese eaters might be no different than that of the non-cheese eaters; any variation in maze running time appears within each group and thus is unrelated to cheese eating. Any differences among the maze runners would be due just to residual factors unrelated to cheese-eating. Cheese eating does not account for any variation in maze running time, and we would have to conclude that it is not related to maze running. All variation is due to "error" or "residual" factors that we don't know about. This is bad, very disappointing for our research.

Notice that the logic of ANOVA is similar to the logic of R-squared (the coefficient of determination) for the regression analysis. We compare the proportion of "good" variation related to our IV to the "bad" or "error" variation related to residual influences that we don't know about. In fact, the significance of R-squared is tested with ANOVA, as you can see if you look at the computer output for our regression examples. (See the "How To?" section for more about this.)

Experimental design in its simplest form has two IV-groups, experimental and control. But we can use ANOVA when there are more than two groups, and we can apply it to samples collected in the field as well as to experimental designs. Being able to use it with more than two groups makes ANOVA more flexible than t-tests.

The actual calculation for ANOVA is a bit cumbersome. An F-test is performed that compares the between-groups and the within-groups variability by computing the ratio of the former to the latter. The null hypothesis is that all the group means are equal, in other words, that there is no between-group variation. We actually test whether the F-ratio is sufficiently larger than one. (If it's less than 1, it's pretty clear that the between-group variation is very small compared to the within-group variation).

F is tested to see if it sufficiently big to indicate that there is enough "between-groups" variability to enable us to conclude that variation in the DV is not simply due to the "error" factors. If it is sufficiently large, we can conclude that there probably is a relationship of the IV-groups variable to the DV. The computation of this ratio is a bit tricky, but if you follow the point of ANOVA, you can follow the calculations described in the "How To?" section.

- The between-group variation is calculated as variation of the group means from the overall mean. This is variation predicted from the IV categories (the "groups").

- The within-group variation is defined as variation of individual scores from the mean of their group, and it is computed for all the groups. This is the "bad," "error," or "residual" variation that we cannot predict from the groups/IV categories.

- The total variation is defined as variation of individual scores from the overall mean.

As in any variance problem, we first subtract appropriately to find the differences. Then we square these differences to get rid of negatives, producing a sum of squares. Next, we divide appropriately—and this is gets a bit tricky—to find the mean squares. For between-group variation, we divide by $k - 1$, where k is the number of groups. For within-group variation, we divide by $N - k$, and for the total variation, we divide by $N - 1$, where N is the total sample size. The F-ratio is computed by dividing the between-group mean sum of squares by the within-group mean sum of squares; it is tested for significance with a table of the F-distribution (see Appendix). A large F-ratio (relative to degrees of freedom for both the between- and within-groups variance) will have a low p-value that allows us to reject the null hypothesis.

If there are more than two groups, when F turns out to be significant, we are left with the problem of figuring out which means are different from each other; see a more comprehensive text or software manual for details concerning how to test this with a multiple comparisons procedure.

Empirical Examples

A one-way ANOVA was carried out for General Social Survey data on TV watching habits. The research question is whether having a college degree is related to hours of TV watching per day.

Figure 24: ANOVA—Hours per day watching TV by college degree (GSS data)

Descriptives 1

	N	Mean	Std. Deviation	Std. Error	95% Confidence Interval for Mean	
					Lower Bound	Upper Bound
No college degree	1140	3.17	2.39	709E-02	3.03	3.31
College degree	346	1.99	1.22	6.54E-02	1.86	2.11
Total	1486	2.89	2.23	5.79E-02	2.78	3.01

Descriptives 2

	Minimum	Maximum
No college degree	0	24
College degree	0	10
Total	0	24

ANOVA

	Sum of squares	df	Mean square	F	Sig.
Between groups	371.947	1	371.947	78.525	.000
Within groups	7029.253	1484	4.737		
Total	7401.201	1485			

We first see a display of the descriptives: People without a college degree report watching more TV than those with a degree (a mean of 3.17 hours in contrast to one of 1.99 hours). There clearly is a difference. Is it significant?

In the ANOVA box, we see the calculation of the two types of variance, between-groups variance (contrasting college degree holders and others) and the residual, within-groups variance. (Look at the "How To?" section, and you can follow the calculation.) The F-ratio is tested for significance and turns out, in this case, to be highly significant, with $p < .001$. It is very unlikely, then, that in a sample of 1486 people, a difference in means of the two sub-groups that is this great would come about by chance in sampling. We can conclude that people with college degrees are significantly different from other folks in the number of hours a day they report watching TV. As always, the definitive results merely open up new questions—why are they different?

To end on a light-hearted note, we use GSS data to test whether astrological sign is significantly related to family income.

Figure 25: ANOVA—Family income in dollars by astrological sign (GSS data)

Descriptives

| | N | Mean | Std. Deviation | Std. Error | 95% Confidence Interval for Mean | |
					Lower Bound	Upper Bound
Aries	120	35308.33	25675.04	2343.80	30667.38	39949.29
Taurus	94	35340.43	25107.11	2589.60	30197.99	40482.86
Gemini	119	35934.87	26809.34	2457.61	31068.14	40801.61
Cancer	134	38930.97	26275.62	2269.87	34441.26	43420.68
Leo	135	36755.56	25557.16	2199.61	32405.11	41106.00
Virgo	101	37353.96	26922.26	2678.86	32039.17	42668.75
Libra	98	32744.90	24823.24	2507.53	27768.15	37721.64
Scorpio	101	37886.14	25442.96	2531.67	32863.38	42908.90
Sagittarius	115	32506.52	25929.06	2417.90	27716.69	37296.36
Capricorn	102	32911.76	22771.65	2254.73	28438.99	37384.54
Aquarius	106	35511.79	25848.28	2510.61	30533.72	40489.86
Pisces	133	35860.90	24756.36	2146.65	31614.62	40107.19
Total	1358	35678.39	25515.48	692.39	34320.11	37036.67

ANOVA

	Sum of squares	df	Mean square	F	Sig.
Between groups	5.17E+09	11	470320512.47	.721	.719
Within groups	8.78E+11	1346	652516584.35		
Total	8.83E+11	1357			

In the descriptives table, we see that there are indeed differences in the mean family income of people in the twelve astrological-sign groups. But the test of significance yields a very low F-ratio (.721) with a high p-value (.719) that is nowhere near significant. We fail to reject the null hypothesis that sign of the Zodiac and family income are unrelated. The differences in means we saw in the descriptives table are probably just the result of sampling variability.

SECTION FOUR: LOGISTIC REGRESSION

In this section, we will do a regression for odds ratios that expresses the relationship between IVs and a dichotomous (binary) DV or "outcome variable."

This data analysis technique is especially useful in medical research where the outcome is disease or no disease, and we are curious which IV (such as diet, heredity, or vaccines) contribute to the no-disease outcome.

Let's use an example from political science or political sociology.

The DV is the likelihood of voting Republican in the US presidential elections vs. voting for another party. On the basis of recent elections and opinion polls, we can say that this split is about 50/50 overall for the electorate. Based on exit polls or public opinion data, we hypothesize that several IVs are associated with differences in voting preferences. In this research hypothesis, we identify "high values" of each variable with greater odds of voting Republican, using variables that are either continuous or binary. (Remember that we can dummy other types of variables into binary variables.) Of course, this is arbitrary, and we could identify the high and low values the other way around.

Here is our list of variables and our identification of the "high" values.

- Gender: Male (rather than female).

- Race: White (rather than other).

- Economic class: (Wealth or income in $, treated as a continuous variable).

- Religion: Conservative Protestant (rather than other).

We plan to test these hypotheses with a data set. As in a multiple regression, we have to control for the interaction of these variables. For example, males might also be more likely to be wealthy, so we need to control for gender as we look at the effect of wealth on the odds ratio.

We first compute the overall odds ratio of voting Republican.

$$OR = \frac{p}{1-p}$$

In our example, $OR = \dfrac{.50}{1 - .50} = 1$

Now we want to know if, based on our data, each IV is associated with a different level of the odds ratio.

Warning: Up to this point, the logic of the question is straightforward; now, however, the math gets a little rough.

We actually do the regression using the natural log of the odds ratio, rather than the base 10 log. The natural log—*ln* for short—is in base e, where $e = 2.718$ ... and the decimal expansion goes on forever. This is a very special irrational number that also appears in the formula for the normal curve; if you want to learn more about it, there are a number of good math websites. (Most software allows us to make this transformation or does it automatically in a logistic regression.)

The expression for the natural log of the odds ratio is $ln\left(\dfrac{p}{1-p}\right)$

If the odds ratio is $\dfrac{.50}{.50} = 1$ (even odds), then *ln* will be 0.

(Remember from high school math that the log of 1 is 0.)

If the odds ratio is low, like $\dfrac{.10}{.90}$, then *ln* will be large and negative

(−2.20 in this case). This expresses a low likelihood of voting Republican. For example, on the basis of past election data, we might hypothesize that women, people who are not conservative Protestants, and persons of colour have relatively lower odds of voting Republican.

If the odds ratio is high, like $\dfrac{.90}{.10}$, then *ln* will be large and positive

(+2.20 in this case), expressing a high likelihood of voting Republican. We might hypothesize that males, conservative Protestants, and whites have relatively higher odds.

The log-odds transformation allows us to treat the equation as a linear additive function of independent variables, as in linear regression. (However, the best-fit model—the constant and coefficients—is not found with an Ordinary Least Squares method, but with a series of estimates or iterations, called MLE (maximum likelihood estimation). Check out an intermediate or advanced text for the details, e.g., Tabachnick and Fidell (2001) or Bohrnstedt, Knoke, and Mee. (2002).)

The computer output shows the logistic coefficients, each tested for significance.

Positive coefficients show that, in this data, based on our variable definitions, high values of the IV are associated with high values of the DV, and low IV values are associated with low DV values.

Negative coefficients show that high values of the IV are associated with low values of the DV, and low values of the IV are associated with high values of the DV. This would also be called an inverse relationship.

Notice that we have to keep a careful record of how we coded all our variables in order to make sense of the output.

Most software also shows the exponents, exp(B), which can be read as how many times higher the odds of occurrence of the DV high value are for each one unit increase in the independent variable.

We can substitute in the regression equation to find out precisely what the predicted odds are based on our data for individuals with combinations of characteristics to vote Republican—for example, the odds of voting Republican for individuals who are wealthy, white, male, conservative Protestants, or the odds for individuals who are white, female, poor, and conservative Protestants, and so on for all the possible combinations. We substitute the values of the independent variables into this equation.

$$\text{Odds} = \text{Exp}\,(A + b_1X_1 + b_2X_2 + b_3X_3 \,...)$$

This formula can be rearranged to compute the probability of a person with these characteristics voting Republican, based on our data.

Empirical Example

Let's look at a logistic regression. Emphasis is on reading and interpreting it, rather than doing calculations. The author used a large data set to explore the well-being of youngsters in families with a stepfather. The data were collected in the United States, and the set is referred to as Wave 1 of the National Longitudinal Study of Adolescent Health. There are 3103 cases in the regression. (Tait Runnfeldt Medina, "Emotional Wellbeing and Parenting Processes in Stepfather Families Compared to Intact Original Families: The Adolescent's Perspective," DePaul University, unpublished paper, 2004.)

Medina decided to use the adolescent's report of suicidal thoughts as one of her outcome variables. This variable was dichotomized on the basis of the adolescent's answer to this question: "During the past 12 months, did you ever seriously think about committing suicide?" She then carried out a logistic regression to see which other variables were significantly related to this outcome variable and therefore might serve as predictor variables. Once again, it is important to keep in mind that Medina is not making any claim of causality as she identifies the predictor variables.

The results of her logistic regression are displayed in a table that she has labelled "Table 12." This table contains a lot of information:

- Along the left side, we see the variables that Medina is testing as independent variables. They include family type, several child characteristics, several parent characteristics, and perceptions of the parenting process. Some of these variables are continuous, such as age or income. In the case of income, she used the natural log transformation to make the variable more suitable for use in the regression. In the case of race, she "dummied" a six-category variable into a series of five 0/1 dummy variables. "White" is not really omitted, but is used as the baseline (or reference) racial/ethnic group.

- Across the top of the table, we see that she is testing four models. Each model is located in a column. Each successive model includes additional groups of variables. Model 1 only includes family type, model 2 adds child characteristics, model 3 adds parent characteristics, and model 4 adds perceived parenting processes.

- For each model, she reports the regression coefficients (designated "b") and the exponentiated coefficient ("e^b"). The exponentiated coefficient compares the odds of reported suicidal thoughts for cases with the targeted independent variable characteristic compared to the baseline of 1 for the omitted reference category or the overall sample. All of these coefficients are unstandardized, as the author tells us in a note at the bottom of the table. A negative coefficient means a negative or inverse relationship to the outcome variable. A negative coefficient is always associated with an exponentiated coefficient that is less than 1 because, if the relationship is negative, the odds are below 1, in other words, the odds fall below the baseline value of 1. It is generally difficult to give a simple, real world explanation of these coefficients in terms of empirical units of measurement, such as metres or degrees of temperature.

- Independent variables are marked with asterisks if they are significant. One asterisk (*) means significant at the .05 level, two (**) at the .01 level, and three (***) at the .001 level. The author explains this notation in a note at the bottom of the table. As we "eyeball" the table, we see that many of the tested variables did not turn out to be significantly related to the outcome variable, reported suicidal thoughts, once their relationships to the other independent variables were controlled for.

- Finally of note is the pseudo R-squared reported in the last row of the table. This measure is similar to the R-squared in regular regression.

So what are we to make of all these numbers?

Here are a few main ideas:

- Once the author adds perceived family support to her model, the relationship between family type and suicidal thoughts is no longer significant! We can see this by looking at the row "Family type—stepfather" and then following that row to the right across the table. When we get to model 4, we see that the coefficient ("b") no longer has an asterisk. This finding is important because it suggests that it is not "stepfather family" per se that is related to suicidal thoughts (as it appears to be in models 1, 2, and 3). Rather, the lower level of perceived family support, which may tend to be associated with stepfather families, might be the significant factor. Notice that in model 4, perceived family support has a highly significant (***) negative relationship to suicidal thoughts; we can see the relationship is negative or inverse from the minus sign. The exponentiated coefficient is less than one, also displaying the inverse or negative relationship between perceived family support and suicidal thoughts. The key result here is that, as long as perceived family support is present, the stepfather family type is not significantly more likely to be associated with suicidal thoughts.

• We note a couple of interesting significant relationships of reported suicidal thought to the child characteristics. Being female is related positively to reporting suicidal thoughts in three models; and so is biracial race/ethnicity. Being African American is related negatively to reporting suicidal thoughts in three models. These results would require further analysis and probably additional data—perhaps qualitative data—for a good interpretation.

• While the pseudo-R-squared does not seem overwhelming as a proportion of explained variance, it does increase from model 1 to model 4. With pseudo-R-squared = .072, there is still a lot of variation in reported suicidal thoughts that has not yet been explained.

Just to familiarize ourselves with the lingo, let's see how the author herself discusses the table. One more thing to notice: at the end of the discussion she refers to the fact that "two interaction terms were tested...." Remember our discussion of three-variable relationships at the beginning of Chapter Four? When she refers to interaction terms, she is asking the question whether the negative relationship between parenting processes and suicidal thoughts is equally strong in stepfather and intact families—and her conclusion is that there is no difference in the family types in terms of that relationship. The children are "equally protected" from suicidal thoughts by good perceived parenting processes, whether they are in a stepfather family or an intact family. The parenting-process/suicidal-thought relationship is equally strong for the two categories of the family type variable (stepfather and intact).

Suicidal Thoughts

To disentangle the relationship between family type, child and parent characteristics, parenting processes, and adolescent suicidal ideation, I use a multivariate logistic regression. Because I am testing if parenting processes mediate the relationship between family type and suicidal thoughts, it does not make sense to include those stepchildren whose parents were not yet together during the period for which they report having suicidal thoughts. To deal with this I exclude from the analysis children whose parents have been in a relationship for less than 1 year. In doing this I lose 9 cases (a loss of 0.3% of cases).* A listwise deletion of cases with missing values on these variables results in a sample size of 3,103 (a loss of 3% of cases).

Model 1 in Table 12 (next page) shows that the coefficient between family type and thoughts of suicide (focal coefficient) is significant. The exponentiated coefficient indicates that the odds of having seriously thought about committing suicide for an adolescent in a stepfather family is 1.43 times greater than the odds for an adolescent in an intact original family. In other words, adolescents in stepfather families have approximately 43% higher odds of having seriously thought about committing suicide compared to adolescents in intact original families.

In Model 2 I add child characteristics. The focal coefficient is for the most part unaffected, and actually increases slightly. In Model 3 I add parent characteristics; again the focal coefficient is for the most part unaffected and slightly rises. This suggests that child and parent characteristics, although related to suicidal thoughts and/or family type at the bivariate level, are not leading to a spurious relationship between the focal variables and in fact might actually have a slight suppressor effect on the relationship between family type and adolescent wellbeing. In Model 4 I add in parenting processes: adolescent perceived residential father warmth and family support. I do not include marital stability in this analysis because it is not associated with suicidal thoughts and therefore cannot mediate the focal relationship.[†] The addition of adolescent perceived residential father warmth and family support, net of child and parent characteristics, reduces the focal coefficient by 46% (.367 to .198), making it nonsignificant. The coefficient for perceived residential father warmth is not significant, suggesting that perceived family support has the strongest effect in mediating the relationship between family type and suicidal ideation. Net of parenting processes, and primarily perceived family support, adolescents in stepfather families do not have a significantly greater chance of having seriously thought about committing suicide compared to adolescents in intact original families. To sum up, family type per se does not seem to influence the odds of having seriously considered suicide. Instead the adolescent's perception of family support, which is differentially associated with family type, is significantly related to suicidal ideation.

In addition to reducing the coefficient to nonsignificance, the addition of parenting processes increases the fit of the model. Both the likelihood ratio and the Pseudo-R^2 increase substantially between Model 3, which includes child and parent characteristics and Model 4, which includes parenting process. The Pseudo-R^2 suggests that Model 3 explains approximately 1.8% of the variance in suicidal thoughts whereas Model 4 explains approximately 7% of the variance in suicidal thoughts. This is a substantial increase in explanatory power. Two interaction terms were tested to see if children in these two family types receive the same returns on perceived residential father warmth and family support. Neither interaction term was significant suggesting that children in both family types receive equal returns on parenting processes.

* Please note that earlier in the paper it is reported that length of marital relationship is not significantly related to suicidal ideation.

† Please note that marital stability is included in an earlier analysis as a predictor of adolescent depression.

Table 12: Logistic Regression Predicting Suicidal Thoughts, Add Health, Wave 1, 1995, (N = 3103)

Independent variables		Model 1		Model 2		Model 3		Model 4	
		b	e^b	b	e^b	b	e^b	b	e^b
Family Type	Intact Original	omitted		omitted		omitted		omitted	
	Stepfather	.359*	1.432	.364*	1.439	.367*	1.444	.198	1.219
		(.154)		(.156)		(.157)		(.1767)	
Child Characteristics	Female			.508***	1.662	.501***	1.651	.515***	1.674
				(.117)		(.117)		(.122)	
	Age			.094**	1.099	.095**	1.099	.045	1.047
				(.033)		(.033)		(.036)	
Race	White			omitted		omitted		omitted	
	Black			-.433*	.649	-.431*	.650	-.449*	.638
				(.190)		(.191)		(.199)	
	Asian			-.226	.798	-.245	.782	-.384	.681
				(.359)		(.361)		(.371)	
	Latino			-.314	.731	-.438	.645	-.534	.586
				(.210)		(.224)		(.233)	
	Other			.194	1.214	.127	1.135	.093	1.097
				(.494)		(.498)		(.510)	
	Biracial			.612**	1.844	.607**	1.835	.586*	1.797
				(.246)		(.247)		(.256)	
Learning Disability				.306	1.357	.271	1.312	.318	1.374
				(.171)		(.172)		(.180)	

	Model 1		Model 2		Model 3	
Parent Characteristics						
Household Income (natural log)			−.003 (.049)	.997	−.013 (.052)	.987
Income Missing			−.352 (.195)	.703	−.383 (.203)	.682
Maternal Education: Less than HS			.355 (.201)	1.426	.297 (.208)	1.346
HS			.025 (.153)	1.026	−.047 (.159)	.954
Some College			−.046 (.155)	.955	−.127 (.161)	.881
College Degree			omitted		omitted	
Parenting Processes						
Perceived Residential Father Warmth					−.043 (.024)	.958
Perceived Family Support					−.247*** (.026)	.781
Constant	−3.841***		−3.822***		1.452*	
Model G^2 (df)	5.129* (1)		56.457*** (14)		233.006*** (17)	
Pseudo–R^2	.002		.018		.072	

* $p \leq .05$, ** $p \leq .01$, *** $p \leq .001$
Coefficients are unstandardized. Standard Errors in parentheses.

This example completes our discussion of logistic regression. The overall logic is not hard to follow: As in a regular multiple regression, we try to identify independent variables that are significantly related to the outcome variable after we control for their interrelationships with each other. We are looking for independent variables with a "net" significant relationship with the outcome variable—"net" of their interrelationship with each other. The outcome variable is dichotomous/binary.

At this point, it should be possible for you to tackle reading a research article that includes a logistic regression, although to do one yourself requires more study at the intermediate level and access to statistical software because the calculations are complicated. For this reason, the "How To?" section does not include the formulas for calculating coefficients for a logistic regression.

Conclusion

In this chapter, we have summarized the logic of different types of data analysis techniques. In the conclusion of this chapter, we review the basic steps of reading and interpreting data analysis output for the simpler, bivariate techniques we encountered in the chapter as well as for the *t*-tests covered at the end of Chapter Three. These are useful steps to go through when you interpret statistical output from a software package for a particular empirical research question, and they can serve as a study guide or review of the chapter material.

Check List for Data Analysis Output

1. What is the research question?

2. Is this the best data analysis technique for the variables considering their level of measurement as well as the research question? Remember that categoric variables can be "dummied" for a regression analysis.

3. Bivariate Crosstabs:

a. Which is the IV, and which is the DV?
b. Is the table arranged and percentaged correctly?

   c. What do the percentages suggest about the relationship of the two variables?

   d. Are the results statistically significant? (chi-square, *df*, *p*-value)

   e. Was a measure of association computed for the strength of the relationship; was it selected and interpreted correctly?

   f. What do you conclude about the research question?

4. One-way ANOVA

   a. What are the groups (IV categories)? What is the DV?

   b. Are the results statistically significant? (*p*-value for the *F*-test)

   c. What does this mean in plain English, referring to the research question?

5. *T*-test

   a. If this is a one-sample *t*-test, what is the test value and why was it chosen? The test-value is the standard or baseline used in the null hypothesis.

   b. If this is an independent-samples *t*-test, are the means for the two samples significantly different?

   c. Given this result, how would you answer the research question?

6. Bivariate Linear Regression Analysis

   a. Which is the IV, and which is the DV?

   b. Is the scatterplot arranged correctly to match the IV/DV choice?

   c. What does the scatterplot suggest about the relationship of the variables? (The strength of the relationship is judged by tightness of fit along the regression line; the positive or negative relationship is judged by the slope)

   d. What does the correlation coefficient tell us? Describe the relationship as "no relation, weak, moderate, strong, very strong," and identify it as positive or negative.

   e. What does R-squared tell us? What proportion of the variation in the DV was predictable from the IV? Was R-squared significant?

   f. Can you write the equation of the regression line? The slope can be interpreted as "for every one-unit increase in X, we expect a ___ unit increase/decrease in Y." What do we learn from the equation with the beta weights, the standardized coefficients for the Z-scores?

  g. What does the regression analysis tell you about the research question? Can you write a sentence or two of "plain English" about it?

7. What ideas do you get from the bivariate relationship for adding variables to elaborate the analysis?

8. For multiple regressions, which variables in the model were significant?

Key Terms

bivariate relationship
predictor variable
association, correlation
regression analysis
    correlation coefficient
    average product-moment
    regression coefficients
    slope
    y-intercept, constant
    coefficient of
       determination
       (R-squared)
    beta weights (standardized
       regression coefficients)
    multiple regression,
       adjusted R-squared
ANOVA
    compare means
    between-groups variance
    within-groups variance
    F-ratio

multivariate relationships
    spurious relationship
    intervening variable
    interaction effect
crosstabs/contingency tables
    cells
    row and column totals
       (marginals)
    expected counts
    chi-square test of
       significance
    measures of association
    percentaging in the
       direction of the IV
logistic regression
    binary outcome variable
    odds ratio
    natural log of the odds-
       ratio
    logistic regression
       coefficients
    exponentiated coefficient

Conclusion

Looking at multiple regression and logistic regression has taken us right to the edge, to the take-off into intermediate statistics. At this point you can deepen your understanding of introductory statistics in several ways: checking out rigorous mathematical treatments, learning to use computer software such as SPSS, SAS, or STATA (widely used stats packages for the social sciences and other research applications), or reading a comprehensive text to become familiar with fine points in the use and interpretation of the basic techniques. You can combine an in-depth review of introductory statistics with a move into intermediate applications (more multivariate statistics, such as multiple and logistic regression) because (almost paradoxically) foundational knowledge is firmed up and starts to look easier as you forge ahead.

This completes our short tour of statistics for the social sciences. At this point you can use software to run your own data analysis, check out details of techniques in more comprehensive texts, go on to intermediate statistics, and begin to read research articles. Whatever you decide to do, keep up the mindset that goes with statistics:

- A sceptical attitude about hype, claims, anecdotal evidence, and all the misinformation with which we are bombarded on a daily basis. Very little of this garbage can pass careful scrutiny and rigorous testing, and statistics as a form of reasoning helps us to resist it.

- Limitless curiosity as each empirical finding leads into new questions and possibilities. "Significant results" are rarely the end of the story and usually stimulate us to begin a new round of inquiry.

- A playful and imaginative feeling about statistical concepts such as variability, risk, probability, chance, discrepancy, randomness, and order.

How To?

The purpose of this section is to provide more detail about specific procedures, including calculations, explanations, and selection of techniques. For each basic concept in bivariate analysis, "How To?" will take you from a common-sense notion about relationships in the real world to the algorithm and formula. Consequently, we will look at when to use a concept, the common-sense notion on which it is based, a few simple examples, a precise formulation of the question the concept can answer, a precise statement of how it is calculated, the actual algorithm in words for the procedure, the formula, and tips for interpreting it. Please keep in mind that some of these procedures can be applied to only certain types of data and distributions; once you have a general idea what to do, it may be wise to check the detailed specifications for the procedure in a more comprehensive textbook or software manual.

CHOOSING A DATA ANALYSIS TECHNIQUE

This short guide helps in the selection of a data analysis technique based on the level of measurement of the variables in the study:

- Remember that variables can be converted to different levels of measurement: Continuous variables can be broken up into ordinal-categoric variables, although we lose information. Categoric variables can be "dummied" into several dichotomous variables that can be used in a multiple or logistic regression.

- Also keep in mind that interval-ratio variables are often treated as continuous, even if they are really discrete and sometimes even if they are constructed scales. Be careful!

Independent Variable(s)	Dependent Variable	Data Analysis Technique
Categoric	Categoric	Crosstabs, with chi-square and measures of association
Categoric (defines groups)	Continuous	ANOVA If only two groups, also *t*-test
Continuous and dummied categoric	Continuous	Regression Analysis; correlation
Continuous and dummied categoric	Dichotomous	Logistic Regression, odds ratio

REGRESSION ANALYSIS

Pearson's Correlation Coefficient

WHEN DO WE USE IT?

Use it when looking at the strength of the relationship between two (or more) interval-ratio variables.

COMMON-SENSE NOTION

Are the distributions of two characteristics matched in such a way that knowing about one can be used to predict the other? Are the variables "proportionate" to each other?

EXAMPLE

Does knowing people's heights improve the prediction of their weights? If I know someone's height can I make a better guess about his or her weight than if I don't know the height?

PRECISE WORDING OF THE QUESTION

Are the Z-scores for the two variables lined up in such a way that knowing the Z-scores for one variable enables us to make consistently good predictions for the Z-scores of the other variable?

PRECISE PROCEDURE

Multiply the Z-scores of the two variables (Z_x and Z_y) together for each case, add up the products, and divide by the number of cases. This number, the average product moment, has a range from −1 to +1. A value at or near 0 means that the relationship is weak or non-existent.

FORMULA

$$R = \frac{\Sigma(Z_x Z_y)}{N}$$

INTERPRETATION

This number will always be between −1 and +1.

The maximum, at +1, means a perfect positive correlation. The distributions are perfectly matched. If we made a scatterplot for the standardized data, all the points would be exactly on a 45-degree line with positive slope. For all cases, $Z_x = Z_y$.

The minimum, at −1, means a perfect negative or inverse correlation. The distributions are perfectly matched, with high values of the one corresponding to low values of the other one. If we made a scatterplot for the standardized data, all the points would be exactly on a 45-degree line with negative slope. For all cases, $Z_x = -Z_y$.

If $R = 0$, it means that the match is very bad. Knowing the Z-scores for one variable tells us **nothing** about the Z-scores of the other variable. Our best guess for a Y is still just the mean of the y-distribution. The best-fit line for the standardized data would be a horizontal line drawn through the mean of Y.

How do we describe the relationship when we know the **absolute value** of R? The following chart tells us.

> **Algorithm:**
>
> **1.** Find the mean and SD of the x-distribution.
>
> **2.** Find the mean and SD of the y-distribution.
>
> **3.** Compute the Z-score for each case in the x-distribution.
>
> **4.** Compute the Z-score for each case in the y-distribution.
>
> **5.** Multiply Z_x and Z_y for each case, producing N products, $Z_x Z_y$.
>
> **6.** Sum these N products.
>
> **7.** Divide by N (or N − 1). This number is the correlation coefficient.

R-value	Relationship
.8 to 1.0	very strong relationship
.6 to .8	strong relationship
.4 to .6	moderate relationship
.2 to .4	weak relationship
0 to .2	no relationship

Notice that R is symmetrical: It doesn't matter which variable is being treated as the predictor variable.

Alternative formula: R = covariance of X and Y divided by the product of the standard deviations of the x-distribution and the y-distribution.

$$R = \frac{\left\{ \Sigma \left[(X - \overline{X})(Y - \overline{Y}) \right] / N - 1 \right\}}{S_x S_y}$$

R can be tested for significance. The null hypothesis is usually that *rho* (the population parameter for the correlation coefficient) is equal to 0.

If the correlation coefficient in the population is 0, that would mean that there is no relationship between the variables.

The test statistic that is used to test this null hypothesis is the Z-distribution, although in practice, usually a t-test is performed.

The Bivariate Regression Equation

WHEN DO WE USE IT?

Use it to find the equation (especially the slope) of the regression line for two interval-ratio variables for a particular data set, preferably after a scatterplot suggests the relationship is somewhat linear.

COMMON-SENSE NOTION

Based on the data we have available, how much difference does a unit increase in the independent variable make in the dependent variable? "How much bang do I get for my buck?"

EXAMPLES

If I grow an inch, how much heavier am I likely to get, based on observations of people's heights and weights? If a province spends $1 more on textbooks, how much will its incarceration rate decline, based on data from all the provinces?

PRECISE WORDING OF THE QUESTION

Given the observed data (the math is not magic!—it is based on a real-world set of observations!), what are the slope and constant term of the ordinary-least-squares regression line—the best line we can fit through the data? By OLS regression line, we mean that we minimize the sum of the squared deviations from the line—each observed Y may be a bit "off" the line, but altogether we have found the minimum amount by which they are "off" when their deviations are squared and added. We can find the equation of this line either for the standardized scores (in which case there is no constant term, since the line passes through (0,0), the point at the means of the two standardized distributions) or for the un-standardized scores.

It requires calculus to show how to find the coefficients in general, so is a bit beyond our scope, but here is the procedure for computing the coefficients:

Precise wording of the procedure for finding the slope, usually called "b."

The slope of the regression line (usually designated "b") is the covariance of X and Y divided by the variance of the X-distribution. This makes sense in terms of "rise over run," since the slope equals the amount that X and Y vary together for each unit of variation in X. If the absolute value of covariance is high relative to the variance of X, the slope is steep; if covariance is relatively low in absolute value, the slope is sort of flat.

Algorithm:

To find the slope of the line, b_{yx},

1. Compute the covariance of X and Y.

    1.1 For each case and its ordered pair, subtract the mean of the Y-distribution from Y and the mean of the X-distribution from X.

    1.2 Multiply these differences together.

    1.3 Sum for all pairs (X, Y).

    1.4 Divide by $(N - 1)$. This quotient is the covariance.

2. Divide the covariance by the variance of X (the average of the squared deviations of the X scores from the mean of the X-distribution. Remember, we found the variance of X earlier, when we were doing univariate analysis).

3. As we divide the covariance by the variance, $(N - 1)$ cancels out since it appears in the denominator of both the covariance and the variance of X.

FORMULA

$$R = \frac{(\text{covariance of } x \text{ and } y)}{(\text{variance of } x)} = \frac{S_{yx}}{S_x^2}$$

The regression coefficient is the ratio of the covariance of X and Y to the variance of X.

$$R = \frac{\left\{ \Sigma\left[(X - \overline{X})(Y - \overline{Y}) \right] / (N - 1) \right\}}{S_x^{2}}$$

(the covariance, divided by the variance of x)

Alternative formula for the regression coefficient

$$b_{yx} = (R)\,\frac{S_y}{S_x}$$

(the correlation coefficient times the SD of the
Y-distribution, divided by the SD of the X-distribution.)

If we are working with standardized scores (Z-scores), the slope in the bivariate regression is identical to the correlation coefficient. In a regression with standardized scores, the constant term is always 0. The regression coefficient in a regression with standardized scores is called a beta or a "beta weight."

The computational formula for b_{yx} is

$$b_{yx} = \frac{\left[N\Sigma yx \right] - (\Sigma y)(\Sigma x)}{N\Sigma x^2 - (\Sigma x)^2}$$

$$a = \overline{Y} - b\overline{X}$$

(Once b_{yx} is computed, a can be computed by substituting the means in the formula.)

This formula just manipulates the terms of the "ratio of the covariance of X and Y to the variance of X" formula in such a way as to speed up computation.

Constant term: If we are not using standardized scores, here is the formula for the constant term:

a = (mean of the Y-distribution) – b (mean of the X-distribution).

If the scores are not standardized, notice that the regression coefficients are not symmetrical. The line looks different depending on whether we use X or Y as the independent variable. (The correlation coefficient expressing the strength of the relationship is, however, symmetrical.)

It is helpful to remember that in real-world data, only a segment of this regression line makes sense. Often the y-intercept falls into a stretch of the line that "doesn't make sense" in the real world, for example, having 0 height. So most researchers don't pay a lot of attention to the constant term.

INTERPRETATION

With the coefficients (slope and constant term), we can write the regression equation that predicts what Y will be for every given X for the model that we have developed using our data. The Y that we compute with this equation is an estimated Y. It is not necessarily the real, observed Y-value associated with that particular X in the data set. The regression line is a highly idealized model of the relationship of the variables. A positive slope means a positive relationship and a negative slope means a negative or inverse relationship.

Unless we are working with standardized scores, the exact value of the slope of the line really doesn't tell us much about the strength of the relationship, since it is highly dependent on the units in which the two variables were measured. It does, however, tell us how much of an increase we get in the dependent variable for every unit increase in the independent variable.

The slope and constant term can be tested for significance if we are working with sample data. The null hypothesis is that the population parameter for the slope coefficient is 0. ("For every additional buck of IV, we get 0 additional units of bang in the DV.") The population parameter for the slope is called "beta," which is very unfortunate because this beta is not at all the same beta or "beta weight" that refers to the regression coefficient for the standardized slope. Sorry, there is a shortfall of Greek letters! The test-statistic for testing the significance of the slope coefficient is based on the standardized normal distribution (Z-scores), but in practice a t-test is usually performed.

In multiple linear regression, we compute a constant term for the line and a b (or beta) for each independent variable.

$$\hat{Y} = a + b_1 X_1 + b_2 X_2 + b_3 X_3 \ldots$$

The independent variables are controlled for their relationship with each other.

A significance test using a t-test is carried out for each slope coefficient, with the null hypothesis usually being that the beta (the population parameter for the slope for that particular IV) equals 0. If the slope coefficient is significant, we can conclude that this particular IV is significantly related to the DV, controlling for its relationship with the other IVs.

Coefficient of Determination (aka "R-squared")

WHEN DO WE USE IT?

Use this to determine the PRE (proportional reduction in error) in a regression analysis involving two (or more) interval-ratio variables. It is another way of measuring the strength of the relationship, closely related to the correlation coefficient and almost always reported with it.

COMMON-SENSE NOTION

Does knowing something about one characteristic improve my guess about the other characteristic? Exactly how much does it improve the guess, overall, for all cases?

EXAMPLE

By what percent is my overall prediction about a weight distribution improved by knowing the same people's height distribution?

PRECISE WORDING OF THE QUESTION

What proportion of all the variation in the DV can be predicted from the regression analysis, i.e., from knowing about the distribution of the IV (predictor variable)?

PRECISE PROCEDURE

Compare (by a division) the variance in the DV predicted from the regression equation to the total variance in the DV. The proportion of total variance in the DV that is predicted from the regression equation is "good variance" or explained variance, while the rest of the total variance in the DV is "error," "residual" or "bad—unexplained" variance.

Algorithm:

The shortcut is just to square R. The long way:

1. To compute the numerator (variation in Y predicted from the regression):

    1.1 Subtract the mean of the y-distribution from each **estimated** Y (the number computed in the regression equation). This will produce N numbers, each one representing the difference between an estimated Y computed from the regression equation and the mean of the y-distribution.

    1.2 Square all these differences.

    1.3 Add all the squared differences to get a sum of squares. This number represents the variation between the values of Y estimated from the regression equation and the mean of the Y-distribution—the "good variation" that we can predict from our data.

2. To compute the denominator (total variation in the Y-distribution):

    2.1 Subtract the mean of the Y-distribution from each **observed** Y. This produces N numbers representing the difference between each observed Y and the mean of the Y-distribution.

    2.2 Square all these differences.

    2.3 Add all the squares to form the sum of squares representing the total variation in the Y-distribution for this data.

3. Now complete the division. The result is the proportion of variation in the Y-distribution that we were able to predict on the basis of the regression analysis.

FORMULA

$$R^2 = \frac{\Sigma(\hat{Y} - \overline{Y})^2 / (N - 1)}{\Sigma(Y - \overline{Y})^2 / (N - 1)}$$

(the regression sum of squares divided by the total sum of squares)

The computational formula for R^2 is as follows:

$$R^2 = \frac{S_{yx}^2}{S_x^2 S_y^2}$$

(the ratio of the squared covariance to the product of the variances.)

Yes, just in case you were wondering, we are actually looking at the proportion of the total **variance** in Y that was predicted from the regression equation. To get the variance, we would have to divide each sum of squares—the one in the numerator and the one in the denominator—by $N - 1$. We didn't bother to do this step, since the two ($N - 1$) divisions would have cancelled out in the final division.

INTERPRETATION

The coefficient of determination can range from 0 to 1. It is always a positive number or 0, never negative (since we are squaring the correlation coefficient).

- 1 means that our regression equation predicts all the variation in the DV. Our predictor variable predicts all variation in the dependent variable—Yeah!

- 0 means that our predictor variable predicts none of the variation in the dependent variable—it is all "error" or "residual" variation due to variables that we don't know—Boohoo!

The coefficient of determination can be read as a proportion or even (with the decimal place moved two places to the right) as a percentage. "The predictor variable accounts for ___% of the total variation in the dependent variable." Values near 0 suggest a non-existent relationship, values from .1 to .2 a weak one, values from .2 to .4 a moderate one, values from .4 to .6 a "strong moderate" one, values from .6 to .8 a strong one, and values from .8 to 1 a very strong one.

We can think of the coefficient of determination as a way of testing the model of the relationship expressed in the regression equation. If R-squared is low, this model does not predict very much about the dependent variable in the real world.

If we are working with sample data, R-squared can be tested for significance using an F-test for the ratio of variances. It will be labelled "ANOVA" in some software output, such as SPSS. The null hypothesis is usually that *rho*-squared (the population parameter for *R*-squared) is 0, in other words, that the IV does not allow us to improve our estimate of the DV variation at all.

A multiple *R*-squared, the coefficient of determination for a multiple regression, shows how much of the total variation in the DV was predicted or accounted for by the combination of several predictor/independent variables. In a multiple regression analysis, it is best to use the adjusted *R*-squared.

CROSSTABS AND RELATED PROCEDURES

Computing Chi-Square

WHEN DO WE USE IT?

Use this procedure for the proportional distribution of categoric variables.

COMMON-SENSE NOTION

Are groups different in the proportion in each group that has a certain characteristic? If so, we can say that groups differ in this characteristic. An alternative wording is that the variables are related.

EXAMPLE

Are men and women different in their proportions of smokers and non-smokers?

PRECISE WORDING OF THE QUESTION

How different are the proportional distributions of the dependent variable in the categories of the IV (predictor variable) from the proportions that we would expect to find if the IV categories are not different in their DV distributions, in other words, if the two variables are independent and not related to each other?

We can also do a "univariate chi-square" looking at whether the proportional distribution of a single variable corresponds to a hypothetical distribution. For instance, are there equal numbers of births in all four seasons of the year?

PRECISE PROCEDURE

Compute what the proportions would be if there were no differences among the categories (the null hypothesis), and then test if the observed data are close to the hypothetical expected values.

Algorithm:

1. Compute the expected counts (E) in each cell if the hypothesis of "no difference in the proportions" were true. In each cell,

$$E = \frac{(\text{row total})(\text{column total})}{N}.$$

2. Compute chi-square, a test statistic that expresses the difference between these hypothetical, expected counts and the observed counts we found in the data.

2.1 In each cell, subtract the expected count (computed in Step 1) from the observed count in the data.

2.2 Square the difference.

2.3 Divide by the expected count for the cell.

2.4 Sum all the values found in step 2.3; that is, add together all the values for all the cells. (This will be a "big" number if the observed and expected counts are consistently different from each other.)

Formula: chi-square = sum for all cells $\left(\dfrac{(\text{Observed} - \text{Expected})^2}{\text{Expected}} \right)$

$$\chi^2 = \sum \left(\frac{(O - E)^2}{E} \right)$$

3. Ascertain the degree of freedom of chi-square. $df = (r - 1)(c - 1)$ where r and c are, respectively, the numbers of row categories and column categories. For a univariate chi-square, it is $k - 1$, where k is the number of categories for the variable.

INTERPRETATION

Look up the computed chi-square in a table of the chi-square distribution, and see if its p-value is less than or equal to .05. If $p \leq .05$, we can reject the null hypothesis that there is no relationship (i.e., the null hypothesis of the same proportional distribution of the DV for all categories of the IV).

If the *p*-value for chi-square is less than or equal to .05 we can say that there is a significant difference in the proportional distribution of the DV for the different categories of the IV. The variables are probably related to each other and not independent of each other.

Joint and Marginal Distributions

Here we explore further the joint distribution of two categoric variables. For any two variables with given distributions, there is usually more than one possible joint distribution. Look carefully at the following tables; at first they may seem "believe it or not." It seems surprising to see how many different joint distributions there can be for the same two fixed or given marginal distributions. The row and column marginal distributions represent the distributions of the two variables separately, before we know anything about the joint distribution.

Table 13: GPA by drinking habits—Distribution of each variable separately

| | Drinking habits | | |
GPA	Low	High	Total
High			75
Low			25
Total	60	40	100

Table 14: GPA by drinking habits—The null hypothesis

| | Drinking habits | | |
GPA	Low	High	Total
High	45	30	75
Low	15	10	25
Total	60	40	100

Table 15: GPA by drinking habits—Low drinkers are good students

	Drinking habits		
GPA	Low	High	Total
High	60	15	75
Low	0	25	25
Total	*60*	*40*	*100*

Table 16: GPA by drinking habits—Low drinkers are good students

	Drinking habits		
GPA	Low	High	Total
High	55	20	75
Low	5	20	25
Total	*60*	*40*	*100*

Table 17: GPA by drinking habits—High drinkers are good students

	Drinking habits		
GPA	Low	High	Total
High	35	40	75
Low	25	0	25
Total	*60*	*40*	*100*

In Table 13, we have only the two variables separately from each other. We do not yet know what their joint distribution looks like. It turns out a number of joint distributions are possible.

In Table 14, we see the joint distribution for the **null hypothesis**. This distribution (or one close to it) represents the situation in which the two variables are unrelated. The low drinkers have a 75% to 25% split into high and low grades, and the high drinkers have a 75% to 25% split into high and low grades. Drinking habits make no difference in the DV distributions; the DV distributions are identical for the two drinking-habits groups. We cannot improve our prediction of a person's grade average from knowing her or his drinking habits. The two variables are independent of each other.

Tables 15 and 16 represent two situations both of which would lead us to the conclusion that low drinkers are more likely to have high grade averages than high drinkers.

Finally, Table 17 represents a joint distribution that suggests that high drinkers tend to be better students—every single one of them has a high GPA.

The point of this example is to show how knowledge of the two variable distributions alone does not tell us much about the joint distribution, and that for any given two variable distributions, a number of joint distributions may be possible. Each one of these represents a distinct relationship (or lack thereof) among the variables.

More about Running Percentages

Why do we have to run percentages in the direction of the independent variable? What is so awful about running them in the direction of the dependent variable?

When we run percentages in the direction of the independent variable, we can answer our research question directly. If we run percentages in the direction of the dependent variable, we confound or confuse our research question with information about the relative sizes of the independent variable categories.

Here is a simple example. A small college, with a total of 600 students, has 400 students from suburban communities, 100 students from cities, and 100 students from rural areas. Our research question is whether pet ownership, the DV, is related to home location, the IV. Are there differences in the rate of pet ownership among the three home-location categories? Do suburbanites, city kids, and rural kids have different rates of pet ownership?

Table 18: The counts

Pet Owner	Home location			
	Suburban	City	Rural	Total
Yes	300	25	50	375
No	100	75	50	225
Total	400	100	100	600

In Table 19, the percentages are run correctly, by IV, which, in this case, means down the columns.

Table 19: Correct percentaging, in the direction of the IV

Pet Owner	Home location			
	Suburban	City	Rural	Total
Yes	75%	25%	50%	62.5%
No	25%	75%	50%	37.5%
Total	*100%*	*100%*	*100%*	*100%*

We can immediately and easily answer the research question. Suburbanites are most likely to own pets (75% do), city kids are least likely to own pets (only 25% do), and rural kids are intermediate (50% do). The percentages we see in the table give a direct answer to the question: Are there different rates of pet ownership among kids from different home-locations?

Now let's see what happens when we run percentages the wrong way, by DV, which in this table means across the rows. Remember that we are still trying to answer the same research question: "Are there different rates of pet ownership (DV) among the three home-location categories (IV)?"

Table 20: Incorrect percentaging, by dependent variable

Pet Owner	Home location			
	Suburban	City	Rural	Total
Yes	80%	6.67%	13.33%	100%
No	44.4%	33.3%	22.2%	100%
Total	*66.67%*	*16.67%*	*16.67%*	*100%*

We can see that city kids are "under-represented" among pet owners, with a lower proportion among pet owners (6.67%) than their overall proportion (16.67%). Suburban kids are over-represented among pet owners with a higher proportion (80%) than their overall proportion (66.67%). While Table 19 clearly shows a 50%/50% split between pet owners and non-owners among the rural kids, it is almost impossible to read that from Table 20. Notice that suburbanites are the modal category for both pet owners and non-owners, because they are such a large majority of the overall enrolment. Overall, we can see that this table cannot answer the original research question directly and simply. To answer it, we have to go through a number of steps, asking if the IV categories are "under-" or "over-" represented within the pet owners categories relative to their proportion in the college as a whole, and then we have to figure out some way of expressing this under- or over-representation precisely. Table 20 really answers a different question: What is the proportion of suburban, city, and rural kids among pet owners and non-owners? The answer to this question strongly reflects the different proportions of students from different home-locations at this college. It is very hard to go from Table 20 to the answer to the original question, whereas it was straightforward to answer that question from Table 19.

Measures of Association

This chart is designed to help you select and interpret a measure of association for crosstabulated data.

To use the chart, we need to determine the level of measurement of the two categoric variables—nominal or ordinal.

The ranges of these measures are different and call for close attention in interpretation.

A symmetrical measure is one that is the same regardless of which variable is selected as the IV and which as the DV. Several of these measures are not symmetrical; if we flip the IV and DV, we have to re-calculate the measures and may come to a different conclusion about the strength of the relationship.

PRE measures can be read as a proportion (or percentage) of the decrease in error that takes place when we use the IV to predict the category that a case falls into on the DV. (If the computed value is negative, we need to look at the absolute value to gauge proportional reduction in error.)

Table 21: Selecting Measures of Association

If both variables are ordinal (includes 0/1 dichotomous variables)

Name	Range	Symmetric?	PRE?	Comments
Gamma	−1 to +1	yes	yes	runs high; Yules Q for 2 × 2 table
Somers Dyx and Dxy	−1 to +1	no	yes	use Dyx if the DV is in the rows
Tau-b	−1 to +1	yes	yes	square tables only
Tau-c	−1 to +1	yes	yes	

If one or both variables are nominal

Name	Range	Symmetric?	PRE?	Comments
C	0 to <1	yes	no	
Cramer's V	0 to 1	yes	no	
Phi	0 to 1	yes	yes (Phi-squared)	For $2 \times k$ or $k \times 2$ table
Lambda	0 to 1	no	yes	0 unless DV modes are different

Let's actually compute a couple of these measures, just to see how they are quite different from each other and present problems of interpretation.

Our first one is Yules Q, a measure that is similar to the correlation coefficient. It can only be used for 2×2 tables, i.e., crosstabulations of dichotomous variables. It is a special case of a more general measure of association called gamma that is used for ordinal data.

Yules Q can range from –1 to +1.

We arrange the table carefully, placing higher values of the IV further to the right in the table and higher values of the DV higher up in the table. Notice that the table follows the layout of the X-Y plane, with larger X values to the right and larger Y values upwards.

Table 22: Weight by height

Weight	Height	
	Short	**Tall**
Heavy	a 20	b 50
Light	c 50	d 20

Notice how the "tilt" of the table resembles a positive regression line. Larger values of weight tend to go with larger values of height, and smaller values of weight go with smaller values of height. The major concentrations of cases are on the "positive slope" diagonal. Each cell has been identified with a letter (a, b, c, d).

Here is the formula: Yules $Q = \dfrac{(bc - ad)}{(bc + ad)}$

$$\text{Yules } Q = \frac{(2500 - 400)}{(2500 + 400)} = \frac{2100}{2900} = .724$$

This result is considered strong and positive. In this data, height and weight are positively related.

Lambda (Λ) is a measure of association with a different logic and a different formula. The formula is:

$$\Lambda = \frac{(E1 - E2)}{E2}$$

$E1$ represents the errors we make in predicting the DV from its mode without any information about the IV. With no other information about the data, our best guess for the DV is its modal category, but all cases that fall into other categories would then lead to errors in prediction.

$E2$ represents the errors we make in predicting the DV categories when we know what the DV modes are for the IV categories.

We will compute lambda for our data about pet ownership at Valley View College. Here is Table 18 again.

Table 18: The counts

Pet Owner	Home location			
	Suburban	City	Rural	*Total*
Yes	300	25	50	*375*
No	100	75	50	*225*
Total	*400*	*100*	*100*	*600*

If we have to guess whether a student at Valley View College is a pet owner or not, we have to guess that she or he is a pet owner because that is the modal category. Given no other information, and forced to bet "yes" or "no" for any individual, we have to guess the mode and say "yes." With this decision, how often would we make errors? We would be right 375 out of 600 times and wrong 225 out of 600 times. $E1 = 225$.

Let's see if our errors decrease—if there is a "proportional reduction in error"—when we know something about an IV, when we can use information from the joint distribution.

So now,

- For suburbanites, we guess "yes" (the suburban pet ownership mode), and we will be wrong 100 times (the 100 suburban non-pet owners).

- For city kids, we guess "no" (the city pet ownership mode), and we will be wrong 25 times (the 25 city pet-owners).

- For rural kids, we can guess either category, and whichever way we do it, we will be wrong 50 times.

Therefore, $E2 = 100 + 25 + 50 = 175$.

Now we stick these values into the formula:

$$\Lambda = \frac{(225 - 175)}{225} = \frac{50}{225} = .222$$

Lambda (Λ) ranges from 0 to 1. Our computed value of lambda suggests a weak to moderate relationship with a .222 reduction in error.

Lambda is not symmetrical. We can calculate lambda "the other way" for this table, reversing the IV and DV and asking this research question: "Do pet owners and non-owners (IV) have different home locations (DV)?"

$E1 = 200$. We guess "suburbs" as the answer to what is the home location because suburb is the mode; and we turn out to be wrong 200 times, for the city and rural kids.

$E2$ is calculated by including the pet ownership information and using the modal location for each category of pet ownership separately.

- For pet owners, we guess "suburban," and we turn out to be wrong 75 times (the 25 city and 50 rural kids who are pet owners).

- For non-owners, we also guess "suburbs" because it is the modal category for non-owners as well as owners, and we turn out to be wrong 125 times (the 75 city kids and the 50 rural kids who are non-owners).

When we put these two groups of errors together, we get $E2 = 75 + 125 = 200$.

$$\Lambda = \frac{(200 - 200)}{200} = 0$$

Ugh, we did not reduce our error one bit! Lambda is 0 because the DV modes of the two IV categories are the same. In this case, the modal

DV category for both pet owners and non-owners is "suburbanites." If the modes are not different, lambda will always be 0.

We have to be very careful how to interpret lambda because we can observe substantial, important, and statistically significant percentage differences, and still have lambda equal 0.

Here is a simple example:

Table 23: Illness by vaccination

	Vaccinated?	
Ill?	No	Yes
Yes	49	10
No	51	90

This table shows an obvious, major difference in illness rates between the vaccinated and unvaccinated; if you compute chi-square, you will see it is statistically significant. Yules Q shows a strong negative relationship between vaccination and illness, if you use the formula to compute it:

$$\text{Yules } Q = \frac{(510 - 4410)}{4920} = -.79$$

This makes sense in terms of the percentages in the table because it seems quite clear that the vaccinated are much less likely to become ill than the unvaccinated.

Yet lambda would be 0, because the DV modes are the same ("no, not ill" for both the vaccinated and the unvaccinated).

ANOVA AND THE *F*-TEST

WHEN DO WE USE IT?

Use these for examining the relationship between a categoric IV ("groups") and an interval-ratio DV (for which we can compute a mean and a variance). ANOVA and the *F*-test must be used if there are more than two groups; if there are only two groups, a *t*-test for the difference in means can be computed, producing the same conclusion as the *F*-test.

COMMON-SENSE NOTION

Are the groups different in terms of their average scores on some numerical variable? How much of the difference in scores is due to being in one or another of the groups?

EXAMPLES

Are men taller than women, on the average? How much of the difference among people's heights is due to gender and how much is due to something else we haven't identified (e.g., diet or genetic factors) that operate across gender lines? Is race or ethnicity a good predictor of income or is people's income affected by many different variables, so that there is a lot of variation within each racial or ethnic category?

PRECISE WORDING OF THE QUESTION

How much of the total variation in the DV is associated with the categoric IV (the "groups" or categories of the IV)? How much is associated with "residual" variables we have not identified that produce variation within the groups?

PRECISE PROCEDURE

Compare these two types of variance by a division—that is, compute the ratio of DV variance between groups (the "good variance") to the variance of the DV within groups (the "residual" or "error" variance). The between-groups variance is variance associated with the predictor variable, the IV-groups variable. The within-groups variance is residual variance, not associated with the predictor variable; it produces variation within each group, variation from the group mean (For example, not all women are the same height just because they are women.) If this ratio is large, it means a lot of the total variance is associated with the groups-variable and thus is predicted in our model. If this ratio is relatively low, it means there is a lot of residual variation and the IV-groups variable does not account for much of the total variation.

(Yeah, this computation is a big hassle, and, fortunately, it is usually done with a computer.)

Algorithm:

1. For the numerator, compute the mean sum of squares for between-group variance.

    1.1 To compute the between-groups sum of squares:

        1.1.1 Subtract the overall mean from each group mean,

        1.1.2 Square the difference, and

        1.1.3 Add all the squared differences for the sum of squares. This represents total variation between group means and the overall mean.

    1.2 Compute the between-groups mean sum of squares by dividing the between-groups sum of squares by its degrees of freedom, $k - 1$, where k is the total number of groups.

2. For the denominator, compute the within-groups mean sum of squares for within-group variance.

    2.1 To compute the within-groups sum of squares:

        2.1.1 Subtract each score from its group mean,

        2.1.2 Square this difference, and

        2.1.3 Add all of these squares.

    2.2 Compute the within-group mean sum of squares by dividing the sum of squares by its degrees of freedom: $df = n - k$, where n is the total sample size and k is the number of groups. Here we are obtaining a sort of average of the variability within the groups.

3. Divide the numerator by the denominator, the between-groups mean sum of squares (numerator) by the within-groups mean sum of squares (the denominator). This is the F-ratio.

FORMULA

$$F = \frac{(\text{mean sum of squares "between"})}{(\text{mean sum of squares "within"})}$$

INTERPRETATION

We now look up the value of F in a table that shows the degrees of freedom of both the numerator and the denominator. If the p-value of F is less than or equal to .05, we conclude that the relationship is significant. The groups-variable is associated with a between-groups variance that is substantially large compared to the "residual" within-group variance. We can reject the null hypothesis that the two variables are independent.

If there are more than two groups, further procedures (multiple comparison procedures) are required to identify exactly which group means are different from each other.

T-TESTS

In general, *t*-tests are used to determine if the difference or discrepancy between two values is sufficiently large to be considered statistically significant. In one-sample *t*-tests, we compare an observed sample value to the value that is expected under our null-hypothesis. In independent-samples *t*-tests, we compare the difference in means of two samples to the expected value of this difference under the null hypothesis that there is no difference; the expected value under the null hypothesis is 0. This *t*-test is a little more difficult to set up and compute than the one-sample *t*-test because the groups' sample sizes and/or the standard deviations may differ.

One-Sample *T*-test

WHEN DO WE USE IT?

Use a one-sample *t*-test for testing for a significant difference between a value in observed sample data (often a mean or a proportion) and an expected value under a null hypothesis that expresses a baseline amount or "test-value" that is being compared to the observed value.

COMMON-SENSE NOTION

Is this value I found in my data really very different from my baseline value?

EXAMPLES

My light bulbs seem to have a very short life. Is the manufacturer lying about their 1000-hour life? The kids taking the new reading curriculum had a higher mean score than the national baseline established in the past. Is it significantly higher or basically no different? A vegetable supplier claims that each package contains a kilo of frozen broccoli. These packages seem very light to me, so am I being short-weighted?

PRECISE WORDING OF THE QUESTION

Is there a significant difference between the value in the observed sample data and the test-value or baseline value specified as the expected value in the null hypothesis? Is this discrepancy sufficiently large that it is unlikely to be the result of only sampling error? Is the difference in values relative to the standard error a very large amount, so that it is in the "tails" (or one tail) of the t-distribution that represents the discrepancy of sample outcomes in standard error units?

PRECISE PROCEDURE

Find the difference (by subtraction) of the observed value and the null-hypothesis expected value, and compare it (by division) to the standard error. This computes the t-test statistic. The standard error is computed on the basis of sample size and the population standard deviation. Population standard deviation is estimated from the sample standard deviation.

Note: If we knew the population standard deviation and had a sample of 100 or more, we could compute a Z-statistic and use the standardized normal distribution; usually, however, one or the other of these conditions—especially the first one—isn't met. So we have to use the t-distribution with its "fatter tails" and "lower peak." With fat tails and low peak for the distribution, the t-test value has to be a little larger (in absolute value)—a little more "excessive"—for the result to be considered significant at a particular alpha level, such as .05.

Algorithm:

1. To calculate the numerator, find the difference between the observed sample value and the expected value under the null hypothesis. (This measures difference or discrepancy in whatever units the variable is in.)

2. The denominator is the estimated standard error. Dividing by the estimated standard error expresses the discrepancy in standard error units, the standard deviation of the sampling distribution. In other words, it compares the difference we computed in the numerator to the units of the sampling distribution, the standard error. How likely was a difference "this big" relative to the standard error?

3. To calculate the estimated standard error to use in the denominator, divide the sample standard deviation by the square root of sample size.

To do a *t*-test, we should have an underlying distribution that is more or less normal, although, in practice, researchers are sometimes careless about this, especially if sample size is large.

The difficult part of the one-sample *t*-test is to set up the value for the null hypothesis correctly. We have to figure it out from the wording of the problem—for example, using a manufacturer's claim about a product or a baseline measure for a medical or educational test.

FORMULA

$$T = \frac{(\text{observed sample value} - \text{expected null hypothesis value})}{\text{standard error}}$$

$$T = \frac{\left(\overline{X} - \mu_{H_0}\right)}{\left(s / \sqrt{N}\right)}$$

- $\overline{X}$ is the mean computed for sample data.

- *Mu* (μ_{H_0}) is the value specified for the population mean under the null hypothesis.

- *s* is the sample standard deviation, which is used to estimate the population standard deviation.

- $\sqrt{N}$ is the square root of the sample size.

The computed value of *t* is then looked up in a table of the *t*-distribution (see Appendix), and if its absolute value exceeds the critical value listed in the table for the correct degrees of freedom ($N - 1$), we can say it is "significant at the *p*-value" indicated in the table. This *p*-value or level of significance is usually the .05 or .01 level. If the computed value of *t* fails to exceed the critical value listed in the table, we fail to reject the null hypothesis. The discrepancy was not big enough, and it is quite probable that the null hypothesis is true.

We use a one-tailed test when we are interested in discrepancy in a certain direction (Did the bulbs' life fall short of the manufacturer's claim? Did the kids' mean reading score exceed the state norm?) We use a two-tailed test if we are interested in discrepancy in either direction.

Independent Samples *T*-test

WHEN DO WE USE IT?

In this situation, we have two samples (or sub-samples in a larger sample that was randomly selected). These samples were drawn in such a way that inclusion in one sample was independent of inclusion in the other sample. This means that cases were not assigned to the two samples on the basis of matching or pairing; nor are the two sets of observations based on the retesting of the same individuals. We are interested in knowing whether the values in the populations from which the samples were drawn are significantly different.

COMMON-SENSE NOTION

Do these two groups really have different means or proportions?

Notice that if the question concerns proportions, the problem could probably also be tackled with a crosstabs procedure. If it concerns means, we could probably use ANOVA.

EXAMPLES

Do the students in the two reading programs have the same mean performance? Are people who were randomly assigned to take a daily aspirin equally likely to develop adenomas (pre-cancerous growths in the intestine) as those who were randomly selected to take a placebo? Do Canadians and citizens of the United States score differently on a violence scale?

PRECISE WORDING OF THE QUESTION

Is there a significant difference between the two values observed for the two groups? Is the discrepancy in these values likely to be a product of sampling error—in which case it is not significant—or is it great enough to suggest that the population values are actually different?

PRECISE PROCEDURE

In this type of problem, the null hypothesis value is almost always set at 0. In other words, the expected value in the population for the difference in means is 0—no difference. We compare the difference

Algorithm:

To find the **numerator**, subtract one observed sample mean from the other observed sample mean. What is implicit here is that this difference is significantly different from the difference between the two population means under the null hypothesis, which we set at 0. All this stuff can be left out of the actual formula, since it is all 0, and we only need to actually compute the difference in observed means.

The **denominator** is the estimated standard error of the difference in means.

1. Calculate the standard error of the difference.

$$S_{\bar{X}_1 - \bar{X}_2} = \sqrt{\frac{S_1^2}{N_1} + \frac{S_2^2}{N_2}}$$

2. Calculate t.

$$t = \frac{(\bar{X}_1 - \bar{X}_2) - 0}{\sqrt{\frac{S_1^2}{N_1} + \frac{S_2^2}{N_2}}}$$

When we have calculated t, we look it up in the t-table and decide if the result is statistically significant. If so, we can reject the null hypothesis and conclude that the means of the two groups are significantly different. If not, we fail to reject the null hypothesis and fail to conclude that the differences are significant. Note: For the independent samples t-test for difference in proportions, see the section entitled "Exercises" for the formula.

in observed means for the two samples to this null hypothesis value of 0. This is the difference computed in the numerator of the t-test statistic. In the denominator, we place the standard error of the difference in means. Once again, we are comparing the difference in the numerator to the standard error, i.e., converting the discrepancy into a t-score to see if it was a likely result in the sampling distribution of the difference.

The really tricky part in the procedure is computing the estimated standard error of the difference in means. To do this, we have to take into account the likely possibility that the two independent samples have different sample sizes, N_1 and N_2, and that they have different standard deviations. Computer software actually checks for significant differences in the sample standard deviations. All this makes the formula for the estimated standard error of the difference a bit of a bear.

Other *T*-tests

This basic logic can now be varied for other kinds of data. For example, we can do t-tests for proportions. Just remember that the variance of a proportion is defined as pq, where p is the proportion of some outcome and $q = (1 - p)$, where q is the proportion that did not have the given outcome (like voting Republican or not voting Republican). The standard deviation of the proportion is the positive square root of the variance. This type of problem could also be tackled using a 2 × 2 crosstab and chi-square.

We can also carry out t-tests for matched or paired samples. Check out a comprehensive statistics text for more details on these procedures.

Exercises

There are different types of exercises: discussion questions, word problems, interpretation exercises, and small research projects or field experiments. **Discussion questions** are for reflection and conversation, and they have no single right answer. **Word problems** involve setting up a calculation and finding an answer. While there may be several ways to set them up, there is generally a single correct answer, which the text provides, so you can check your work. **Interpretation exercises** ask you to discuss conclusions based on data analysis output, and **small research projects or field experiments** ask you to collect and analyse data. For these, there are correct techniques, but obviously the results will vary and there is no single right answer. If you don't have the time to actually collect the data, you can, in many cases, do a "thought experiment" and try out your project with hypothetical data.

Questions

CHAPTER ONE EXERCISES

Question One: Operationalizing Variables

Part I: For each variable, suggest a valid and reliable measurement procedure. Specify how the value for each case would be ascertained. Given your suggested operationalization of the variable, at what level of measurement would the data be collected?

- Individual's wealth

- Individual's academic performance

- College quality

- Country's standard of living

- Country's level of respect for human rights

- Individual's political party preference

- Individual's racial/ethnic identity

Part II: Identify some conceptual variables that present interesting challenges to operationalization and discuss them.

Question Two: Level of Measurement

For each variable, suggest ways of collecting data so that the data are at the nominal, ordinal, interval-ratio, and dichotomous/binary levels of measurement. Note any situations that present problems. Notice the overlap with the problem of operationalizing variables.

- Shoe size

- City homicide rates

- Intensity of religious belief (for individuals)

- Racial/ethnic identity (of individuals)

- A country's level of educational disparities within the population

- A community's level of affluence

Question Three: Independent and Dependent Variables

Part I: For the following list, identify the best choice for an independent and a dependent variable, taking into account the type of case for which data was collected. Explain your choice. Remember that, in some cases, either variable could be the IV or the DV.

a) Individuals: college grade point average and family income

b) Countries: infant mortality rate and number of doctors per capita

c) Individuals: attitude on the death penalty and attitude on abortion

Exercises

d) States or provinces: high school dropout rate and crime rate

e) Individuals: religion and attitude on same sex marriage

f) Countries: majority religion and whether or not the country has the death penalty

g) Cities: crime rate and the number of police officers per capita

h) Countries: homicide rate and percentage of the population in poverty

i) States or provinces: average performance of high school students on standardized tests and poverty rate

Part II: Come up with your own examples of pairs of variables (and the cases for which they are defined) that pose interesting problems in identifying the best choice of the IV and the DV.

Part III: Class exercise on formulating hypotheses with an independent and dependent variable: Each person writes on a slip of paper the name of a variable that could be used to characterize college students, for example, eye colour, major, gender, location of home. Pair off, and, in each pair, develop a hypothesis that links your two variables in a plausible research hypothesis with an independent and dependent variable. Now repeat the exercise, but this time use variables that characterize colleges or universities rather than individual students, for example, percentage of female enrolment, number of students, or annual tuition.

CHAPTER TWO EXERCISES

Question One: Frequency Table

Create a frequency table, with percentages (rounded to one decimal place) for the following information.

"On one day, the college bookstore sold 200 math and science books, 30 law texts, 50 novels and plays, and 300 social science and psychology books."

Question Two: Descriptive Statistics— Thinking about Distributions

For the following data and for each beach,

- Create a frequency table of its recorded wave heights.

- Find the mean, median, and mode.

- Find the variance and standard deviation (use $N - 1$ in the division step).

- Find the range.

a) On Playa Mansa, a sample of fifty waves had the following wave heights: 20 waves were .25 metres, 3 waves were .35 meters, 22 waves were .40 meters, and 5 waves were .30 meters.

b) On Playa Brava, a sample of 40 waves had the following heights: 30 were .1 meters, 3 were .15 metres, 3 were .2 metres, and 4 were 2 meters.

c) At which beach would you feel more secure?

d) For an uncertain swimmer, which is the best information about wave heights? Mean, median, mode, standard deviation, or maximum?

Question Three: Discussion Question—Distributions

Italians use the expression "a la Romana" to mean that a total restaurant bill is divided equally among all the diners in a group, regardless of how much each individual ordered. At what level of disparity (or dispersion) in individual orders do you think people would object to this way of dividing the bill? Use the terms "standard deviation" and "Z-score" in discussing your answer.

Question Four: Distributions

A university department has the following distribution of salaries in dollars: (The list also shows the years at the university for each person.)

Abe	27,000	4
Bella	40,000	4
Carl	48,000	5
Dalia	48,000	4
Edo	54,000	3
Fred	60,000	3
Gina	60,000	10
Harry	65,000	8
Ilaria	74,000	8
Jonah	80,000	10
Ke'An	86,000	8
Leila	90,000	8

a) What is the mean salary? Median salary? Modal salary?

b) An observer looking at these figures says that the first person on the list, who is the department's technical assistant but not part of the teaching faculty, should not be included in the salary listing. If Abe's salary is removed from the distribution, how does this affect the mean? The median? The modal salary?

c) Consider the listing without Abe's salary. Which salaries have positive Z-scores and which have negative Z-scores? How can you tell?

d) Compute the standard deviation and Z-scores for the distribution with and without Abe's salary.

Question Five: Class Exercises in Describing Variable Distributions

1. **Nominal variable:** Record everyone's eye colour and create a frequency table, a pie chart, and a one-variable bar chart to display the information.

2. **Numerical variable:** Each person provides information about his or her mother's age at the time of that person's (the respondent's) own birth. Find the mean, median, mode, range, variance, and standard deviation of this distribution. Chart it in a histogram and in a boxplot. Discuss how the boxplot and the histogram are different.

Question Six: Measures of Dispersion Problem

Calculate the range, variance, and standard deviations. Use $N - 1$ in the division step for the variance and standard deviation.

a) 2, 5, 8, 10, 12.

b) –1, 0, –3, 4, 5.

c) 5, 5, 5, 5, 5, 5, 5.

d) 10, 20, 30, 40, 500.

e) –2, –3, –4, –5.

Question Seven: A Problem in Thinking about the Standard Deviation

a) Can the standard deviation ever be 0?

b) Can it ever be a negative number?

c) What is the effect of a small number of extreme values or "outliers" on the standard deviation? (Hint: look at item 4 in the preceding exercise.)

d) The standard deviation of women's heights in the United States is about 3 inches. How could it be that small when there are millions of women in the US?

CHAPTER THREE EXERCISES

Question One: Standard Error

I. For each sample size and sample standard deviation, calculate the estimated standard error.

a) $N = 100$, s = 20.

b) $N = 100$, s = 5.

c) $N = 400$, s = 20.

d) $N = 36$, s = 5.

e) $N = 1200$, s = 20.

II. Discuss the patterns you see in the calculated standard errors. What does this tell you about sampling error and variability in sampling?

Question Two: Confidence Intervals—Proportions

Joe Candidate's polling organization finds that in a random sample of 900 voters, 500 prefer Joe to his rival candidate in a two-person race. In your calculations, round answers to two decimal places.

a) What proportion of voters prefers Joe?

b) Compute the variance and standard deviation of the proportion. What is the standard error?

c) What are the UCL and LCL for a 95% confidence interval for the proportion preferring Joe? What do you predict about the race?

d) What are the UCL and LCL for a 99% confidence interval for the proportion preferring Joe? What do you predict about the race?

e) Would your conclusion be different if the sample size were 400 and the proportion were the same as in the original problem? (Carry out this calculation to three decimal places.) What about a sample of 1600?

f) What would you conclude if the sample size were 900 but the number of respondents who favour Joe were (i.) 460? (ii.) 700?

Question Three: Confidence Intervals—Means

We are trying to estimate how long it takes to prepare a school lunch. In a test kitchen, a sample of 100 school lunches was prepared. The average time per lunch was 10 minutes. Assume that we know the population standard deviation (sigma) and that it is 3 minutes. (This allows us to use the Z-distribution, instead of t). Find the lower confidence limit and upper confidence limit for a 95% confidence interval.

In this problem, instead of using 1.96, for convenience we will round off the Z corresponding to the 95% confidence level to 2. This will give us a slightly wider interval.

Question Four: Distributions

a) In any distribution, how probable is it to find a score that falls 3 or more standard deviations from the mean? (Hint: a probability is expressed as a fraction from 0 to 1.)

b) If the distribution is normal, what is the probability of encountering a score that is 3 or more standard deviations from the mean?

c) Why are the probabilities different in parts 1 and 2?

Question Five: The Normal Distribution

At Pleasant Valley High, a very large school, math test scores are distributed normally with a mean of 50 points and a standard deviation of 20 points.

a) What percentage of scores fall between 30 points and 70 points? What percentage of scores falls between 10 and 90 points?

b) If we drew a random sample of 100 students' scores, what is the expected value for the mean of the sample?

c) Considering all possible samples of 100 (sampling with replacement makes this an infinite number of samples), what is the expected value for the mean of all the sample means? What is the standard deviation of this distribution of sample means? What term is used for this special type of standard deviation?

Question Six: Reading the Z-distribution Chart

I. Use the chart in the Appendix to find Z-scores that correspond to the following values for alpha:

a) .05 for a one-tailed test.

b) .01 for a one-tailed test.

c) .05 for a two-tailed test.

d) .01 for a two-tailed test.

II. Now do the same for the t-distribution with 60 df (in other words, for a sample of 61).

a) .05 for a one-tailed test.

b) .01 for a one-tailed test.

c) .05 for a two-tailed test.

d) .01 for a two-tailed test.

Question Seven: One-Sample T-test

I. A manufacturer claims that battery life is 80 hours. Since we know that not all batteries will last exactly 80 hours, we understand that the claim really is that the mean life is 80 hours. Do we have reason to doubt this claim after we test 25 batteries and find that the mean life for the sample was 70 hours with a standard deviation of 20 hours?

a) State the null hypothesis as a precise formula

b) Why would we use a one-tailed t-test, with an alpha of .05 for this problem? Explain in your own words why these are good choices.

c) What are the degrees of freedom?

d) Carry out the calculation of t (the test statistic), explaining each part of the formula.

e) What is the critical value to which we compare the computed value of t? Explain what the critical value means.

f) Did the absolute value of the computed t exceed the critical value?

g) What is your conclusion about the batteries—and explain it in plain English.

II. Redo this problem with the following values; change the values one at a time, keeping the other information the same.

a) Sample means: 79, 60, and 75.

b) Sample standard deviations: 5, 15, and 30.

c) Sample size: 49, 100, and 1600. (Remember to change the degrees of freedom accordingly!)

d) Alpha set at .01.

Question Eight: Field or Thought Experiment on Sampling

Select a current issue for which opinions can be dichotomized (example: yes or no on same sex marriage). Ask twenty people what their views are and record each person's name and opinion. Compute the proportion that answers "yes." This will be the parameter pi, the population proportion in our experiment.

Now draw (pseudo) random samples of ten people from the population of twenty. You can do this by assigning each person a number, writing these numbers on a piece of paper, and then pulling ten of the numbers from a hat to form a (sort of) random sample. For each random sample, look at your list of names and record what proportion of the ten people in the sample said "yes" This proportion is the sample statistic. Throw all the numbers back in the hat to simulate sampling with replacement before you draw out your next sample. More simply, you can just write people's names on scraps of paper and draw ten of them out of the hat each time, and record how many of the ten had answered, "yes" to your question. Then put the scraps back in the hat and draw a new sample.

Keep doing this until you have recorded the results (sample statistic) from a lot of samples. Record each sample proportion.

What is the range of sample proportions?

When you take the mean of the sample proportions for all your samples, what is it?

Make a histogram of your sample outcomes. What does it look like?

If you are doing this as a class experiment, compare your results to those of others.

Does the value of the population parameter make a difference in the sampling distribution of outcomes? (At what value of the population parameter do you get the greatest variability in sample outcomes?)

You can simulate this experiment by "creating" your own initial population with its proportion of "yes" answers. You can also experiment by "creating" or actually surveying **a larger population and by varying sample size.**

CHAPTER FOUR EXERCISES

Question One: Problem in the Selection of Data Analysis Techniques

Select a good data analysis technique for the following variables and explain your choice. Briefly describe how you would do the analysis and what you might propose as a research hypothesis. Remember, for each set of variables, you are asked to determine three things: **data analysis technique**, **reason for choice of this technique**, and a **research hypothesis**.

a) IV: father's income in dollars.
   DV: respondent's income in dollars.

b) IV: religious affiliation.
   DV: political party preference.

c) IV country's literacy rate.
   DV: country's birth rate.

d) IVs: income, age, number of years of education, and race ("dummied").
   DV: whether or not the person votes.

e) IVs: income, age, years of education, and race ("dummied").
   DV: score on a multipoint scale measuring liberal/conservative orientation.

f) IV: country's level of inequality—high, medium, low.
   DV: country's human rights record—good, medium, poor.

g) IV: city (or state or province) homicide rate.
   DV: city (or state or province) suicide rate.

h) IV: exposure to a violent movie, i.e., yes or no on exposure to an experimental condition.
   DV: score on an aggression scale.

Question Two: Regression Problem

Mario insists that tall men receive higher wages than short men. To test his hypothesis, he collects height and hourly wage data from a random sample of ten men. Here are the data. (Keep in mind they are entirely fictitious!)

Name	height in meters	hourly wage in dollars
Ahmed	1.7	7
Bertrand	1.6	6
Cheng	1.8	8
Darren	1.9	10
Eduardo	2.0	10
Fabrizio	2.0	12
Gus	1.5	6
Henri	1.8	7
Immanuel	1.7	8
Jaime	1.7	8

a) Compute the mean and the standard deviation for each variable. Since this is a sample, divide by $N - 1$ when you calculate the variance.

b) Compute each man's height Z-score and wage Z-score. (You can round off to one decimal place.)

c) Use graph paper to plot the data in a scatter plot. Put height on the x-axis and wages on the y-axis. (Why?)

d) Compute the correlation coefficient using the average product-moment formula. Write a sentence or two of interpretation.

e) Compute R-squared and write a sentence of interpretation.

f) Find the slope for the OLS regression line and use the information provided to find the y-intercept (hint: when $x = 0$).

g) Write the regression equation. If Gus grew a centimetre, how much more would we expect him to earn per hour?

h) Do you agree with Mario? Why or why not?

(If you have access to a computer and statistical software, you can do this problem on the computer.)

Question Three: Chi-Square Problem—One Variable (Birth Season)

We are testing whether babies are born in equal proportions in all birth seasons (spring, summer, fall, winter). We have a sample of 200 children in which 50 were born in the spring, 50 in the summer, 60 in the fall, and 40 in the winter. Determine the following:

a) Null hypothesis,

b) Expected value,

c) chi-square,

d) *df*,

e) Critical value of chi-square for 3 degrees of freedom for the .05 level, and

f) Whether the distribution is significantly different statistically from the counts specified in the null hypothesis.

Question Four: ANOVA Problem

Here are the music achievement scores for three groups of kids.

No Preparation	Conventional Music Instruction	Experimental Plan
4, 3, 4, 5	5, 5, 4, 6	5, 6, 7, 8

Are these three groups performing at significantly different levels? Are the group means significantly different?

a) Find the overall mean.

b) Find the mean for each group.

c) Calculate the between-groups sum of squares.

d) Calculate the within-groups sum of squares.

e) Calculate the mean sum of squares between groups. (What is the *df*?)

f) Calculate the mean sum of squares within groups. (What is the *df*?)

g) Calculate the *F*-ratio and evaluate it against the null hypothesis that the three population means are equal. (Use the chart in the Appendix.)

Write a couple of sentences of interpretation.

Question Five: Regression Problem— Thinking about Findings

Analysing data from a large sample of countries (over 100), we find a .96 correlation of male life expectancy and female life expectancy.

a) How would you interpret this? Is it surprising? Do you think it is a causal relationship? Are the two variables based on data from the same individuals?

b) Draw the regression line that shows the slope (a rough graph suffices). Put male life expectancy on the X-axis.

c) Nepal is a case that lies below the regression line. What does this tell us about Nepal's male and female life expectancy?

Question Six: Research Project—Regression

This project is best carried out if you have access to a computer and statistical software because the calculations for the regressions are rather long. Collect men's and women's heights and weights, from samples of 30 men and 30 women. Which variable is best to use for the IV? Why?

What is the correlation coefficient, r, for men's heights and weights? For women's?

Can you write the regression equation for each sex?

What did you find? How would you explain it? If you are working with classmates, compare your findings to theirs.

If you found a major difference between the correlations, notice that this could be considered an example of an interaction effect: The height-weight relationship is different for different values of the variable "sex category" (men and women).

Question Seven: Gender, Seniority, and Salaries

I. Discussion Question

Imagine a debate in a large firm with hundreds or even thousands of employees about whether there is gender bias in the distribution of salaries. There is indeed a significant difference between men's and women's mean salaries, but some of the managers argue that this difference is just a result of seniority differences—men have worked at the firm longer, on average, than women, so they earn more. Discuss how you would examine this issue using data analysis techniques.

II. Data Analysis Question

Go back to Question Four of Chapter Two and look at the faculty salaries. (Do not include Abe's.) Remember that these are fictitious data! Answer the following:

a) Is gender a predictor variable for salary? (Hint: After looking at the data and coming up with an estimate, use ANOVA to make your conclusion precise.)

b) Is there a relationship between salary and seniority? Do this data analysis with a regression analysis (scatterplot, correlation, regression).

(For convenience, enter salary in tens of thousands of dollars, e.g., 10 = $10,000.)

Question Eight:
Statistical Significance—Is this a
Statistically Significant Difference?

I. Gender Ideology

In a study of sexual attitudes and behaviours in the Chicago area (Edward O. Laumann et al., *The Sexual Organization of the City*, Chicago: University of Chicago Press, 2004, p. 78), the researchers found that for a sample drawn from all of Cook County (where Chicago is located), 31.6% of 190 men and 35.9% of 286 women expressed agreement with a traditional gender ideology that husbands should earn a living and wives should stay home and take care of the family. Is there a statistically significant difference between men and women in their responses?

a) Explain in your own words what "statistically significant difference" means in this context.

b) What is the null hypothesis in words?

c) Create a crosstab for this information, correctly laid out with the IV in the columns. Show the percentages and the counts (rounded off to the nearest person).

d) What are the expected cell counts under the null hypothesis? Show the corresponding crosstab.

e) What is the computed value of chi-square? What are the degrees of freedom?

f) Is the difference statistically significant or not? Explain the steps you went through to find your answer.

g) How would you explain your conclusion to a person who is not acquainted with statistics?

h) As measures of association, compute Yules-Q and lambda, and discuss the results.

i) Suggest three variables (other than sex category) that you might use in a logistic regression to find variables that could be used to predict whether or not a person agrees with traditional gender ideology.

j) This problem could also be worked using an independent samples *t*-test for differences between sample proportions. Use the steps explained below to compute the *t*-test statistic and discuss your conclusion. If you are in a class, you can have half the group use a crosstabs/chi-square technique and the other half use the independent samples *t*-test and compare your results.

Steps: *T*-test for difference between sample proportions

P_1 is the proportion in the first sample.

P_2 is the proportion in the second sample.

N_1 is the size of the first sample and N_2 is the size of the second sample.

First, we have to compute the standard deviation of the sampling distribution of differences in proportions (the standard error). This in turn involves three steps.

1. Estimating the population proportion, using the formula:

$$P' = \left(N_1 P_1 + N_2 P_2\right) / \left(N_1 + N_2\right)$$

2. Computing the estimated standard deviation for the population:

$$s' = \sqrt{P'(1 - P')}$$

3. Computing the standard error, the standard deviation of the sampling distribution:

$$SE = (s') \sqrt{(N_1 + N_2)(N_1 N_2)}$$

Second, for the t-test, we divide the difference in proportions by the standard error of the difference.

$$t = \left(P_1 - P_2\right) \big/ SE$$

$$t = \left(P_1 - P_2\right) \bigg/ \left[(s') \sqrt{\frac{1}{N_1} + \frac{1}{N_2}} \right]$$

(Comment: the denominator is just a simplification of the formula for the SE displayed above, and it is more easily handled with a calculator.)

Use this formula to compute t, substituting the values given in the problem. Find the degrees of freedom and compare the computed value of t to the critical value.

k) What do you conclude? Is your conclusion the same for the t-test and chi-square? Does it make sense to you empirically?

II. "Heterosexual Friends Only?"

In the same study, researchers compared respondents from different neighbourhoods. For a sample of 175 men from Shoreland (a predominantly white middle class neighbourhood with a large gay and lesbian population), 24% reported that their friends were all heterosexual, while for a sample of 81 men from Erlinda (a predominantly Hispanic/Puerto Rican working class neighbourhood), 87% reported that their friends were all heterosexual. Is this a statistically significant difference or is the difference probably just the result of sampling error?

Perform an independent-samples t-test for difference in proportions to see if this difference is statistically significant.

Answers

CHAPTER ONE ANSWERS

1 and 2. These problems in Chapter One are discussion questions, and the answers will vary.

3.   This question is also a discussion question. However, for Question Three, Part I, the following choices would be the most plausible: **a)** "family income" as the IV if it is thought of as preceding GPA in time, **b)** "number of doctors per capita" as the IV, **e)** "religion" as the IV, **f)** "majority religion" as the IV. In the other items, a plausible case can be made either way.

CHAPTER TWO ANSWERS

1.   Book Types Sold

Type	Frequency	Relative frequency (%)
Math-Science	200	34.5
Law	30	5.2
Novels and Plays	50	8.6
Soc Sci/Psych	300	51.7
Total	*580*	*100.0*

2.   a) Playa Mansa

Height	Frequency	%
.25	20	40
.30	5	10
.35	3	6
.40	22	44
Total	*50*	*100*

The mean is .3270, the variance is .005, the standard deviation is .07014, and the mode is .40 with a modal frequency of 22. The range is .4 − .25 = .15.

The median is .325. The median is the wave height at the middle of the distribution. Since the number of waves in the distribution is even, the mean is computed as the mean of the wave height for the 25th and 26th waves in the distribution. Median = (.30 + .35) / 2 = .325.

b) Playa Brava

Height	Frequency	%
.1	30	75
.15	3	7.5
.2	3	7.5
2.0	4	10
Total	*40*	*100*

The mean is .3013—actually lower than that at Playa Brava—but the variance is .330 and the standard deviation is .574. The range is 1.90 and the maximum is 2.

The median is .1—considerably lower than at Playa Mansa. The median is found by computing the mean of the wave heights of the 20th and 21st waves in the distribution, both of which have a height of .1. The mode is .1 as well, with a modal frequency of 30.

c) One would almost certainly feel more secure at Playa Mansa because, although the mean wave height is slightly higher, its waves are more uniform, and it has no really high ones. Playa Brava has an occasional wave of two metres; although these waves are not frequent, they are very high.

d) The maximum wave height would probably be best. The mean, median and mode can be very deceptive; even the standard deviation does not "warn" us very well against the worst case scenario of a really big wave.

Descriptive Statistics for MANSA and BRAVA

	N	Range	Minimum	Maximum	Mean	Std. Deviation	Variance
MANSA	50	.15	.25	.40	.3270	.07014	.005
Valid N (listwise)	50						

	N	Range	Minimum	Maximum	Mean	Std. Deviation	Variance
BRAVA	40	1.90	.10	2.00	.3013	.57418	.330
Valid N (listwise)	40						

3. Answers will vary. Many people may feel that diners whose individual bills are more than one standard deviation below the mean ($Z < -1$) might object. A situation in which the standard deviation is small—most people's orders were quite similar—will bring about fewer objections. Some people may want to talk about cultural differences; in some cultures, it might be considered rude to object to the equal division of the bill.

4. **a)** With Abe's salary, the mean is $61,000, the median is $60,000 (the mean of the middle two salaries), and the modes are $48,000 and $60,000.

   b) Without Abe's salary, the mean is $64,090, the median is still $60,000 (Gina's salary), and the two modes remain $48,000 and $60,000.

c) The Z-scores are displayed in the following tables. For the salary Z-scores, check the column labelled "z-SALARY."

d) With Abe's salary, the variance is 363.46, and the standard deviation is 19.06. Without Abe's salary, the variance is 273.69, and the standard deviation is 16.54.

University Salaries

	SALARY	SENIORITY	z-SALARY	z-SENIORITY
1	27.00	4.00	−1.78342	−.84360
2	40.00	4.00	−1.10152	−.84360
3	48.00	5.00	−.68190	−.46867
4	48.00	4.00	−.68190	−.84360
5	54.00	3.00	−.36717	−1.21853
6	60.00	3.00	−.05245	−1.21853
7	60.00	10.00	−.05245	1.40600
8	65.00	8.00	.20981	.65613
9	74.00	8.00	.68190	.65613
10	80.00	10.00	.99662	1.40600
11	86.00	8.00	1.31134	.65613
12	90.00	8.00	1.52115	.65613

	SALARY	SENIORITY	GENDER	z-SALARY	z-SENIORITY
1	40.00	4.00	1.00	−1.45621	−.91017
2	48.00	5.00	.00	−.97264	−.53936
3	48.00	4.00	1.00	−.97264	−.91017
4	54.00	3.00	.00	−.60996	−1.28098
5	60.00	3.00	.00	−.24728	−1.28098
6	60.00	10.00	1.00	−.24728	1.31469
7	65.00	8.00	.00	.05495	.57307
8	74.00	8.00	1.00	.59897	.57307
9	80.00	10.00	.00	.96165	1.31469
10	86.00	8.00	1.00	1.32432	.57307
11	90.00	8.00	1.00	1.56611	.57307

5. Answers will vary.

6. **a)** Range is 10, variance is 15.800, and standard deviation is 3.97492.

b) Range is 8, variance is 11.500, and standard deviation is 3.39116.

c) Range is 0, variance is 0, and standard deviation is 0.

d) Range is 490, variance is 45250.000, and standard deviation is 212.72047.

e) Range is 3, variance is 1.667, and standard deviation is 1.29099.

Except for the ranges, which are calculated by subtracting the minimum from the maximum value is each case, a computer program generated these answers. Each set of observations was entered into a computer, and the "Descriptives" table shows the number of observations, the minimum and maximum values, means, standard deviations, and variances.

Data Table

Number of observations	var a	var b	var c	var d	var e
1	2.00	−1.00	5.00	10.00	−2.00
2	5.00	.00	5.00	20.00	−3.00
3	8.00	−3.00	5.00	30.00	−4.00
4	10.00	4.00	5.00	40.00	−5.00
5	12.00	5.00	5.00	500.00	
6			5.00		
7			5.00		

Descriptives

	N	Minimum	Maximum	Mean	Std. Deviation	Variance
var a	5	2.00	12.00	7.4000	3.97492	15.800
var b	5	−3.00	5.00	1.0000	3.39116	11.500
var c	7	5.00	5.00	5.0000	.00000	.000
var d	5	10.00	500.00	120.0000	212.72047	45250.000
var e	4	−5.00	−2.00	−3.5000	1.29099	1.667
Valid N (listwise)	4					

7. a) Yes, if all the observations are equal.

b) No. The deviations from the mean are squared, so their sum is always positive. The smallest the standard deviation could ever be is 0, if all the observations are equal.

c) As in computation of the mean, a number of extreme values have an effect on the standard deviation, making it larger.

d) The standard deviation is based on the variance, which is computed as a **mean for the number of cases.** Although each case may "put in" a certain amount of deviation from the mean of the heights, this deviation is squared and then averaged over the total number of cases when we compute the variance. The more cases there are, the higher the N in the denominator, and the answer gives us the amount of squared deviation "per case."

Exercises

CHAPTER THREE ANSWERS

1. **I.** **a)** $SE = 20/10 = 2$ **c.** $SE = 20/20 = 1$ **e.** $SE = 20/34.64 = .577$

     b) $SE = 5/10 = \dfrac{1}{2}$ **d.** $SE = 5/6$

II. In general, the larger the sample, the lower the standard error. The smaller the standard deviation, the lower the standard error. In any case, the standard errors are always considerably lower than the corresponding sample standard deviations. The sample statistics are unlikely to deviate extremely from the population parameter.

2. **a)** The proportion of voters supporting Joe is $500/900 = .56$.

b) The variance of this proportion is $(.56)(1 - .56) = (.56)(.44) = .25$. The standard deviation is the square root of the variance, in other words, $.5$. The $SE = .5/30 = .017$. The denominator of the standard error is the square root of sample size; $N = 900$, so the square root of $N = 30$.

c) The Z-score that corresponds to a 95% confidence interval is 1.96. The UCL $= .56 + (1.96)(.017) = .56 + .032 = .592$ or 59.2%. The LCL $= .56 - (1.96)(.017) = .56 - .032 = .528$ or 52.8%. In other words, the 95% confidence interval is between 52.8% and 59.25%, so we predict a victory for Joe. The interval does not include 50%, so it is unlikely that Joe will lose.

d) For a 99% confidence interval, $Z = 2.58$. The other information remains the same. The UCL $= .56 + (2.58)(.017) = .56 + .04 = .60$ or 60%. The LCL $= .56 - (2.58)(.017) = .56 - .04 = .52$ or 52%. We predict that Joe will be the winner of the election; once again, the confidence interval does not include 50%. The higher confidence level widens the confidence interval, however.

e) If the sample were 400, rather than 900, the SE would be $.5/20 = .025$. For a 95% confidence interval, the UCL $= .556 + .049 = .605$ or 60.5%. The LCL is $.556 - .049 = .507$ or 50.7%. Here we are rounding the proportion to three rather than two decimal places. We are still predicting a victory for Joe, but now it's very close. The smaller sample size widens the confidence interval.

f) **i.** When first varying the sample proportions in favour of Joe, the sample size $= 900$ and 460 favour Joe, so $P = 460/900 = .511$. The variance $= (.511)(.489) = .25$. The standard deviation is the square root of the variance or $.5$. The $SE = .5/30 = .017$. The UCL $= .511 + .032 = .543 = 54.3\%$, and the LCL $= .511 - .032 = .479 = 47.9\%$. The 95% confidence interval now includes a lower value than 50%, so the race is too close to call with this sample size.

ii. When varying the sample proportions in favour of Joe the second time, the sample size $= 900$, and 700 favour Joe, so $P = 700/900 = .78$. The variance $= (.78)(.22) = .18$. The standard deviation $= .41$. $SE = .41/30 = .014$. The UCL $= .78 + (1.96)(.014) = .780 + .027 = .807 = 80.7\%$, and the LCL $= .78 - (.027) = .753 = 75.3\%$. Notice that with a higher proportion in favour of Joe, the SD and the *SE* are a little smaller. There is little doubt that Joe will win the election.

3.　The *SE* = 3/10 (standard deviation divided by the square root of sample size). The *UCL* = 10 + (2 × $3/10$) = 10.6 minutes, and the *LCL* = 10 – (2 × $3/10$) = 9.4 minutes.

Comment: Questions two and three in this chapter are about confidence levels and confidence intervals. Constructing an interval for a 95% confidence level is like making a bet based on the mathematical probability that 95% of sample outcomes (mean, proportion) are within plus or minus 1.96 standard errors of the population parameter. This probability corresponds to the confidence level (95%). The width of the interval is 1.96 times the standard error. Only 5% of the sample outcomes are so far "off" from the population parameter that the intervals we construct around them would fail to include the population parameter. How do we know this probability? The Central Limit Theorem tells us so—sampling error is normally distributed! Unfortunately, once we compute the confidence interval using a specific sample outcome, we don't know whether it is one of the 95% of "good" intervals that contain the population parameter or one of the 5% of "bad" intervals that missed it.

4.　**a)** $P <= 1/9$. By Chebycheff's Inequality, a score that is three or more standard deviations from the mean has a probability of no more than 1/9 in any distribution.

　　b) In a normal distribution, the probability of a score that is 3 or more standard deviations from the mean is .003, and 99.7% of all scores in a normal distribution are within 3 standard deviations, plus or minus, from the mean, so the probability of an observation falling beyond this interval is (1 – .997) = .003.

　　c) The two probabilities are different because Chebycheff's Inequality applies to all distributions, whereas the normal distribution is a special distribution in which scores are mostly close to the mean. In the normal distribution, the probability of encountering a very "deviant" observation is lower than it is for distributions in general.

5　**a)** About 68% of all scores are between 30 and 70 points (within plus or minus one standard deviation from the mean of 50). About 95% of all scores fall between 10 and 90 points (within plus or minus 2 standard deviations from the mean of 5).

　　b) The expected value for the sample mean is 50 points.

　　c) The expected value of the mean of all sample means is 50 points.

The standard deviation of the distribution of sample means is called the standard error, and, in this problem, it is $20/\sqrt{100}$ = 20/10 = 2.

Notice that the standard error for samples of 100 is considerably smaller than the standard deviation. By the time our sample size is up to 100, there is just not that much sampling error (variability in sample outcomes). A random sample of 100 students would usually give us a very good estimate of the mean score for all the students.

6. **I. a)** 1.65 **b)** 2.33 **c)** 1.96 **d)** 2.58

 II. a) 1.67 **b)** 2.39 **c)** 2.0 **d)** 2.66

Notice that for the *t*-test we have to consider sample size. The larger it is, the closer the *t*-distribution is to the Z-distribution. When *df* = 60 (i.e., N = 61), the critical values for the *t*-distribution are slightly larger than those for the Z-distribution. All other things being equal, it is a little "harder" for the results to be statistically significant in a *t*-test than in a Z-test.

7. **I.** One-sample *t*-test for battery life.

a) The null hypothesis is that *mu* (μ) = 80.

b) We will do a one-tailed test because we are concerned with battery life falling short of the claim. We chose .05 because it is a common cut-off point. We do not want to be embarrassed in making a complaint; we want to be fairly sure that we are justified in complaining. An alpha level of .05 means that there is only a $5/100$ chance that this large a disparity came about due to sampling error.

c) *df* = N − 1 = 24. (Remark: this is a rather small sample!)

d) $t = (70 - 80)/(20/5)$. The numerator expresses the difference between the observed mean and the claimed value specified in the null hypothesis. The denominator is the estimated standard error, found by dividing the observed standard deviation by the square root of sample size. The formula as a whole is a measure of the disparity of the observed mean from the null hypothesis claim, compared to the variability of sample outcomes.

$$T = -10/4 = -2.5$$

e) The critical value is 1.71. We read this from the *t*-table, looking for 24 degrees of freedom, an alpha level of .05, in a one-tailed test. The disparity must be greater—in absolute value—than this number in order for the observed data to be considered significantly different statistically from the null hypothesis value (the manufacturer's claim).

f) Yes, the absolute value of our computed *t*-statistic is greater than the critical value: 2.50 > 1.71.

g) We therefore can reject the null hypothesis. The observed value is significantly different statistically from the manufacturer's claim.

II. Changing values in the one-sample *t*-test for battery life.

a) Varying the sample means, while keeping the standard deviation and sample size the same:

If the sample mean is 79: $t = (79 - 80)/4 = -.25$. The absolute value does not exceed the critical value. The difference is not statistically significant. The observed value is not significantly different from the null hypothesis value.

If the sample mean is 60: $t = (60 - 80)/4 = -20/4 = -5$. The absolute value of the disparity exceeds the critical value. This is a very large disparity. The difference is statistically significant; the manufacturer's claim is almost certainly not accurate.

If the sample mean is 75: $t = (75 - 80)/4 = -1.25$. We cannot reject the null hypothesis. The observed value is not significantly different from the null hypothesis value.

Notice that the larger the difference in means, all other things being equal, the more likely that the difference is statistically significant.

b) Varying sample standard deviations, while keeping sample size at 25.

$s = 5$. $SE = 5/5 = 1$.
$t = (70 - 80)/1. = -10$. This is statistically significant.

$s = 15$. $SE = 15/5 = 3$.
$t = (70 - 80)/3 = -10/3 = -3.33$. This is statistically significant.

$s = 30$. $SE = 30/5 = 6$.
$t = (70 - 80)/6 = -10/6 = 1.66$. The absolute value does not exceed the critical value; the result is not statistically significant.

Notice that the larger the standard deviation, all other things being equal, the less likely the difference is statistically significant. A larger standard deviation increases sampling error.

c) Varying sample size, while keeping the standard deviation at 20.

$N = 49$.
$SE = 20/7 = 2.86$
$t = (70 - 80)/2.86 = -3.49$.
The df is 48, and the critical value is 1.68 for a one-tailed test at the .05 level of significance. Hence this is a statistically significant difference.

$N = 100$.
$SE = 20/10 = 2$.
$df = 99$, and the critical value is 1.66.
$t = (70 - 80)/2 = -10/2 = -5$. This is statistically significant.

$N = 1600$.
$SE = 20/40 = .5$.
$df = 1599$, and the critical value is 1.64.
$t = (70 - 80)/.5 = -20$. This is statistically significant.

Notice that the larger the sample size, all other things being equal, the more likely the difference is to be statistically significant. By the Central Limit Theorem, a larger sample size reduces the sampling error.

Exercises

d) If alpha is set at .01, with sample size = 25, the critical value for a one-tailed test is 2.49 for 24 *df*, instead of 1.71. It is therefore "harder" for the observed disparity to be significant. We are applying a more rigid standard to decide statistical significance, namely allowing a probability of only 1/100 for Type I error (that is, a mistaken rejection of a true null hypothesis).

8. Results will vary. Population proportions closer to 0 or 100% will have less variability in sampling outcomes. Larger samples will have less variability.

CHAPTER FOUR ANSWERS

1. **a)** Regression because both variables are continuous; Possible research hypothesis is a positive correlation between these two variables. Wealthier fathers tend to have wealthier children.

b) Crosstabs because there are two categoric variables; Possible research hypotheses are that Fundamentalist Christians might be more likely to vote for conservative political parties or that people from minority religions (e.g., Jews, Muslims, Hindus) and atheists might be more likely to vote for liberal parties. Answers will vary depending on how the variables are operationalized and on what categories are defined.

c) Regression because both variables are continuous; Possible research hypothesis is that there is a negative correlation between the two variables. Countries with higher literacy rates might have more women in the paid labour force and be less rural, both characteristics that would lead to lower birth rates.

d) Logistic regression because of the binary outcome variable and the multiple predictor variables. Possible research hypothesis is open for discussion. Discussion question! Answers may vary.

e) Multiple regression because there are multiple independent variables and a numeric dependent variable that can be treated as continuous. Possible research hypothesis is open for discussion. Discussion question! Answers may vary.

f) Crosstabs because both variables are ordinal (categoric); Possible research hypothesis is that countries with a lot of inequality will tend to have worse human rights records; there might be more class conflict, more is at stake in social conflicts, and people in the lower classes might be more vulnerable, have less access to political and legal resources.

g) Regression because both variables are continuous; Possible research hypothesis is open for discussion. Answers may vary. In nineteenth century Europe, these variables had an inverse relationship, but that may not be the case here and now.

h) ANOVA because of the 2-category independent variable and the numeric dependent variable that can be treated as continuous. Independent samples *t*-test for difference in means is also OK. Possible research hypothesis is that seeing violent movies makes people more aggressive—a positive relationship between the variables.

2. Answers may be found by consulting the included tables and graph, which were generated by a computer program.

a) Height: mean = 1.77 meters. S = .1634 meters. Variance = .027
   Hourly wage: mean = 8.2. S = 1.932. Variance = 3.73

b) See the first table.

c) See the graph. It is plotted this way because Mario is testing the research hypothesis that taller men receive higher wages, so height is the IV and wage is the DV.

d) r = .900. This is a very strong positive correlation. Height and hourly wage are strongly and positively related. Taller men receive higher wages.

e) R-square = .809 (.81 if you round off). About 81% of variation in hourly wage can be predicted from height.

f) W = −10.6 + 10.6H. We can read this from the table labelled "Coefficients," and compute it by the following formula.
   The slope coefficient: $b = R (s_y/s_x)$
   In this case, b = .9 (1.93/0.1634)= .9 × 11.81 = 10.6
   Constant term: When x = 0, y = −10.6

g) From the equation, if Gus grew a centimetre (.01 meters), we would expect a $0.106 increase in his hourly wage—a dime more per hour.

h) From Mario's data, his hypothesis looks correct. However, this is a very small sample. Even though R and b are statistically significant, we would be wise to carry out the study with a larger sample and to think about repeating it in other places.

	HEIGHT	HOURWAGE	z-HEIGHT	z-HOURWAGE
1	1.70	7.00	−.42777	−.62106
2	1.60	6.00	−1.03887	−1.13861
3	1.80	8.00	.18333	−.10351
4	1.90	10.00	.79443	.93159
5	2.00	10.00	1.40553	.93159
6	2.00	12.00	1.40553	1.96669
7	1.50	6.00	−1.64997	−1.13861
8	1.80	7.00	.18333	−.62106
9	1.70	8.00	−.42777	−.10351
10	1.70	8.00	−.42777	−.10351

Exercises

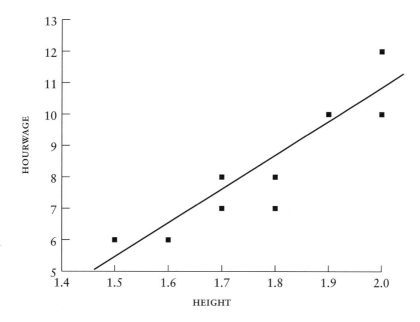

Descriptives

	N	Minimum	Maximum	Mean	Std. Deviation	Variance
HEIGHT	10	1.50	2.00	1.7700	.16364	.027
HOURWAGE	10	6.00	12.00	8.2000	1.93218	3.733
Valid N (listwise)	10					

Correlations

		HOURWAGE	HEIGHT
HOURWAGE	Pearson Correlation	1	.900**
	Sig. (2-tailed)	.	.000
	N	10	10
HEIGHT	Pearson Correlation	.900**	1
	Sig. (2-tailed)	.000	.
	N	10	10

** Correlation is significant at the 0.01 level (2-tailed).

Regression Tables

Variables Entered/Removed[b]

Model	Variables Entered	Variables Removed	Method
1	HEIGHT[a]	.	Enter

a. All requested variables entered
b. Dependent Variable: HOURWAGE

Model Summary

Model	R	R Square	Adjusted R Square	Std. Error of the Estimate
1	.900[a]	.809	.785	.89489

a. Predictors: (Constant) HEIGHT

ANOVA[b]

Model		Sum of Squares	df	Mean Square	F	Sig.
1	Regression	27.193	1	27.193	33.956	.000[a]
	Residual	6.407	8	.801		
	Total	33.600	9			

a. Predictors: (Constant) HEIGHT
b. Dependent Variable: HOURWAGE

Coefficients[a]

Model		Unstandardized Coefficients B	Unstandardized Coefficients Std. Error	Standardized Coefficients Beta	t	Sig.
1	Constant	−10.602	3.239		−3.273	.011
	HEIGHT	10.622	1.823	.900	5.827	.000

a. Dependent Variable: HOURWAGE

3. **a)** Null hypothesis: All birth seasons have the same number of births: 200/4 = 50.

b) Expected value: 50 for each season.

c) chi-square = $0/50 + 0/50 + 100/50 + 100/50 = 4$.

d) df = (categories − 1) = 4 − 1 = 3.

e) The critical value of chi-square for 3 degrees of freedom for the .05 level is 7.82.

f) No, the test statistic did not exceed the critical value. We cannot conclude that the distribution is statistically significantly different from the equal counts specified in the null hypothesis.

4. NB: You may find some variation in answers due to rounding.

a) Overall mean: 5.167.

b) Group means: No prep 4.0; conventional 5.0; experimental 6.5.

c) Between-groups sum of squares: 12.67.

d) Within-groups sum of squares: 9.00.

e) Between-groups mean square: 6.33 and 2 *df*.

f) Within-groups mean square: 1.00 and 9 *df*.

g) $F = 6.333/1.000 = 6.33$, with 2 *df* for the numerator and 9 *df* for the denominator. The critical value from the *F*-table is 4.25 for the .05 level and 8.02 for the .01 level. We conclude that the results are significant at the .05 level but not the .01 level. If we run this problem on the computer, we will see that the *p*-value is .019. Yes, we can conclude that the three groups have significantly different means, although we cannot say (without further tests) which group or groups are different.

This problem can be done on the computer and the results of doing this follow.

Descriptives

Descriptive Statistics

	N	Minimum	Maximum	Mean	Std. Deviation
SCORE	12	3.00	8.00	5.1667	1.40346
Valid N (listwise)	12				

Oneway

ANOVA

SCORE

Model	Sum of Squares	df	Mean Square	F	Sig.
Between Groups	12.667	2	6.333	6.333	.019
Within Groups	9.000	9	1.000		
Total	21.667	11			

Oneway

Descriptives

SCORE

	N	Mean	Std. Deviation	Std. Error	95% Confidence Interval for Mean	
					Lower Bound	Upper Bound
.00	4	4.0000	.81650	.40825	2.7008	5.2992
1.00	4	5.0000	.81650	.40825	3.7008	6.2992
2.00	4	6.5000	1.29099	.64550	4.4457	8.5543
Total	12	5.1667	1.40346	.40514	4.2750	6.0584

Descriptives

SCORE

	Minimum	Maximum
.00	3.00	5.00
1.00	4.00	6.00
2.00	5.00	8.00
Total	3.00	8.00

5. a) R = .96 suggests a very strong positive relation. This is not surprising since the same social forces that affect male life expectancy positively also affect female life expectancy positively. It is probably not a causal relationship—the levels of both variables are caused by other variables, such as health care quality, available resources, nutrition, income level, and level of equality. The two variables are not based on data from the same people—one is based only on males, the other only on females. These variables pertain to countries—the cases are countries, not individuals.

   b) The regression line has a positive slope, very close to the 45-degree line.

   c) Nepal: If a case lies below the regression line, its female life expectancy is lower than what we would predict from its male life expectancy.

6. Answers will vary. If you find differences, you may want to consider whether different variables impinge on the height-weight relationship for men and women.

7. I. **Discussion Question:** This issue calls for an analysis with two independent variables—gender and seniority. We want to look at the 0-order relations first: gender and salary (perhaps using a ANOVA or a *t*-test) and seniority and salary (perhaps doing a regression). We could do a one-way ANOVA in which four groups are defined as senior women, senior men, junior women, and junior men. This is a way of including two predictor variables (gender and seniority) in a one-way ANOVA.

   After that, we can try different three-variable techniques. For instance, we could change the level of measurement of seniority into a categoric variable, and then do a two-way ANOVA, using seniority and gender as our two independent variables. Alternatively, we could "dummy" gender and do a multiple regression with seniority and gender as the IVs to see if either one of them has an effect on salary "net" of the other. Remember that, if gender has no significant relation to salary net of seniority, we still need to think about why women have less seniority. Or we could even convert all the variables into categoric variables—we would lose quite a bit of information this way—and do a three-variable crosstab.

Finally, we might want to run the seniority-salary regression separately for men and women, and look for an interaction effect—is the relationship similar in strength for men and women.

After these steps we could try a multiple regression with additional variables—if the firm provides the information—such as years of education or (as dummied categoric variables) job title or family structure (e.g., "childless" and "with children" as categories).

II. **Data Analysis Question:** The tables and graph that follow give details.

a) When we do ANOVA for salary (DV) by gender (IV), we find that the results are not significant. (See the second table.) Gender is not a good predictor for salary in this (fictitious) data set.

b) When we do the regression analysis for salary by seniority (or, as some say "salary regressed on seniority"), we find a strong correlation—$r = .680$—that is significant at the .05 level ($p = .021$). We can see from R-squared that about 46% of the variation in salary can be predicted from seniority. (See the table labelled "Model Summary.")

	SALARY	SENIORITY	GENDER	z-SALARY	z-SENIORITY
1	40.00	4.00	1.00	−1.45621	−.91017
2	48.00	5.00	.00	−.97264	−.53936
3	48.00	4.00	1.00	−.97264	−.91017
4	54.00	3.00	.00	−.60996	−1.28098
5	60.00	3.00	.00	−.24728	−1.28098
6	60.00	10.00	1.00	−.24728	1.31469
7	65.00	8.00	.00	.05495	.57307
8	74.00	8.00	1.00	.59897	.57307
9	80.00	10.00	.00	.96165	1.31469
10	86.00	8.00	1.00	1.32432	.57307
11	90.00	8.00	1.00	1.56611	.57307

Oneway

ANOVA: GENDER (IV) and SALARY (DV)

SALARY

Model	Sum of Squares	df	Mean Square	F	Sig.
Between Groups	66.376	1	66.376	.224	.647
Within Groups	2670.533	9	296.726		
Total	2736.909	10			

Descriptives

Descriptive Statistics

	N	Minimum	Maximum	Mean	Std. Deviation	Variance
SALARY	11	40.00	90.00	64.0909	16.54361	273.691
SENIORITY	11	3.00	10.00	6.4545	2.69680	7.273
Valid N (listwise)	11					

Correlations

Correlations

		SALARY	SENIORITY
SALARY	Pearson Correlation	1	.680*
	Sig. (2-tailed)	.	.021
	N	11	11
SENIORITY	Pearson Correlation	.680*	1
	Sig. (2-tailed)	.021	.
	N	11	11

* Correlation is significant at the 0.05 level (2-tailed).

Regression

Variables Entered/Removed[b]

Model	Variables Entered	Variables Removed	Method
1	SENIORITY[a]	.	Enter

a. All requested variables entered
b. Dependent Variable: SALARY

Model Summary

Model	R	R Square	Adjusted R Square	Std. Error of The Estimate
1	.680[a]	.463	.403	12.78013

a. Predictors: (Constant) SENIORITY

ANOVA[b]

Model		Sum of Squares	df	Mean Square	F	Sig.
1	Regression	1266.923	1	1266.923	7.757	.021[a]
	Residual	1469.986	9	163.332		
	Total	2736.909	10			

a. Predictors: (Constant) SENIORITY
b. Dependent Variable: SALARY

Coefficients[a]

Model		Unstandardized Coefficients		Standardized Coefficients	t	Sig.
		B	Std. Error	Beta		
1	Constant	37.151	10.412		3.568	.006
	SENIORITY	4.174	1.499	.680	2.785	.021

a. Dependent Variable: SALARY

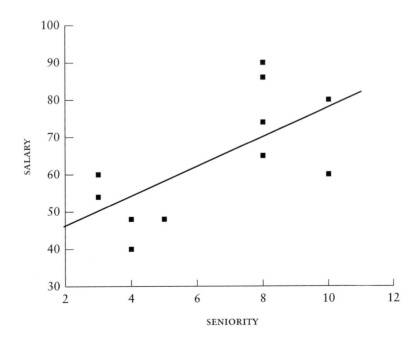

8. **I. Gender-ideology**

As we look at the data, we can see that there is not really a huge difference between men and women in the proportion agreeing with traditional gender ideology. For both, it is around 33%. This initial estimate suggests that the difference found in the sample data may not be significant; it may turn out to be hard to dismiss the null hypothesis that men and women in Cook County feel pretty much the same way. The observed difference is probably just due to sampling error, inherent variability in sample outcomes.

We will test this in two different ways. First we will set up a crosstab, establish a table of expected counts for the null hypothesis that there is no difference is proportions between men and women, and compute chi-square.

After that, since we have only two samples (men and women) and a proportion for a dichotomous variable (agree or disagree), we can also carry out an independent-samples *t*-test for differences in proportions.

a) The difference between the proportions of men and women who agree with the statement is said to be statistically significant if it is extremely unlikely that the difference is just the result of sampling error, of having drawn a random sample that happened to have an outcome that is discrepant from the condition of "no difference" which actually prevails in the population.

b) The null hypothesis is that there is no difference in proportions between men and women.

c) Our crosstab table with percentages and observed counts looks like this:

Table 24: Gender ideology by sex category—Observed values

Attitude	Men	Women	Total
Agree	60 (31.6%)	103 (35.9%)	163 (34.2%)
Disagree	130 (68.4%)	183 (64.1%)	313 (65.8%)
Total	*190 (100%)*	*286 (100%)*	*476 (100%)*

d) Our null hypothesis expected count table is created by using the overall split between 34.2% and 65.8% in the totals column of the observed counts table and applying this percentage split to both men and women. The expected count table looks like this:

Table 25: Expected values for the null hypothesis

Attitude	Men	Women	Total
Agree	65 (34.2%)	98 (34.2%)	163 (34.2%)
Disagree	125 (65.8%)	188 (65.8%)	313 (65.8%)
Total	*190 (100%)*	*286 (100%)*	*476 (100%)*

e) The computed chi-square is: $25/65 + 25/98 + 25/125 + 25/188 = .973$.

The degrees of freedom is $(r-1)(c-1) = 1$.

f-g) The critical value for 1 degree of freedom for the .05 level of significance is 3.84. Our computed value for chi-square does not exceed the critical value. We fail to reject the null hypothesis. The difference is not statistically significant. We cannot conclude that men and women in Cook County have different proportions responding "yes" to traditional gender ideology.

h) Measures of association for gender-ideology crosstab:

Yules-$Q = (ad - bc)/(ad + bc)$

$YQ = (10{,}980 - 13{,}390)/(10{,}980 + 13{,}390) = -2410/24370 = -.098$

This is a very weak Yules-Q. Its sign is not very meaningful since this is not really ordinal data.

Lambda is equal to 0 because the modal categories are the same—"not agree" for both men and women.

i) What three other variables might be related? Answers will vary and might include age, educational level or years of schooling, religious affiliation, and liberal/conservative political orientation.

j) The t-test procedure:

First our givens for the women are $P_1 = 35.9\% = .359$, and $N_1 = 286$, and for the men they are $P_2 = 31.6\% = .316$, and $N_2 = 190$.

First step: Compute the standard error, the standard deviation of the sampling distribution of the differences in proportions. This step has several sub-steps.

First sub-step: Compute the pooled population proportion:

$P' = (N_1 P_1 + N_2 P_2)/(N_1 + N_2) = (60 + 130)/476 = .342$

Second sub-step: The standard deviation of this proportion—the estimated population standard deviation—is

$s' = \sqrt{P'(1 - P')} = \sqrt{.342(1 - .342)} = .474$

Third sub-step: The standard error, calculated using a simplification of the formula for SE, is

$SE = (s')\sqrt{\dfrac{1}{N_1} + \dfrac{1}{N_2}} = (.474)(0.0935) = .0447$

Second step: Now we are ready to find t, which is computed as the difference in the observed sample means divided by the standard error.

$$t = (P_1 - P_2)\big/SE = (.359 - .316)\big/.0447 = .043\big/.045 = .955$$

Since the critical value for t is 1.98 at 474 degrees of freedom for a two-tailed test with a .05 level of significance, we find that the computed t does not exceed the critical value.

k) We conclude that we cannot reject the null hypothesis. Indeed, men and women in Cook County may well have the same level of agreement with traditional gender ideology. We cannot conclude that there is a statistically significant difference in their response rate. Our initial hunch about the data—that this difference in proportions does not look very big and might well be the result of sampling error—was supported by our calculation.

(Note: We have slightly simplified the formula. For a t-test, when we compute the estimated standard error, we should really subtract 1 from each of the Ns, the sample sizes. However, if the combined sample is greater than 100, this simplification will not make a big difference.)

II. "Heterosexual Friends Only?"

Here we do a t-test for difference in proportions. We can see at a glance that there is a hefty difference between the two neighbourhoods in the proportion of men who claim to have only heterosexual friends. It would seem unlikely that this large a difference is just a result of sampling error and that the two neighbourhoods really have the same proportions prepared to make this claim.

Let's use an independent samples t-test for difference in proportions to check this out. The formula is a bit of a bear, and we need to work it in steps.

Our first step is to set up our given information:

$P_1 = 24\% = .24$, and $N_1 = 175$.

$P_2 = .87\% = .87$, and $N_2 = 81$.

Our next step is to compute an estimated standard deviation for the population. This step has several sub-steps:

First, we compute an estimated population proportion if there were no difference:

$$P' = (N_1 P_1 + N_2 P_2)\big/(N_1 + N_2) = (42 + 70.47)\big/262 = 112.47\big/262 = .429$$

Notice that this is similar to figuring the expected proportion in the crosstabs null hypothesis.

Second, we compute the estimated standard deviation for the population:

$$s' = \sqrt{P'(1 - P')} = \sqrt{(.43)(.57)} = .495 \text{ or } .5 \text{ if we round off.}$$

Now that we have the estimated standard deviation for the population, we compute the standard error—the standard deviation of the sampling distribution of the difference in proportions.

$$SE = (s')\sqrt{\frac{1}{N_1} + \frac{1}{N_2}} \ = \ (.5)\sqrt{.018} \ = \ .5(.134) \ = \ .068$$

Now we are ready to compute t!

$t = (.87 - .24)/.068 = .63/.068 = 9.27$.

The critical value for a two-tailed test at 262 degrees of freedom ($df = N_1 + N_2 - 2$) is 1.98 for the .05 level and 2.6 for the .01 level. We are doing a two-tailed test because we are just interested in difference.

Our computed t exceeds the critical value by a lot! We can reject the null hypothesis. The difference is highly statistically significant. It is very unlikely that these two neighbourhoods really have the same proportion of men who have only heterosexual friends. The differences are statistically significant—provided everyone is telling the truth!

We need to point out that we simplified the formula a tiny bit. If we are doing a t-test rather than using Z, we really should use $N - 1$ in computing the expected proportion, but it makes very little difference once the combined sample is over 100.

You can also do this analysis using crosstabs and a chi-square test of significance. You should get the same result, the conclusion that the difference is statistically significant.

Math Refresher

The next pages are designed to refresh memories of arithmetic and math. The treatment is focused on ideas and terms that will be useful in statistics, either as the basis of statistical concepts or for computations and procedures.

TIPS FOR STUDYING MATH

- **Relax:** Put on music you like, work in a comfortable place, and keep refreshments handy. Don't let math make you feel stressed or anxious. Yes, there is only one right answer, but usually there are many ways of thinking about a problem and of reaching that answer.

- **Take your time:** Math requires thinking, and a math book cannot be read at the same pace as a novel. You need to stop and reflect on what you are reading. Don't let your eyes glaze over or the reading become mindless and mechanical. Keep paper and pencil handy to take notes and work examples.

- **Visualize:** Many great mathematicians work by visualizing a problem and possible solutions first, rather than by directly manipulating a formula. The number line and coordinate plane will help us picture what we are doing in stats.

- **Experiment—try simple examples:** When you see a formula, concept, procedure, or rule, try it out with simple examples using whole numbers. Use a calculator if needed. Make up story or word problems to illustrate the concept.

- **Math is about concepts:** Remember that a formula is just precise shorthand for stating a concept, conclusion, or procedure that can be expressed in words. The words and concepts are more important than the formula.

- **Talk to other people:** Cooperative learning, study groups, and just short conversations are helpful in understanding concepts. Math does not have to be lonely.

- **The calculator:** Tool, not crutch! Some teachers prohibit the use of calculators, but a calculator can be useful for longer computations and for experimenting with examples. Don't let it substitute for learning concepts, and don't rely on it needlessly—everyone should know the multiplication tables and rules for multiplying and dividing fractions. Dividing $\frac{1}{2}$ by $\frac{1}{4}$ should **not** be done with a calculator, but dividing 3.768 by 12.93 is much better done with a calculator than by hand!

- **Don't be afraid to ask questions:** Chances are that many of your classmates have the same questions in mind and will not resent your asking the professor or TA. Instructors may not realize that what seems easy to them is hard for beginners. They rely on feedback from you to know at what level to pitch the material. Pretending to "get" math is tempting, but pretty pointless—it's hard to fake. This is another reason for insisting that the instructor explain math clearly.

Estimating

Estimating the answer to a problem is a very important skill in applied math (and basic statistics is applied math). Estimating brings together math skills with a "feel" for the real world.

Before doing a long calculation, make an educated guess about what the result will be. How big will the number be? In what "ball-park" do we expect it? What units (if any) should it be in? What result would raise a "warning flag" that we made a mistake in calculation or didn't understand the concept?

For example, if I tell you that I calculated that the average height of the Bulls NBA team is 10 inches, you would be puzzled—something went wrong! Maybe I don't understand the meaning of "height" or the concept "average." Maybe I made a major calculation error. As soon as you heard "average height" of a group of tall men, you probably expected to hear a number between 6 and 7 feet. Your estimate led you to see immediately that 10 inches could not be a good answer to the question "what is the average height of the Bulls team?"

Let's say I tell you their average height is 6.5%. Wait a minute—shouldn't a question about height be answered in feet, meters, inches, etc.? Why would a % be part of the answer? Let's say I tell you the answer is 77. Is this plausible? What did I calculate?

This example gives you a sense of how important estimating is. Estimating means understanding what is going on and anticipating the result. It means not just mindlessly doing steps in a calculation, but understanding the concepts, the real world, and the math operations. Always think about what you expect the answer to look like: In what units (if any)? What "ballpark"—how large or small? Will my answer by a positive or negative number?

QUESTIONS—ESTIMATING

1). Answer the following without a calculator!

a) Which of the following would be a plausible answer to this question: What was my car's gas mileage on the trip from Chicago to Washington DC?

1000 kilometres	800 miles
25 miles per gallon	38.3%
300 miles per gallon	48

b) Which of these is a plausible answer to this question: What is the per capita income in Japan? (What does "per capita" mean?)

120 million	$5 billion	$300
$20,000	20%	

c) In a store, I see there is a 40% markdown on winter coats. Chicago has an 8.75% sales tax. A coat that was originally priced at $200 will end up costing how much, approximately?

$160	$129	$88	$186
$209	$165	$169	

d) Japan's population decreases but its total national income remains the same. What happens to the per capita income?

decreases   increases   remains the same

e) Here's a question for baseball fans. What, approximately, was Ted William's lifetime batting average? (Explain "batting average.")

2.80	7	3000	5.04
.350	.100	70	

From Common Sense to Formula

In basic statistics, a formula is often just a very precise way of stating a common sense idea. For example, we often talk about "average," "expectation," "volatility," and "variation."

- Are men taller than women, "on average"?

- How long does it take to drive from Toronto to New York: What is my "expected time of arrival"?

- On a visit to a casino in the state of Illinois, a gambler can expect to lose $104. (Yes, this is a fact.)

- The waves at Playa Azul are very unpredictable—some are high, some are small, and there is a lot of "variation in wave height."

- Stock prices have been "volatile" lately, with many ups and downs.

These ordinary, everyday expressions are turned into precise concepts that can be expressed in mathematical formulas. The vague general notions that we all use in everyday speech are transformed into clear and precise concepts or procedures, which in turn are expressed in math symbols. It is helpful to think about ideas or procedures in words before tackling the formula. Think about each step or part of a formula or procedure verbally.

THE NUMBER LINE

Here is a good way to visualize all the numbers we commonly encounter. Think of all the numbers we know lined up along a line. In the middle is 0. A little bit to the right of 0 is 1. As we move further to the right, the numbers get bigger and bigger. All the numbers to the right of 0 are positive. They include fractions between 0 and 1, such as $\frac{1}{4}$, $\frac{1}{2}$, $\frac{2}{3}$, and so on; positive integers (whole numbers), such as 1, 2, 3, 410, and 5,678; numbers that are composites of whole numbers and fractions, such as $3\frac{1}{2}$. They also include a lot of less familiar numbers, which cannot be expressed as fractions—the irrational numbers, such as *pi* and the square root of 2.

To the left of 0 are the negative numbers. They are very much like the positive numbers, but they have a negative sign and values of less than 0. If we think of numbers as representing money, the positive numbers represent our assets and the negative ones our debts.

GREATER AND LESSER

We use > to mean "greater than," reading from left to right, and < to mean "less than," reading from left to right. For example, 6 > 2 and 2 < 6. As we move right from 0 along the number line, numbers become larger. So 4 is bigger than 2, and 55 is bigger than 4, and so on. As we move left from 0 along the number line, the numbers become smaller. So –5 is less than –2, and –781 is less than –5. (If we had a debt of $781, we would have less money than if our debt were $5.)

We want to give special attention to the interval between 0 and 1, the interval of numbers less than 1 and more than 0. Here it can be a little tricky to tell which of two fractions is larger. If we have two fractions $\frac{a}{b}$ and $\frac{c}{d}$, we can compare them easily once we put them over a common denominator (the denominator is the "bottom" of the fraction). The simplest way of finding a common denominator is by multiplying the two denominators. The product is the common denominator. We then convert each fraction to the new common denominator.

$$\frac{a}{b}\left(\frac{d}{d}\right) = \frac{ad}{bd} \qquad \text{and} \qquad \frac{c}{d}\left(\frac{b}{b}\right) = \frac{cb}{db}$$

Now we have fractions rewritten, so they have the same denominator, and we can decide which is larger just by comparing the numerators (the "top" numbers), ad and cb.

Let's try it with a real example. Is $\frac{5}{8}$ bigger or smaller than $\frac{2}{3}$?

$$\frac{5}{8}\left(\frac{3}{3}\right) = \frac{15}{24} \qquad \text{and} \qquad \frac{2}{3}\left(\frac{8}{8}\right) = \frac{16}{24}$$

Now we can see that $\frac{16}{24}$ is greater than $\frac{15}{24}$, so we know $\frac{2}{3}$ is bigger than $\frac{5}{8}$.

Don't bother to go through the procedure of finding the common denominator if it's obvious which one is greater, for example, when comparing $\frac{3}{4}$ and $\frac{1}{2}$!

If numbers are composites of whole numbers (integers) and fractions, we first compare the integer parts, and, if they are the same, we compare the fractional parts.

QUESTIONS—GREATER OR LESSER THAN

1. Place the following numbers on the number line:

   −5.5   +3   +1500   −10.12   −785 $\frac{3}{4}$ $\frac{1}{2}$ +1.8

2. Which is greater?

   a) $\frac{3}{4}$ or $\frac{5}{8}$ b) $\frac{7}{8}$ or $\frac{14}{16}$ c) $\frac{39}{40}$ or $\frac{18}{21}$ d) $2\frac{1}{2}$ or $1\frac{1}{2}$

ABSOLUTE VALUE

In the preceding section, we saw that 2 is a larger number than –220. This is because +2 is further to the right on the number line and represents a positive value ("assets") while –220 is further to the left and is negative ("debts"). However, looking at these two numbers, we still might feel that in some way –220 is "bigger"—it seems heftier or weightier.

This feeling is made precise by the concept of absolute value. A number has an absolute value, a size regardless of its positive or negative sign. Absolute value is symbolized by an upright line on each side of the number, like $|2|$ or $|-220|$.

If a number is positive, its absolute value is equal to the number. If a number is negative, its absolute value is equal to the positive value of the number. The absolute value of 0 is 0.

Finding the absolute value of a number is like flipping all the negative numbers into their positive "mirror images" on the right hand side of the number line, to the right of 0. It's like folding the number line over on itself at 0. Zero and the positive numbers stay put, while all the negative numbers "flip over" to their positive equivalents. Consequently, –2 goes to +2 and –3.81 goes to +3.81 and minus *pi* goes to plus *pi* and so on. With absolute values, "small" means near 0 and "big" means further away.

This makes sense in real life. We talk about a person having "big debts," which means the debt has a large absolute value—it is a big number, in absolute terms.

QUESTIONS—ABSOLUTE VALUE

What are the absolute values of the following numbers?

a) –.3   b) –5.5   c) –35.7   d) $-3\frac{1}{4}$ e) $3\frac{1}{4}$

f) 0   g) 565   h) 1   i) $\frac{1}{2}$ j) –.50

FRACTIONS AND OTHER PROPORTIONS

Here are a few more tips about fractions. A fraction can be written in several ways.

It can be written as $\frac{a}{b}$, with a numerator (the top, which enumerates the pieces) and a denominator (the bottom, which names the pieces).

For example, when we see $\frac{4}{9}$, we know that the pieces are named ninths, and we've got four of them. Pieces of what? Pieces of one whole thing. Think of a pie. Mom or Dad has cut a pie into nine pieces and given us four of them—that's what $4/9$ means. The whole thing—the totality—has been cut into nine pieces, and the part or proportion we have is four of those pieces. **To think about fractions, always picture someone cutting up a pie!**

To add or subtract fractions, put them over a common denominator and add or subtract the numerators.

$$\frac{a}{b} - \frac{q}{r} = \left(\frac{a}{b}\right)\left(\frac{r}{r}\right) - \left(\frac{q}{r}\right)\left(\frac{b}{b}\right) = \frac{ar}{br} - \frac{qb}{br} = \frac{(ar - qb)}{br}$$

(In putting them over a common denominator, we multiply by $\frac{r}{r}$ and $\frac{b}{b}$, respectively, which is OK, since, in each case, it is the same as multiplying by 1.)

To multiply fractions, multiply the numerators and divide their product by the denominators multiplied together: $\left(\frac{a}{b}\right)\left(\frac{q}{r}\right) = \frac{aq}{br}$.

To divide fractions, invert the divisor and multiply the fractions:

$$\frac{a}{b} \div \frac{q}{r} = \frac{a}{b} \times \frac{r}{q} = \frac{ar}{bq}$$

("Invert the divisor" means flip around the numerator and denominator.)

QUESTIONS—OPERATIONS WITH FRACTIONS

a) $\dfrac{2}{3} + \dfrac{4}{5}$ b) $\dfrac{4}{7} - \dfrac{8}{9}$ c) $\dfrac{3}{4} \times \dfrac{1}{2}$ d) $\dfrac{5}{6} \times \dfrac{3}{11}$

e) $\dfrac{5}{9} \div \dfrac{5}{4}$ f) $\dfrac{5}{7} \div \dfrac{5}{6}$ g) $\dfrac{2}{3} + \dfrac{3}{2}$ h) $\dfrac{4}{7} + \dfrac{8}{3}$

Decimal Fractions

Another way we can write a fraction is as a decimal fraction. Decimal fractions are easier to use in calculations because they are added, subtracted, multiplied, and divided like whole numbers; but they are sometimes less precise than regular fractions. When we convert a fraction into a decimal fraction, we are cutting our pie into decimal wedges—tenths, one-hundredths, and so on.

To convert a fraction into a decimal fraction, divide the bottom (denominator) into the top (numerator). When we do this, we get a number with a decimal point in it. To the left of the decimal point is the whole number (if any). To the right of decimal point are the tenths. In the next place to the right are the hundredths, and in the third place over to the right of the decimal point are the thousandths, and so on.

one tenth = $\dfrac{1}{10}$ = .1

one hundredth = $\dfrac{1}{100}$ = .01

one thousandth = .001

Examples:

$\dfrac{1}{4}$ = .25   (This number can be read as "twenty-five hundredths" or called "one-quarter.")

$\dfrac{1}{2}$ = .5   (five tenths or one-half) or $\dfrac{3}{5}$ = .6 (six tenths or three-fifths)

When we do the division, we find that some fractions have an infinite repeating decimal expansion, such as $1/3$ = .3333... on and on and $1/9$ = .11111... on and on. These have to be rounded off, and this makes them a little less precise than the fraction in its original form.

Any small calculator is fine for changing fractions into decimal fractions.

Percent

There is one more way of writing a fraction—as a percentage. This means that Dad or Mom has cut the pie into 100 little wedges. A fraction written as a percentage expresses how many of those 100 pieces we have.

If we have half the pie, we have 50 of the 100 little wedges or 50%. If we have a quarter of the pie, we have 25 of the 100 little wedges or 25%.

To convert a fraction into a percent:

1. Divide the bottom (denominator) into the top (numerator), converting the fraction into a decimal fraction.

2. Move the decimal point two places to the right.

3. Stick in the percentage sign to show it's a percentage.

Examples:

$$\frac{1}{4} = .25 = 25\% \qquad\qquad \frac{1}{2} = .5 = 50\%$$

$$\frac{3}{5} = .6 = 60\% \qquad\qquad \frac{1}{40} = .025 = 2.5\%$$

To convert a percent into a fraction, write it as a fraction with 100 in the denominator and reduce to lowest terms.

Example: $80\% = \dfrac{80}{100} = \dfrac{4}{5}$

Percentages are frequently used to express fractions of a collection of things like people (what percentage of Europeans live in cities?) or money (what percentage of the national budget is spent on education?). The total pie—100%—is the entire collection, all the people or all the dollars. The percentage is the fraction or proportion of the total collection in which we are interested.

Knowing fraction-decimal and fraction-percent conversions: Remember that these are just three ways of writing the same number. Each one represents a proportion or part of a totality, whole, or collection. If not otherwise specified, the totality or whole is equal to 1.

It's very useful to memorize some conversions and be able to do them instantly:

$$\frac{1}{2} = .50 = 50\% \qquad\qquad \frac{1}{4} = .25 = 25\%$$

$$\frac{1}{5} = .20 = 20\% \qquad\qquad \frac{1}{3} = .333... = 33.3\%$$

Multiples of these basic conversions should also be committed to memory:

$$\frac{3}{4} = .75 = 75\% \qquad\qquad \frac{2}{5} = .40 = 40\%$$

$$\frac{3}{5} = .60 = 60\% \qquad\qquad \frac{4}{5} = .80 = 80\%$$

QUESTIONS—CONVERTING FRACTIONS

Write each of these fractions in three different ways.

a) .6   b) $\frac{7}{8}$ c) 32%   d) 33.3%   e) 100%

f) $\frac{1}{92}$ g) $\frac{3}{7}$ h) $\frac{3}{9}$ i) .064

Comparing Fractions

A couple of pages ago, we discussed how to compare fractions by converting them to a common denominator. Decimal fractions provide a very easy way to compare fractions. Working with positive fractions less than 1, we begin by comparing the numbers in the tenths place, the place immediately to the right of the decimal point. Whichever fraction has a larger value in the tenths place is greater. If the numbers in the tenths places are equal, compare the numbers in the second place to the right, the hundredths place. If these are the same, go on to the thousandths place, the third spot to the right of the decimal point, and so on.

For example: .6 > .4   (six tenths is greater than four tenths)
.06 < .4   (six hundredths is less than four tenths)
.001 and .005   .005 is greater.
.05 and .001   .05 is greater.
.01 and .005   .01 is greater.

It is very important in a stats course to be able to read and use percentages and to compare decimal fractions!

Percentage Alert!

"x% of y are z" does NOT mean the same thing as "x% of z are y." These are completely different things. The expression cannot be flipped around. For example, even if the statement that half of all Jamaicans are women were true, it would still *not be true* that half of all women are Jamaican! (Think through enough examples to convince yourself that these expressions are **not** the same.) **A lot of people have made fools of themselves with this simple mistake.**

Here is another example of how, in statements about proportions (percentages), the bases **cannot** be flipped around! (The percentage has to be recomputed for a new base.) Studying poverty in the United States, we might be interested in the question of whether different ethnic groups have different poverty rates: Is the proportion of poor people the same among Latinos, African Americans, Asian Americans, Euro-Americans, and Native Americans? This is a completely different question from asking what proportion of the poor are Latino, African American, Asian American, Euro-American, and Native American. For example, even though Euro-Americans have a relatively low poverty rate, they are a large percent of the total US population, and thus account for a large percent of the poor people. In other words, we may find that a small percentage of the total number of Euro-Americans is poor although Euro-Americans make up a large percentage of the total number of those in the US who are poor.

Computing Percent Change and Percentage Point Change

To compute the percent change in a quantity, we subtract the old amount from the new amount and divide the difference by the old amount. This gives a decimal fraction, which we can change into a percent. For example, let's say we had $160 and make an additional $40, for a total of $200.

The percent change in our money is $\dfrac{\$200 - \$160}{\$160} = \dfrac{\$40}{\$160}$

$$= .25 = 25\%.$$

It is important to distinguish between **percent change** (the proportion of increase or decrease, relative to the initial amount) and the **percentage point change** (whether the percentage of something went up or down, and by how many points).

Here is an example to clarify the distinction. Suppose that the % of the US population of Hispanic origin increased from 8% in 1990 to 10% in 2000.

As we've discovered, the **percent change** equals $\dfrac{10\% - 8\%}{8\%} = \dfrac{2\%}{8\%}$

$$= .25 = 25\%$$

However, the **percentage point change** is 2. In other words, there is a change of 2 percentage points (from 8% to 10%).

OPERATIONS

In statistics, we will use the four basic arithmetic operations—addition, subtraction, multiplication, and division.

Addition

Addition is straightforward. When we add two positive numbers, the sum is positive (2 + 3 = 5). We are moving to the right on the number line. When we add two negative numbers, the sum is a negative number with a larger absolute value (−2 + −3 = −5). We move to the left on the number line. When we add two positive fractions, the sum is a larger positive number $\frac{1}{3} + \frac{1}{2} = \frac{5}{6}$.

Addition is commutative: We can switch the order of numbers we are adding and get the same sum: 2 + 3 = 3 + 2.

There is a fancy way of saying "add up the following long series of numbers." It is called the addition operator and symbolized by the Greek capital letter Sigma. Sigma is followed by a series of numbers with subscripts. At the top and bottom of the Sigma are indications where to start and end the sum in terms of these subscripts. When we see a Sigma, we have to add a series of numbers.

$$\sum_{k=1}^{10} = x_1 + x_2 + x_3 \ldots + x_{10} \quad \text{(Here we are asked to add 10 numbers.)}$$

Multiplication

Like addition, multiplication is commutative: $ab = ba$. Multiplication is often expressed by writing numbers or letters next to each other without a times sign.

When we multiply two positive numbers the product is positive (3 times 5 = 15). When we multiply two negative numbers, the product is positive (−3 times −5 = 15).

When we multiply a positive and a negative number, the product is negative (−3 times 5 = −15).

When we multiply a number by a positive number less than one, the absolute value of the product is less than that of the original number; multiplying by a positive number less than 1 brings the product closer to 0. When we multiply two positive numbers that are less than one, the product is smaller than either of the numbers,

Important!

e.g., $\dfrac{1}{4}$ times $\dfrac{1}{8} = \dfrac{1}{32}$.

Remember that, to multiply fractions, we find the product of the numerators and divide it by the product of the denominators:

$$\left(\dfrac{a}{b}\right)\left(\dfrac{c}{d}\right) = \dfrac{ac}{bd} \text{ or, for example, } \dfrac{3}{7} \text{ times } \dfrac{4}{5} = \dfrac{12}{35}.$$

Subtraction

Subtraction is generally related to difference. When we ask if two quantities are different, we often answer the question by subtraction.

Subtraction is not commutative: $a - b$ is **not** equal to $b - a$ and $2 - 5$ is **not** equal to $5 - 2$.

Subtracting a negative number is done by adding the number: $-3 - (-6) = -3 + 6$. If we want to, we can think of subtraction as adding a negative number, the negative of the number we are subtracting. This makes the operation commutative like addition.

$5 - 4 = 5 + (-4) = 1$ (Start at 5; move 4 to the left.)

$5 - (-3) = 5 + (-(-3)) = 5 + 3 = 8$ (Start at 5; move 3 to the right.)

$5 - 6 = 5 + (-6) = -1$ (Start at 5; move 6 to the left.)

Division

Division is the most complicated of the four operations. Division is not commutative: $\dfrac{a}{b}$ does **not** equal $\dfrac{b}{a}$ and $\dfrac{6}{2}$ is **not** equal to $\dfrac{2}{6}$.

We cannot divide by 0!!! When we divide a positive by a positive, the quotient is positive. When we divide a negative by a negative, the quotient is positive. When we divide terms one of which is negative and one of which is positive, the quotient is negative.

Reminder: The rule for dividing fractions is **invert and multiply.**

$$\frac{a}{b} \div \frac{c}{d} = \frac{a}{b} \times \frac{d}{c} = \frac{ad}{bc}$$

Does this make sense? Yes it does! Think about pies. How many half-pies can we fit into one quarter of the pie?

$$\frac{1}{4} \text{ divided by } \frac{1}{2} = \frac{1}{4} \times \frac{2}{1} = \frac{1}{2}.$$

We can fit $\frac{1}{2}$ of the half-pie piece into that quarter wedge.

How many quarter-pies can we fit into one half of the pie?

$$\frac{1}{2} \text{ divided by } \frac{1}{4} = \frac{1}{2} \times \frac{4}{1} = 2.$$

We can fit two of the quarter-pie pieces into the half pie piece.

DIVISION: IS THE QUOTIENT BIGGER OR SMALLER THAN THE ORIGINAL NUMBERS?

Let's think about what happens when we divide one number by another. We can never divide by 0!! When we divide by 1, we get the number we started with. When we divide by a positive number greater than 1, the quotient is smaller than the original number: 2 divided by 1.3 is less than 2, and 2 divided by 50 is less than 2. When we divide by a positive number less than 1, the quotient is bigger than the original number. For example, 2 divided by .5 = 4 (the number of halves that fit into 2) and 2 divided by .1= 20 (the number of tenths that fit into 2).

When we divide a positive by a positive, the quotient is positive. When we divide a negative by a negative, the quotient is positive. When the divisor and the dividend have different signs, the quotient is negative.

THE MEANING OF DIVISION

The problem with division is that this operation is used to express a great many ideas. We can think of division as multiplication by a fraction ("the multiplicative inverse"). As long as y is not equal to 0,

$$\frac{x}{y} = x\left(\frac{1}{y}\right).$$

Division can mean this: How many times can I "fit" this number (the divisor) into this other number (the dividend)? The answer is the quotient. How many times does 3 go into 9? (The answer is 3 times.)

How many times does 9 go into 3? ($\frac{1}{3}$ of 9 can be "fit into" 3, so the answer is $\frac{1}{3}$.)

Division is used to express proportions and fractions. What proportion of Americans are women? (The answer is about half because

$$\frac{\text{women Americans}}{\text{total Americans}} = \frac{1}{2} = .50 = 50\%.)$$

We divided 140 million by 280 million to get $\frac{1}{2}$.

What proportion of our class has brown eyes? We divide the number of brown-eyed students by the total number of students

$$\left(\frac{\text{brown-eyed students}}{\text{all students}}\right).$$

How much of my calorie intake is from fat? We divide the number of fat calories by the number of total calories $\left(\frac{\text{fat calories}}{\text{total calories}}\right)$. So far,

the "top" and "bottom" of these proportions is the same "thing": people (women and people in general), students (brown-eyed students and all students), and calories (fat calories and all calories). In these cases, we can go ahead and carry out the division, coming up with a proportion expressed as a fraction or percent. Notice that the units (e.g., people, calories, etc.) "cancel" out and do not appear in the quotient.

Sometimes the top and bottom of a division do not refer to the same thing, and the units cannot be "cancelled out." For example, we might look at income per capita (dividing total national income by the number of people) or automobile death rates (number of accident fatalities divided by the number of passenger miles travelled). These are rates or averages and they look like proportions, but the units of both the denominator and the numerator must be specified and the quotient cannot be expressed as a percentage.

Proportion Alert!

It is important to understand the relationship between the total number and the proportion and not to confuse the two. **In a comparison, proportions can be the same even though the total numbers are very different.**

For example, about $\frac{1}{2}$ or 50% of all Danes are women. About $\frac{1}{2}$ or 50% of all Japanese are women. The proportion female is the same in both countries. The total number of people in each country does not affect the **proportion** female.

However, Denmark has only about 3 million people, hence about 1.5 million women. Japan has 120 million people, hence about 60 million women. The total number of people in each country—the base figure—and hence the total number of women is very different. But the percent or proportion (the fraction of the population that is female) is the same.

QUESTIONS TO THINK ABOUT

1. Could China and Luxembourg have the same proportion of left-handed people?

2. Is it likely that they have the same number of left-handed people?

It is very important to be alert to what numbers are being used as the base figure in computing a proportion.

Word or Story Problems

Now that we have reviewed the four basic operations, we can say a word about word problems. We will encounter many of these in stats. Because statistics is a way of thinking about the real world, almost all problems in intro stats courses are word problems. Here are a few tips for "translating" words into symbols, so we can set up a formula for solving a problem: Variables, or quantities that can take on different values, are represented by letters like x, y, and a.

"Is" and "is the same as" can be represented by the equal sign (=).

"Sum," "addition," "put together," "received," "increased by," "more than," and "how much larger" are generally terms that refer to addition (+).

"Difference," "subtract," "decreased," "less than," "how much less," and sometimes "compare" are terms that refer to subtraction (–).

"Product" and the expression "of" (as in 5% of) refer to multiplication, including multiplication by a fraction.

"Fit into," "containment," "divided," "shared out among," "proportion of," "fraction of," and sometimes "compare" refer to division.

SQUARING, HIGHER POWERS, AND SQUARE ROOTS

Squaring

When we square a number, we multiply it by itself. Five times five = $(5)(5) = 5^2 = 25$. In general, $yy = y^2$.

The little 2 is a superscript, showing that we are multiplying a number by itself, and it is called an "exponent."
Notice: If the number is positive and greater than 1, its square is a larger positive number.

If the number is 0, its square is 0.
If the number is 1, its square is 1.
If the number is positive and lies between 0 and 1, its square is a positive number that is smaller than the original number, for

example, $\frac{1}{2}$ squared $= \left(\frac{1}{2}\right)\left(\frac{1}{2}\right) = \frac{1}{4}$.

If the number is negative, its square is always positive, because we are multiplying a negative number by a negative number.

It's very useful to memorize the squares of the following numbers that appear frequently so that they will pop into our brains instantly, and we don't have to waste time with a calculator: 1, 2, 3, 4, 5, 6, 7, 8, 9, 10, 11, 12, 15, 20, 25.

QUESTIONS—SQUARING

Square each of the following:

a) 3   b) 39   c) 5.4   d) −5.4

e) $\dfrac{1}{2}$ f) .5   g) .75   h) 1

i) 0   j) −1   k) −.32   l) $-\dfrac{1}{2}$

m) $-\dfrac{1}{4}$ n) +25

Higher Powers

We can multiply a number by itself three times: Y^3 or "Y-cubed." Notice that if Y is a negative number (less than 0), its square is positive, but its cube is negative. However, 0 cubed is still 0, and 1 cubed is still 1. Positive numbers less than 1 produce a smaller number when they are cubed, just as they do when they are squared.

In general, we can multiply a number by itself as often as we want to, raising it to the nth power (square, cube, fourth power, fifth power, etc.). If the number is negative, all the even powers will be a positive number, and all the odd powers will be a negative number.

Adding Exponents: We can **add** exponents as long as the base (the number we are multiplying by itself) remains the same:

$$(y^n)(y^m) = y^{(n+m)}$$

Example: $(x^2)(x^3) = (xx)(xxx) = xxxxx = x^5 = x^{(2+3)}$

Negative exponents: If the exponent is negative, it means we are dividing by a number raised to that power. (Remember that division is like multiplying by a fraction.)

$$x^{-1} = \frac{1}{x} \quad \text{and} \quad x^{-2} = \frac{1}{x^2}$$

Square Roots

When we take the square root of a number, we find a number whose square equals the number we started with. For example, 2 is a square root of 4. Notice that positive numbers have two square roots, a positive one and negative one. The square roots of 9 are 3 and −3 because either one of these numbers, when squared, produces +9.

Notice that many numbers have a square root that is expressed as an infinite, non-repeating decimal, one that cannot be turned into an ordinary fraction. For instance, the square root of 2 is one of these "irrational" numbers. Usually in statistics, which is interested in applied problems, we will round these numbers off to a rational number like a whole number or a fraction. (Negative numbers have "imaginary numbers" as their square root, and we won't encounter those in this course—whew!)

We can write roots with a radical sign $\sqrt{}$ or with a fractional exponent.

So $\sqrt{y}$ = square root of y and $y^{1/3}$ = cube root of y.

Multiplying and dividing with square roots: The square root of a product is the product of the square roots. (The square root of r times s is equal to the square root of r times the square root of s.) The square root of a quotient is the quotient of the square roots. (The square root of x divided by y is equal to the square root of x divided by the square root of y.)

For example, $\sqrt{\dfrac{x}{y}} = \dfrac{\sqrt{x}}{\sqrt{y}}$, so $\sqrt{\dfrac{1}{4}} = \dfrac{\sqrt{1}}{\sqrt{4}} = \dfrac{1}{2} = .5$.

QUESTIONS—SQUARE ROOTS

1. Use a calculator to find the positive square root of the following numbers:

a) 35   **b)** 2   **c)** 151   **d)** .099   **e)** .01   **f)** 289   **g)** .3   **h)** .9

2. When we find the square root of a number between 0 and 1, which is bigger, the number or its square root? Why?

Scientific Notation

Instead of writing out tiny fractions or very big numbers, we express them as a number times a power of 10. If it's a large number, we use a large positive power of 10, and if it's a small fraction, we use a large negative power.

For example:

$10^0 = 1$, $10^1 = 10$, $10^2 = 100$, $10^3 = 1000$ and so on;
so 3.2 times 10^2 = 3.2 times 100 = 320.

For a short cut, you can think of the exponents as numbers of tens multiplied together or numbers of zeros or decimal places after the initial 1, which corresponds to no tens or 10^0. Accordingly, 10^5 equals 100,000 (5 zeros), and 32.2×10^5 = 3,220,000 or 32.2 with the decimal moved 5 spaces to the right. Take a look at the following.

$10^{-1} = .1$, $10^{-2} = .01$, $10^{-3} = .001$; so 3.2 times 10^{-3} = .0032.

Here, because 10^0 equals 1, the negative exponent can be thought of as the number of places that the decimal moves to the left of 1.0. Consequently, 10^5 equals a movement of 5 decimal places left from 1, or .00001. So 32.2×10^{-5} = .000322.

Computer output sometimes uses scientific notation to express very small fractions, written with an E for "exponent" followed by the power of 10, like this: 3.2E-2.

This means 3.2 times 10^{-2} or .032 or 3.2 hundredths or thirty-two thousandths.

MANIPULATING FORMULAS

When we see a formula involving a lot of operations, we have to be careful to do these operations in the correct order.

First of all, there is a set of three rules governing operations:

1. **The commutative law** says that we can switch the order of numbers we are adding or multiplying: $ab = ba$ and $a + b = b + a$.

2. **The associative law** says that we can have the choice of grouping operations in more than one way when we add or multiply— again, order doesn't matter:

$$a + (b + c) = (a + b) + c \text{ and } rq(s) = r(qs)$$

3. **The distributive law** governs how addition and multiplication are combined: $a(b + c) = ab + bc$. Notice that this means we have a choice of first adding the numbers in the parentheses and then multiplying, or of multiplying each number in parentheses by the factor outside the parentheses and then adding the products.

We'll call these rules the "CAD" principles, and we have to be very careful to obey them. Note that they do not apply so easily to subtraction and division; they work only if we think of subtraction as the addition of a negative number and of division as multiplication by the (non-zero) "multiplicative inverse," and we have to be careful when we do this.

Large formulas and expressions almost always have grouping symbols that identify the order of operations. The innermost ones are usually parentheses; next come brackets, then braces. The bar that separates a numerator from a denominator is also a grouping symbol that suggests the numerator and denominator must be simplified separately first, before the division can be carried out.

Safe rules for simplifying an expression that represents a number:

1. Work the procedures separately for the numerator and denominator.

2. Simplify powers, if any.

3. Simplify **within** the innermost grouping symbol, usually parentheses.

4. Raise the simplified term within the grouping symbol to the indicated power (if any).

5. Complete multiplication by an external factor, using the distributive law.

6. Add and subtract external numbers.

7. Proceed in the same order at the next level of grouping symbol.

8. Complete the division; if necessary, invert and multiply if the denominator is expressed as a fraction.

9. Reduce the fraction, if any, to lowest terms.

(Actually it is often possible to carry out some short cuts, like doing a division and reduction to lowest terms earlier in the calculation—"cancelling out" common factors from the numerator and denominator.)

Simplification and order of operations in solving an equation:

Often we will be working with an expression that does not represent an actual number. Rather, we are trying to solve an equation involving an unknown term. Generally we will be working with linear equations that do not contain higher or fractional powers of the unknown term. To solve an equation for an unknown term—let's call it x:

1. Simplify any operations inside parentheses and grouped terms.

2. Collect like terms: If x appears in different places, bring all of these together, so that only one term with x in it appears in the equation.

3. Manipulate the equation in order to move x to one side of the equation and everything else to the other side. This is called "solving for x."

Remember that, in manipulating the equation, we can do anything we want to one side, as long as we do the same thing to the other side. So we can add, subtract, multiply, and divide by numbers or expressions on one side, as long as we do the same thing to the other side.

A couple of examples:

Solve $5x - 6 = 20$.

This means finding a number such that when we multiply it by 5 and subtract 6 from the product we end up with 20.

$5x - 6 = 20$.

$5x = 20 + 6$ (We add 6 to both sides as we begin to isolate x.)

$x = 26/5$ (We complete the addition on the right side, and divide both sides by 5 to complete the isolation of x.)

$x = 5.2$ (We complete the division.)

A more difficult example is solving for q in $\dfrac{1}{q} + \dfrac{1}{r} = \dfrac{2}{p}$. This means

getting q by itself on one side of the equation. Here we will not end up with a number as we did in the previous example but with an expression involving p and r. We are solving for q in terms of p and r.

First, we have to find a common denominator and put all the fractions in this form, so we can add them together. Remember that if we multiply all the denominators together we have a common denominator—qrp is the common denominator here.

We multiply both sides by the common denominator—this is OK as long as we do it to both sides:

$$qpr\left(\frac{1}{q} + \frac{1}{r}\right) = qpr\left(\frac{2}{p}\right)$$

Complete the multiplications on both sides, following the distributive law on the left side.

$$\frac{qrp}{1}\left(\frac{1}{q}\right) + \frac{qrp}{1}\left(\frac{1}{r}\right) = \frac{2qrp}{p}$$

$$\frac{qrp}{q} + \frac{qrp}{r} = 2qr$$

$$rp + qp = 2qr$$

Put the q terms together on the same side, by subtracting qp from both sides:

$$rp = 2qr - qp$$

Use the distributive law to "undistribute" and combine all q terms into a single one:

$$rp = \left(2r - p\right) q$$

Divide to isolate q on one side of the equation, "solving for q."

$$\frac{rp}{(2r - p)} = q$$

THE COORDINATE PLANE, ORDERED PAIRS, AND FUNCTIONS

So far we have been thinking about the number line, moving right ("greater") and left ("smaller"). Adding, subtracting, multiplying, and dividing, we can think of as operations that move us back and forth on the line.

Now let's think about a plane, an enormous—infinite—flat, two-dimensional area defined by two perpendicular number lines. We can identify points or locations in the plane by two numbers, an ordered pair (x, y). The x refers to the horizontal dimension—a line that runs across the plane in the way the horizon divides the sea and sky. The y refers to the vertical dimension—a line that runs "up and down."

This is exactly how we think about a flat map. Usually east-west is horizontal and north-south is vertical. In cities laid out like grids or checkerboards, we can identify locations by cross streets: "State and Madison," "18th and Vine," and "5th Avenue and 42nd Street." Naming two intersecting streets makes a location clear. It is at the intersection of the streets, which are like lines.

At the centre of the plane is (0,0), a point that lies at the 0-position on each line. The plane has four quadrants. The upper left quadrant is negative x and positive y. The upper right quadrant is positive x and positive y. The lower left quadrant is negative x and negative y. And the lower right quadrant is positive x and negative y.

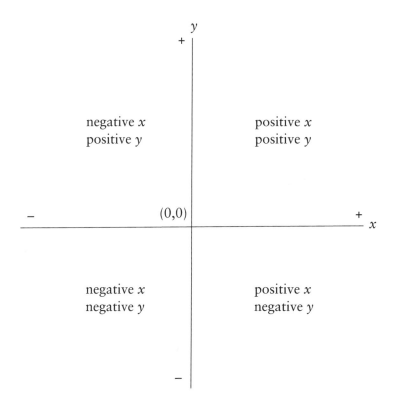

Now we can do several interesting things in the plane. First of all, we can think of a location as representing a case (e.g., a person, place, or object) described in terms of two characteristics. For example, I could represent my height and weight as an ordered pair, (64", 120 lbs). The first number, height, is the x-component, and the second number, weight, is the y-component. We could find the points—the locations represented by the ordered pair—for each person in our class, and plot them on a piece of graph paper, producing a "scatterplot".

Can you picture what this would look like? It would be a cigar-shaped "cloud" of points, one for each person. They would all be located in the upper right quadrant—nobody has a negative height or weight. Tall heavy people are represented by points toward the upper right end of the "cloud" and short light people by points in the lower left end of the cloud. The cloud tilts upward from left to right: Taller people tend to be heavier.

In statistics, as we will soon see, graphing two characteristics like height and weight as ordered pairs is a powerful way of thinking about their relationship.

A function is a special relationship between x and y. A function is expressed in a formula such as $y = F(x)$, which means that we can pick an x, stick it into the formula, and "get out" a y. For example, $y = 5 + 2x$. This is a linear function, involving x but no higher power of x. It is the equation of a specific line. Its slope is 2 (rise over run) and 5 is its y-intercept (the place where the line crosses the y-axis and $x = 0$).

In general, the equation of a line is $y = a + bx$. (In high school, many people learn this formula as $y = b + mx$, but it's the same thing.) The a is the y-intercept, the value of y when $x = 0$, and is sometimes called "the constant term." The b is the slope of the line, the rise over run. The letters a and b are referred to as the linear coefficients in the equation of a line.

Lines stretch off infinitely in each direction, but almost every set of real-world characteristics, such as height and weight, have only a finite range.

Another kind of function is called a quadratic function: $y = x^2$. When we draw the graph, we see that it is not linear. At $x = 0$, $y = 0$. When x is positive or negative, y is positive. When we start plotting points we see that the graph shoots up very rapidly as x moves away from 0. Fortunately, in this course, we will be concerned primarily with linear functions.

QUESTIONS—COORDINATE PLANE

1. Ask 20 friends or classmates for their height and weight. For each person, mark the ordered pair (h, w) on a graph. What does the resulting graph or scatterplot look like?

2. Ask 20 friends how tall they are and how many cigarettes they smoke daily. Plot (h,c). What does the scatterplot look like?

3. Draw the following lines on a piece of graph paper. First put in the x and y axes and at their intersection mark (0,0). For each equation draw the line by graphing a few points, picking a value for x and then computing the corresponding y.

    a. $y = 3 + 2x$
    b. $y = -4 + x$
    c. $y = -5x$

Math Refresher: Answers

Estimating:

1. 25 miles per gallon
2. $20,000
3. $129
4. increases
5. .350

Greater than or lesser than:

1. Numbers should be placed on number line from left to right in the following order:

$-785; -10.12; -5.5; \dfrac{1}{2}; \dfrac{3}{4}; 1.8; +3; +1500$

2. a) $\dfrac{3}{4} > \dfrac{5}{8}$ b) $\dfrac{7}{8} = \dfrac{14}{16}$

   c) $\dfrac{39}{40} > \dfrac{18}{21}$ d) $2\dfrac{1}{2} > 1\dfrac{1}{2}$

Absolute value:

1. a) .3   b) 5.5   c) 35.7   d) $3\dfrac{1}{4}$

   e) $3\dfrac{1}{4}$ f) 0   g) 565   h) 1

   i) $\dfrac{1}{2}$ j) .50

Operations with fractions:

a) $\dfrac{2}{3} + \dfrac{4}{5} = \dfrac{10}{15} + \dfrac{12}{15} = \dfrac{22}{15} = 1\dfrac{7}{15}$

b) $\dfrac{4}{7} - \dfrac{8}{9} = \dfrac{36}{63} - \dfrac{56}{63} = -\dfrac{20}{63}$

c) $\left(\dfrac{3}{4}\right)\left(\dfrac{1}{2}\right) = \dfrac{3}{8}$

d) $\left(\dfrac{5}{6}\right)\left(\dfrac{3}{11}\right) = \dfrac{15}{66} = \dfrac{5}{22}$

e) $\dfrac{5}{9} \div \dfrac{5}{4} = \dfrac{5}{9} \times \dfrac{4}{5} = \dfrac{20}{45} = \dfrac{4}{9}$

f) $\dfrac{5}{7} \div \dfrac{5}{6} = \dfrac{5}{7} \times \dfrac{6}{5} = \dfrac{6}{7}$

g) $\dfrac{2}{3} - \dfrac{3}{2} = \dfrac{4}{6} - \dfrac{9}{6} = -\dfrac{5}{6}$

h) $\dfrac{4}{7} + \dfrac{8}{3} = \dfrac{12}{21} + \dfrac{56}{21} = \dfrac{68}{21} = 3\dfrac{5}{21}$

Converting fractions:

a) .6, $\dfrac{3}{5}$, 60%   b) $\dfrac{7}{8}$, .875, 87.5%

c) 32%, .32, $\dfrac{8}{25}$ d) 33.3%, .333, $\dfrac{1}{3}$

e) 100%, 1, $\dfrac{1}{1}$ f) $\dfrac{1}{92}$, .01086, .01%

g) $\dfrac{3}{7}$, .42857, 42.86%

h) $\dfrac{3}{9}$, .3333, 33.33%

i) .064, 6% (rounded), $\dfrac{3}{50}$

Questions to think about:

1. Yes   2. No.

Squaring:

a) 9   b) 1521   c) 29.16   d) 29.16

e) $\dfrac{1}{4}$ f) .25   g) .5625   h) 1

i) 0   j) 1   k) .1024   l) $\dfrac{1}{4}$

m) $\dfrac{1}{16}$ n) 625

Square roots:

1. a) 5.916   b) 1.414   c) 12.288

   d) .3146   e) .1   f) 17

   g) .5477   h) .94868

2. The square root is bigger because any number between 0 and 1, when multiplied by itself, has a smaller product.

Coordinate plane:

1 and 2. Here is a small data set showing the heights, weights, and number of cigarettes smoked per day for twenty people. (The height and weight data are real, but the "smokes" are just made up to illustrate the point.)

First we have plotted the data, with height in inches as the x coordinate and weight in pounds as the y coordinate. We can see that there is a "loose" positive relationship. Taller people tend to be heavier, and shorter people tend to be lighter. Greater height inevitably means greater volume, and hence more weight, even if the person is very skinny. The cloud of points has a positive tilt. We have drawn the "best fit" line through the data, and this line shows the positive slope, reflecting this positive relationship. However, many points are off the line because the relationship is not all that close. In the little correlation table below the graph, we have computed the closeness of the relationship mathematically. (See Chapter Four for details.) The table shows a correlation coefficient of +.652 on a scale from −1 to +1, meaning a moderate to strong positive relationship between height and weight for this small group of people.

Next we plotted the data with height in inches as the x coordinate and number of smokes as the y coordinate. Here we don't see much relationship at all. Taller people are neither heavier smokers nor less heavy smokers than shorter people. A line drawn through the data points would not have much of a tilt at all. Its slope would be close to 0. Indeed, in the correlation table below this graph, we see that the correlation between height and smokes is −.047, which is very close to 0, meaning no relationship between these two variables at all. Your data set may not look exactly like this one, but if you compare your results with those of your friends, you will probably see similar patterns—very little relationship between height and smoking.

Data Table: Height, Weight, and Smokes

	HEIGHT	WEIGHT	SMOKES
1	66.00	136.00	.00
2	72.00	185.00	1.00
3	72.00	160.00	30.00
4	62.00	125.00	.00
5	63.00	129.00	45.00
6	66.00	164.00	22.00
7	71.00	170.00	10.00
8	63.00	130.00	.00
9	67.00	120.00	.00
10	70.00	175.00	.00
11	66.00	140.00	15.00
12	66.00	135.00	20.00
13	64.00	140.00	5.00
14	68.00	140.00	.00
15	63.00	145.00	14.00
16	63.00	113.00	18.00
17	67.00	210.00	20.00
18	64.00	120.00	.00
19	65.00	140.00	.00
20	67.00	143.00	.00

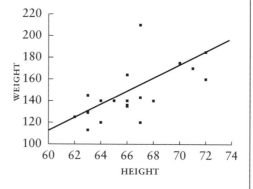

Correlations

		HEIGHT	WEIGHT
HEIGHT	Pearson Correlation	1	.652**
	Sig. (2-tailed)		.002
	N	20	20
WEIGHT	Pearson Correlation	.652**	1
	Sig. (2-tailed)	.002	
	N	20	20

** Correlation is significant at the 0.01 level (2-tailed).

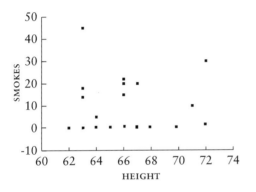

Correlations

		HEIGHT	SMOKES
HEIGHT	Pearson Correlation	1	−.047
	Sig. (2-tailed)		.844
	N	20	20
SMOKES	Pearson Correlation	−.047	1
	Sig. (2-tailed)	.844	
	N	20	20

3. The next graph shows the lines defined by the equations. To graph these equations, we identified two points on the line for each equation and then drew the line to go through the points.

a) $y = 3 + 2x$
   When $x = 0$, $y = 3$. When $x = 2$, $y = 7$.

b) $y = -4 + x$
   When $x = 0$, $y = 4$. When $x = 4$, $y = 0$.

c) $y = -5x$
   When $x = 0$, $y = 0$. When $x = 1$, $y = -5$.

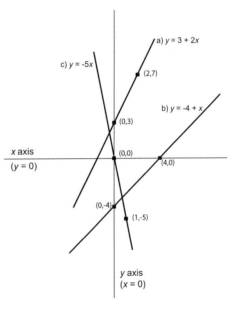

Appendix

Tables of Probability Distributions

The following four tables show values for four probability distributions: the Z-distribution, the *t*-distribution, the chi-square distribution, and the F-distribution. These tables are used to determine whether our observed sample data are sufficiently discrepant from the value we expect under the null hypothesis to allow us to reject the null hypothesis with a low risk of Type I error (rejection of a true null hypothesis). The tables enable us to compare our computed test-statistic with a critical value. The critical value is the value of the test-statistic that has a sufficiently low *p*-value (probability) that we can reject the null hypothesis. In most research, this *p*-value is .05, but you will see that some of the tables also show the critical values for the .10 level of significance. The *p*-value is the probability of Type I error, rejection of a true null hypothesis. It is the probability of obtaining an observed sample outcome by random chance in sampling that is very discrepant from the expected value for the null hypothesis **although the null hypothesis is true.**

Some tests (Z and *t*) can be performed as one-tailed or two-tailed tests. The one-tailed tests are used when we are looking for discrepancy in one direction only (e.g., test results that exceed a certain value) and the two-tailed tests are used when we are looking for discrepancies in either direction.

These tables are arranged for brevity and easy reading. Comprehensive statistics texts often contain more detailed tables with more entries.

TABLE 26: CRITICAL VALUES FOR THE Z-DISTRIBUTION

How to use the Z-table

- When to use it: The Z-table can be used only if both of the following conditions are true: we know the population standard deviation, **and** the sample size is large (at least 30 cases, 100 to be on the safe side). Otherwise, we have to use the *t*-distribution.

- Decide if the problem calls for a one-tailed test (discrepancy in one direction) or a two-tailed test (discrepancy in either direction).

- Compute the Z-statistic for the data as a measure of discrepancy from the expected value under the null hypothesis: (obs. value – exp. value)/(standard error).

- Look up the computed Z-value along the left columns of the table. For a negative Z-value, look up its absolute value.

- When you have found the Z-value, look to the right for either the one-tailed or the two-tailed test.

- Since the computed Z-value may fall between two values, you can either interpolate or (to be on the conservative side), use the smaller value of Z.

- The probabilities are *p*-values that represent the risk of Type I error. If the *p*-value for your computed Z is greater than .05, the null hypothesis cannot be rejected.

Appendix

P-values for the *Z*-distribution

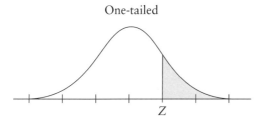

One-tailed   Two-tailed

Z   −Z   +Z

Z-Scores	Probability One-tailed	Probability Two-tailed
.0	.50000	1.00000
.1	.46017	.92034
.2	.42074	.84148
.3	.38209	.76418
.4	.34458	.68916
.5	.30854	.61708
.6	.27425	.54851
.7	.24196	.48393
.8	.21186	.42371
.9	.18406	.36812
1.0	.15866	.31731
1.1	.13567	.27133
1.2	.11507	.23014
1.3	.09680	.19360
1.4	.08076	.16151
1.5	.06681	.13361
1.6	.05480	.10960
1.7	.04457	.08913
1.8	.03593	.07186
1.9	.02872	.05743

Z-Scores	Probability One-tailed	Probability Two-tailed
1.96	.02500	.05000
2.0	.02275	.04550
2.1	.01786	.03573
2.2	.01390	.02781
2.3	.01072	.02145
2.4	.00820	.01640
2.5	.00621	.01242
2.6	.00466	.00932
2.7	.00347	.00693
2.8	.00256	.00511
2.9	.00187	.00373
3.0	.00135	.00270
3.1	.00097	.00194
3.2	.00069	.00137
3.3	.00048	.00097
3.4	.00034	.00067
3.5	.00023	.00047
3.6	.00016	.00032
3.7	.00011	.00022
3.8	.00007	.00014
3.9	.00005	.00010
4.0	.00003	.00006
4.1	.00002	.00004
4.2	.00001	.00003
4.3	.00001	.00002
4.4	.00001	.00001

TABLE 27: CRITICAL VALUES FOR THE *T*-DISTRIBUTION

How to use the *T*-table

- When to use it: Use this if the sample size is small (less than 30 for sure, less than 100 to be on the safe side) **or** the population standard deviation is unknown.

- Decide if the test is one-tailed (tests for discrepancy in one direction) or two-tailed (tests for any discrepancy in either direction).

- Compute the *t*-test statistic for the data. It is a measure of the discrepancy of the observed data from the expected value under the null hypothesis—$(\text{obs} - \text{exp})/SE$.

- Compute degrees of freedom: Degrees of freedom equals the sample size minus 1, namely, $df = N - 1$.

- Select the one- or two-tailed section of the table.

- Look down the left column for the correct df.

- Look across to the entries in that row. Does the computed *t*-value (its absolute value!) **exceed** any of the entries? If yes, the results are significant at the *p*-value indicated at the top of the column. We can reject the null hypothesis, and the *p*-value represents our risk of Type I error (rejection of a true null hypothesis). If the computed *t*-value fails to exceed any of the row entries, we fail to reject the null hypothesis. Note that .05 is a more commonly used *p*-value for rejection of the null hypothesis than is .10.

Appendix

Critical Values for the T-distribution

	One-Tailed Test				Two-Tailed Test		
df	.10	.05	.01	df	.10	.05	.01
1	3.078	6.314	31.821	1	6.314	12.706	63.657
2	1.886	2.920	6.960	2	2.920	4.303	9.925
3	1.638	2.353	4.541	3	2.353	3.182	5.841
4	1.533	2.132	3.747	4	2.132	2.776	4.604
5	1.476	2.015	3.365	5	2.015	2.571	4.032
6	1.440	1.943	3.143	6	1.943	2.447	3.708
7	1.415	1.895	2.998	7	1.895	2.365	3.500
0	1.397	1.860	2.897	8	1.860	2.306	3.356
9	1.383	1.833	2.822	9	1.833	2.262	3.250
10	1.372	1.813	2.764	10	1.813	2.228	3.170
11	1.364	1.796	2.718	11	1.796	2.201	3.106
12	1.356	1.783	2.681	12	1.783	2.179	3.055
13	1.350	1.771	2.651	13	1.771	2.161	3.013
14	1.345	1.762	2.625	14	1.762	2.145	2.977
15	1.341	1.753	2.603	15	1.753	2.132	2.947
16	1.337	1.746	2.584	16	1.746	2.120	2.921
17	1.334	1.740	2.567	17	1.740	2.115	2.898
18	1.331	1.734	2.553	18	1.734	2.101	2.879
19	1.328	1.729	2.540	19	1.729	2.093	2.861
20	1.326	1.725	2.528	20	1.725	2.086	2.846
21	1.323	1.721	2.518	21	1.721	2.080	2.832
22	1.321	1.717	2.509	22	1.717	2.074	2.819
23	1.320	1.714	2.500	23	1.714	2.069	2.808
24	1.318	1.711	2.492	24	1.711	2.064	2.797
25	1.317	1.708	2.485	25	1.708	2.060	2.788
26	1.315	1.706	2.479	26	1.706	2.056	2.779
27	1.314	1.704	2.473	27	1.704	2.052	2.771
28	1.313	1.701	2.467	28	1.701	2.049	2.764
29	1.312	1.699	2.462	29	1.699	2.045	2.757
30	1.311	1.698	2.458	30	1.698	2.043	2.750
35	1.306	1.690	2.438	35	1.690	2.030	2.724
40	1.303	1.684	2.424	40	1.684	2.021	2.705
45	1.301	1.680	2.412	45	1.680	2.014	2.690
50	1.299	1.676	2.404	50	1.676	2.009	2.678
55	1.297	1.673	2.396	55	1.673	2.004	2.668
60	1.296	1.671	2.390	60	1.671	2.001	2.661
65	1.295	1.669	2385	65	1.669	1.997	2.654
70	1.294	1.667	2.381	70	1.667	1.995	2.648
75	1.293	1.666	2.377	70	1.666	1.992	2.643
80	1.292	1.664	2.374	80	1.664	1.990	2.630
85	1292	1.663	2.371	85	1.663	1.989	2.635
90	1.291	1.662	2.369	90	1.662	1.987	2.632
95	1.291	1.661	2.366	95	1.661	1.986	2.629
100	1.290	1.660	2.364	100	1.660	1.984	2.626
Infinity	1.282	1.645	2.327	Infinity	1.645	1.960	2.576

TABLE 28: CRITICAL VALUES FOR THE CHI-SQUARE DISTRIBUTION

How to use the Chi-Square Table

- When to use it: The chi-square test is used for non-parametric data (when we cannot compute a mean and standard deviation), i.e., for distributions of categoric variables.

- Degrees of freedom: $df = (r - 1)(c - 1)$ for a crosstab, where r is the number of categories of the row variable and c is the number of categories of the column variable. If chi-square is being computed for a single variable, $df = k - 1$, the number of categories minus 1; for example, we might be asking if people are born in equal proportions in the four seasons, so $df = 4 - 1 = 3$.

- We compute chi-square. It will always be zero or positive.

- We look down the df column to find the right df. Then we look rightwards along the row to the entries in the next three columns. If the computed chi-square **exceeds** the value in the column, the results can be said to be statistically significant at the p-value indicated at the top of the column. Note that in most research, the .05 level, rather than the .10 level, is considered the p-value that allows rejection of the null hypothesis.

Appendix

Critical Values for the Chi-square Test

	Level of Significance		
df	.10	.05	.01
1	2.71	3.84	6.64
2	4.00	5.99	9.21
3	6.25	7.82	11.34
4	7.78	9.49	13.28
5	9.24	11.07	15.09
6	10.64	12.59	16.81
7	12.02	14.07	18.48
8	13.36	15.51	20.09
9	14.68	16.92	21.67
10	16.99	18.31	23.21
11	1728	19.68	24.72
12	18.65	21.03	26.22
13	19.81	22.36	27.69
14	21.06	23.68	29.14
15	22.31	25.00	30.58
16	23.54	26.30	32.00
17	24.77	27.60	33.41
18	25.99	28.87	34.80
19	27.20	30.14	36.19
20	28.41	31.41	37.57
21	29.62	32.67	38.93
22	30.81	33.92	40.29
23	32.01	35.17	41.64
24	33.20	36.42	42.98
25	34.38	37.65	44.81
26	35.56	38.88	45.64
27	36.74	40.11	46.96
28	37.92	41.34	48.28
29	39.09	42.56	49.59
30	40.26	43.77	50.89

TABLE 29: CRITICAL VALUES FOR THE *F*-DISTRIBUTION

How to use the *F*-table

When to use it: The *F*-distribution is a probability distribution for the ratio of two variances, and it is associated with the data analysis technique called ANOVA (analysis of variance). There are two common situations for its use:

1. When we are comparing means for a variable defined for two or more groups (IV categories) to see if there are statistically significant differences, and we perform this test by computing the ratio of between-groups variability to within-groups variability. In this case, the degrees of freedom of the numerator is the number of categories minus 1 (in mathematical terms, $k - 1$), and the degrees of freedom of the denominator is $N - k$ (total sample size minus the number of categories of the IV).

2. When we are testing the significance of *R*-squared in a regression analysis. *R*-squared is computed as the ratio of regression variance to total variance, which makes it a PRE measure that shows what proportion of total variance can be estimated from the regression. The null hypothesis is that this proportion in the population is 0. But the *F*-ratio that is computed for the significance test is the ratio of regression variance to residual variance. (This may seem confusing, but remember that total variance = regression variance + residual variance, so we are just moving the terms around.) The degrees of freedom for the regression variance (numerator) is the number of independent variables (k), and the degrees of freedom for the residual variance (denominator) is $[(N - 1) - k]$. The degrees of freedom for the total variance is $N - 1$. In the bivariate case, the degrees of freedom work out to 1 *df* for the numerator and $N - 2$ *df* for the denominator.

Appendix

How to read the table: There are three main steps.

- Find the correct *df* for the denominator (within-groups variability) in the left column and for the numerator (between-groups variability) in the upper row. Notice that the numerator degrees of freedom only go up to 12, because it would be unusual to have more than 13 categories in the research design.

- Find the entry in the table that corresponds to the denominator *df* row and the numerator *df* column. This number is the critical value. The computed *F*-ratio must **exceed** this value for the results to be statistically significant. Do this step first in the .05 section of the *F*-table. Then it can be repeated in the .01 section to see if the results are highly significant. Notice that for the .01 level, the critical value that must be exceeded is quite a bit higher than the critical value for the .05 level.

- Notice *F* is always 0 or positive, never negative.

The Joy of Stats

Critical Values for the *F*-distribution

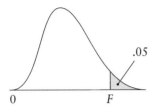

df for the denominator	df for the numerator α = .05							
	1	2	3	4	5	6	8	12
1	161.4	199.5	215.7	224.6	230.2	234.0	238.9	243.9
2	18.51	19.00	19.16	9.25	19.30	19.33	19.37	19.41
3	10.13	9.55	9.28	9.12	9.01	8.94	8.84	8.74
4	7.71	6.94	6.59	6.39	6.26	6.16	6.04	5.91
5	6.61	5.79	5.41	5.19	5.05	4.95	4.82	4.68
6	5.99	5.14	4.76	4.53	4.39	4.28	4.15	4.00
7	5.59	.474	4.35	4.12	3.97	3.87	3.73	3.57
8	5.32	4.46	4.07	3.84	3.69	3.58	3.44	3.28
9	5.12	4.26	3.86	3.63	3.48	3.37	3.23	3.07
10	4.96	4.30	3.71	3.48	3.33	3.22	3.07	2.91
11	4.84	3.98	3.59	3.36	3.20	3.09	2.95	2.79
12	4.75	3.88	3.49	3.26	3.11	3.00	2.85	2.69
13	4.67	3.80	3.41	3.18	3.02	2.92	2.77	2.60
14	4.60	3.74	3.34	3.11	2.96	2.85	2.70	2.53
15	4.54	3.68	3.29	3.06	2.90	2.79	2.64	2.48
16	4.49	3.63	3.24	3.01	2.85	2.74	2.59	2.42
17	4.45	3.59	3.20	2.96	2.81	2.70	2.55	2.38
18	4.41	3.55	3.16	2.93	2.77	2.66	2.51	2.34
19	4.38	3.52	3.13	2.90	2.74	2.63	2.48	2.31
20	4.35	3.49	3.10	2.87	2.71	2.60	2.45	2.28
21	4.32	3.47	3.07	2.84	2.68	2.57	2.42	2.25
22	4.30	3.44	3.05	2.82	2.66	2.55	2.40	2.23
23	4.28	3.42	3.03	2.80	2.64	2.53	2.38	2.20
24	4.26	3.40	3.01	2.78	2.62	2.51	2.36	2.18
25	4.24	3.38	2.99	2.76	2.60	2.49	2.34	2.16
26	4.22	3.37	2.98	2.74	2.59	2.47	2.32	2.15
27	4.21	3.35	2.96	2.73	2.57	2.46	2.30	2.13
28	4.20	3.34	2.95	2.71	2.56	2.44	2.29	2.12
29	4.18	3.33	2.93	2.70	2.54	2.43	2.28	2.10
30	4.17	3.32	2.92	2.69	2.53	2.42	2.27	2.09
40	4.08	3.23	2.84	2.61	2.45	2.34	2.18	2.00
60	4.00	3.35	2.76	2.52	2.37	2.25	2.10	1.92
120	3.92	3.07	2.68	2.45	2.29	2.17	2.02	1.83
∞	3.84	2.99	2.60	2.37	2.21	2.09	1.94	1.75

Appendix

df for the denominator	df for the numerator α = .01							
	1	2	3	4	5	6	8	12
1	4052	4999	5403	5625	5764	5859	5981	6106
2	98.49	99.01	99.17	99.25	99.30	99.33	99.36	99.42
3	34.12	30.81	29.46	28.71	28.24	27.91	27.49	27.05
4	21.20	18.00	16.69	15.98	15.52	15.21	14.80	14.37
5	16.26	13.27	12.06	11.39	10.97	10.67	10.27	9.89
6	13.74	10.92	9.78	9.15	8.75	8.47	8.10	7.72
7	12.25	9.55	8.45	7.85	7.46	7.19	6.84	6.47
8	11.26	8.65	7.59	7.01	6.63	6.37	6.03	5.67
9	10.56	8.02	6.99	6.42	6.06	5.80	5.47	5.11
0	10.04	7.56	6.55	5.99	5.64	5.39	5.06	4.71
11	9.65	7.20	6.22	5.67	5.32	5.07	4.74	4.40
12	9.33	6.93	5.95	5.41	5.06	4.82	4.50	4.16
13	9.07	6.70	5.74	5.20	4.86	4.62	4.30	3.96
14	8.86	6.51	5.56	5.03	4.69	4.46	4.14	3.80
15	8.68	6.36	5.42	4.89	4.56	4.32	4.00	3.67
16	8.53	6.23	5.29	4.77	4.44	4.20	3.89	3.55
17	8.40	6.11	5.18	4.67	4.34	4.10	3.79	3.45
18	8.28	6.01	5.09	4.58	4.25	4.01	3.71	3.37
19	8.18	5.93	5.01	4.50	4.17	3.94	3.63	3.30
20	8.10	5.85	4.94	4.43	4.10	3.87	3.56	3.23
21	8.02	5.78	4.87	4,37	4.04	3.81	3.51	3.17
22	7.94	5.72	4.82	4.31	3.99	3.76	3.45	3.12
23	7.88	5.66	4.76	4.26	3.94	3.71	3.41	3.07
24	7.82	5.61	4.72	4.22	3.90	3.67	3.36	3.03
25	7.77	5.57	4.68	4.18	3.86	3.63	3.32	2.99
26	7.72	5.53	4.64	4.14	3.82	3.59	3.29	2.96
27	7.68	5.49	4.60	4.11	3.78	3.56	3.26	2.93
28	7.64	5.45	4.57	4.07	3.75	3.53	3.23	2.90
29	7.60	5.42	4.54	4.04	3.73	3.50	3.20	2.87
30	7.56	5.39	4.51	4.02	3.70	3.47	3.17	2.84
40	7.31	5.18	4.31	3.83	3.51	3.29	2.99	2.66
60	7.08	4.98	4.13	3.65	3.34	3.12	2.82	2.50
120	6.85	4.79	3.95	3.48	3.17	2.96	2.66	2.34
∞	6.64	4.60	3.78	3.32	3.02	2.80	2.51	2.18

Bibliography, Reading Suggestions, and Works Cited

Overviews of applied statistics, with an emphasis on concepts:

Freedman, David A., R. Pisani, and R.A. Purves. *Statistics*. 3rd ed. New York: W.W. Norton, 1997. (Any edition will do.) Considered by many to be the best non-calculus stats book; goes much further into probability than our text. Problems are drawn from several areas, not only social sciences. Clearly written.

Moore, David S. *Statistics: Concepts and Controversies*. 5th ed. New York: W.H. Freeman, 2001. A good introductory book, lots of problems drawn from many different fields that require thought, not just calculation. Covers probability and related topics in considerable detail.

Comprehensive textbooks in applied statistics for the social sciences, written with a considerable level of mathematical rigor:

Knoke, David, George Bohrnstedt, and Alison Potter Mee. *Statistics for Social Data Analysis*. 4th ed. Itasca, Illinois: Peacock Publishers, 2002. A mathematically rigorous and sophisticated (but non-calculus) stats book that covers introductory material in detail and then develops various multiple regression techniques. Requires a high comfort level with math.

Elifson, Kirk, Richard Runyon, and Audrey Haber. *Fundamentals of Social Statistics*. 3rd ed. New York: McGraw-Hill, 1998. Good coverage of introductory statistics. Attractive graphics.

Lab and software guides with good explanations of applied statistics techniques:

Norusis, Marija J. *SPSS 11: Guide to Data Analysis*. Upper Saddle River, NJ: Prentice-Hall, 2002. More than a lab manual. Explains how to interpret basic stats. Covers the major data analysis techniques for an introductory course in the social sciences. Clearly written. Comes with several data sets. Excellent reference book for anyone going on in research methods.

Sweet, Stephen and Karen Grace-Martin. *Data Analysis with SPSS: A First Course in Applied Statistics.* 2nd ed. New York: Allyn and Bacon, 2003. An excellent manual for learning how to use SPSS for social science data analysis, all the way through multiple and logistic regression. Comes with interesting data sets. Outlines how to write a research report. Very hands-on with exercises in a workbook format. Intelligent discussion of how to think about and interpret "statistical significance."

Statistical arguments and displays, and their pitfalls:

Huff, Darrell. *How to Lie with Statistics.* 1954. New York: W.W. Norton, 1993. A classic little book about how to mislead (or avoid being misled), especially with visual displays. Still very useful.

Tufte, Edward R. *Visual and Statistical Thinking: Displays of Evidence for Decision Making.* Cheshire, CT: Graphics Press, 1997. A fascinating short booklet that shows how visual displays are a key to understanding data. Shows how very poor data display and analysis contributed to the Challenger Shuttle disaster—the displays created before the launch failed to show clearly that O-ring damage was more likely at cold temperatures.

Short conceptual guides for overviews and review:

Cuzzort, R.P. and James S. Vrettos. *The Elementary Forms of Statistical Reason.* New York: St. Martin's Press, 1996. Discursive approach, very little mathematical calculation. Emphasis on the purpose and logic of statistical reasoning, with examples from many fields.

Rowntree, Derek. *Statistics Without Tears: An Introduction for Nonmathematicians.* Boston: Pearson, 2004. This is a discursive guide to statistics with emphasis on statistical inference and statistical reasoning; lots of graphs. It does not go into a lot of data analysis and tends to be very coy about formulas.

Voelker, David H., Peter Z. Orton, and Scott Adams. *Statistics (Cliff Quick Review).* New Jersey: John Wiley & Sons, 2001. One of a number of short, cheap review guides that can be useful. This one has more on *t*-tests than on other techniques—it's very weak on chi-square and crosstabs, and for regression, it does not review the correlation coefficient based on *z*-scores (nor the one based on covariance), only the computational formula. Despite these defects, it can come in handy.

Reading Statistics:

Huck, Schuyler W. *Reading Statistics and Research*. 4th ed. Boston: Pearson, 2004. A wonderful guide to reading statistics in social science research. The author shows the many different ways in which data analysis and statistical results can be displayed in the research literature and helps the reader develop a critical understanding of the material. Indispensable for anyone who is reading social science or social policy research.

Multivariate Statistics:

Tabachnick, B.G. and L.S. Fidell, *Using Multivariate Statistics*. 4th ed. New York: Allyn and Bacon, 2001. A superb and comprehensive book for the intermediate and advanced student, covering a large number of multivariate techniques.

Math for fun: Probability, randomness, chaos, and related topics:

Bennett, Deborah. *Randomness*. Cambridge, MA: Harvard University Press, 1998.

Beltrami, E. *What is Random?* Springer, 1999.

Everitt, Brian S. *Chance Rules: An Informal Guide to Probability, Risk, and Statistics*. New York: Copernicus/Springer-Verlag, 1999.

Three books on probability, chance, randomness, and risk and their role in everyday situations, such as medical tests, gambling, and markets.

Isaac, Richard. *The Pleasures of Probability*. New York: Springer-Verlag, 1995. A thought-provoking foray into probability and related topics for the reader who really enjoys math; no calculus required, but the book is very challenging.

Lowry, Richard. *The Architecture of Chance: An Introduction to the Logic and Arithmetic of Probability*. New York: Oxford University Press, 1989. Discursive coverage of probability and related topics.

Pretty good balance of discussion and numerical examples.

Weaver, Warren. *Lady Luck: The Theory of Probability*. New York: Dover, 1983. A classic that lays out the basics of probability, with lots of examples, many from gambling.

Peitgen, Heinz-Otto, H. Juergens, and D. Saupe. *Chaos and Fractals*. 2nd ed. New York: Springer-Verlag, 2004. A beautiful large tome that covers these fascinating new areas of mathematics. Lavish graphics and colourful computer-generated illustrations. Definitely for the math enthusiast; coverage ranges from fairly simple to advanced.

Gleick, James. *Chaos: Making a New Science*. New York: Penguin, 1988. Easier than Peitgen et al; written for the layperson, to introduce them to development of this field and its basic ideas.

Lipschutz, Seymour and Marc Lipson. *Probability*. 2nd ed. Schaum's Outline Series. New York: McGraw-Hill, 2000. A no-nonsense introduction for folks who like math, with lots of formulas, theorems, proofs, etc. Assumes some familiarity with set theory and calculus.

Other Works Cited

Freedman, David, et al. *Statistics*. 2nd ed. New York: W.W. Norton and Company, 1991.

Hammel, Eugene, P. Bickel, and J.W. O'Connell. "Is there a sex bias in graduate admissions?" *Science* 187 (1975): 398-404.

Hernandez-Arias, Rafael. "Race and Ethnicity as Variables in Health Research." Brandeis University, unpublished paper, 2004.

Laumann, Edward O., et al. *The Sexual Organization of the City*. Chicago: University of Chicago Press, 2004.

Medina, Tait Runnfeldt. "Emotional Wellbeing and Parenting Processes in Stepfather Families Compared to Intact Original Families: The Adolescent's Perspective." DePaul University, unpublished paper, 2004.

Trijonis, John. "Vegas Winners." *Engineering and Science* 2 (2001): 35-41.

Index

absolute value, 289
addition, 296
algebraic formulas
    definition, 23
algorithms and formulas
    ANOVA (F-ratio), 243
    chi-square test, 195
    for converting to Z-scores, 82
    for the correlation coefficient, 169–70, 223
    definition, 19, 23
    index of diversity, 68
    mean, 59
    median, 61
    R-squared, 229
    slope coefficient in regression, 225
    standard deviation, 65
    t-tests, 245–48
    for testing the null hypothesis, 142
    variance, 65
alpha error (Type I error), 135–38
ANOVA (analysis of variance), 155–56, 201–06, 217, 241–44
    between-groups variance, 201–02
    F-ratio, 202–03, 241
    within-groups variance, 201–02
association, 41, 153
associative law, 305
averages. See measures of central tendency

bar graphs, 70, 73
bell curve. See normal curve
Beltrami, E., What is Random?, 114
Bennett, Deborah J., Randomness, 96
"best fit line," 174
beta error (Type II), 135–36
beta weight or standardized regression
    coefficient, 173
    in multiple regression, 188
between groups variance, 155–56, 201–03
biased sampling, 47, 96
bimodal distributions, 109
binary variables. See dichotomous variables

binomial distribution, 122–23
bivariate analysis, 151, 157, 200
bivariate crosstabs, 216
bivariate regression, 173
bivariate regression equation, 224
Bohrnstedt, G. and David Knoke, Statistics for
    Social Data Analysis, 134
boxplots, 74, 77–78

cases
    definition, 29
categoric variables, 33, 67–71
causality, 41–42, 151
    association, 41
    non-spurious relationships, 42
    time-order, 42
cell frequencies, 193–95
Central Limit Theorem, 110–17, 120, 127–28,
    137, 140
central tendency, 58
chaos theory, 114
Chebycheff's Inequality, 83–84, 89, 94, 109,
    114
chi-square, 126, 189, 191–97, 200–01, 231.
    See also significance
    algorithm, 195
    sensitivity to sample size, 197
chi-square table
    how to use, 320
coefficient of determination, 174–76, 228. See
    also R-squared
    in regression analysis, 164
commutative law, 305
compare means, 156, 203
computer-generated random numbers, 96
confidence intervals, 87–88, 127–34
confidence level, 129–30, 132, 134
confounding variables, 153
constructed-scale variables, 34–35
continuous variables, 33, 73
    cutting into intervals, 38
coordinate plane, 308–10

correlation, 153–54. *See also* regression
    analysis
correlation coefficient, 122, 154
    algorithm for, 169–70, 223
    in regression analysis, 164–71
    rule for interpreting, 171
correlation/regression. *See* regression analysis
covariance
    correlation and, 169–70, 172
critical value, 196
crosstabs/contingency tables, 155, 163, 189–
    201, 231–40
    bivariate, 216
    chi-square test, 192–97
    expected value, 192–94, 231–33
    measures of association, 197, 237–40
    percentaging the table, 190, 235–37
    row and column totals (marginals), 190,
        192, 195

data analysis output
    check list for, 216–17
data analysis techniques, 163–216
    ANOVA, 155–56, 201–02, 217, 241
    crosstabs/contingency tables, 155, 163,
        189–90, 192–97, 231
    how to choose, 221
    logistic regression, 156–57, 206–07
    regression analysis, 154–55, 163–76, 184–
        88, 217, 222, 224
decimal fractions, 291
degrees of freedom, 139, 144, 195–96, 203
dependent (DV) variables, 40–41, 43, 151
describing distributions, 29, 55–85
    bar graphs, 70, 73
    boxplots, 74, 77–78
    Chebycheff's Inequality, 83–84
    frequency distributions, 55–57, 78, 92
    histograms, 73–74, 78
    pie charts, 70–71
    stem and leaf chart, 74, 76
    Z-scores, 80–83
descriptive statistics, 45–46, 55
deviation from the mean. *See* standard
    deviation (SD)
dichotomous variables, 35–36, 39, 121, 156,
    206
    dummy, 37, 188

difference, 48
    significant, 49–51 (*See also* significance)
discrete-numerical variables, 34, 56
dispersion
    definition, 58 (*See also* measures of
        dispersion)
distributions. *See* describing distributions;
        probability; sampling distribution
distributive law, 305
division, 297
dummy variables, 37, 188
Durkheim, Emile, 42, 158

ecological fallacy, 43
"error" variation. *See* sampling error
estimates and estimating, 24, 52, 171, 284
expected value, 87, 95, 97–105, 123–25 (for
        proportions), 137, 141, 192–94. *See
        also* probability; sampling distribution
exponentiated coefficient, 210–11

F-ratio, 126, 202–03, 241
F-table
    how to use, 322
formulas, 286, 304–08. *See also* algorithms and
        formulas
    definition, 19
fractions, 290
    math review, 21–22
Freedman, David, *Statistics*, 104
frequency distributions, 56, 78, 92
    categoric variables, 55
    interval-ratio continuous data, 57
frequency polygons, 74, 107

graphing and visual displays of distributions,
        70–78
    guidelines, 79
grouped data, 57
    variance for, 66

higher powers, 302
histograms, 73–74, 78
    of sample means, 91–94, 106–07, 117–19
Huff, Darrell, *How to Lie With Statistics*, 79
hypothesis testing, 88, 127
    null hypothesis, 87–88, 127–28, 134–41,
        144–46, 192, 196

Index

"in-between" variables, 33–34
independent (IV) variables, 40–41, 43, 151
independent samples *t*-test, 146, 156, 217, 247
index of diversity, 69
    algorithm for, 68
index of qualitative variation, 35, 68–69
individual and place-level data, 43
inferential statistics. *See* statistical inference
interaction effect
    in multivariate analysis, 158, 160
interquartile range (IQR), 77
interval-ratio continuous data, 57
interval-ratio variable, 33, 39, 78
intervals, 38
    confidence, 87–88, 127–34
intervening variable, 158, 161

Kun, Béla, 64
kurtosis, 75

Law of Large Numbers, 98, 101–02
laws of probability, 137
least squares. *See* ordinary least squares (OLS)
level of measurement, 31–34, 39
    interval-ratio or scale, 33
    nominal, 32
    ordinal, 32
    selecting, 37–39
level of significance. *See* significance
Likert scale, 34
Lipschutz, S. and M. Lipson, *Probability*, 84
logistic coefficients, 208, 210
logistic regression, 156–57, 206–16
    binary outcome variable, 206
    odds ratios, 206–07
"lurking" variables, 162

margin of error, 127, 129, 133
marginal distributions, 233
marginals. *See* row and column totals
mean, 60–61, 63, 87, 107, 109–10
    algorithm for, 59
    of a dichotomous variable, 36
    sample means, 92, 109–13
measures of association, 201, 237
    gamma and Yules Q, 197, 200, 238–39
    lambda, 197, 239–41
measures of central tendency, 58–63. *See also*

mean; median; mode
    monkey business with, 63 (*See also* "spin")
measures of dispersion and variability, 58, 64
    range, 65
    standard deviation (SD), 65–67
    variance, 65–67
median, 61–63, 69, 107
    algorithm for, 61
misinformation, 219
modal frequency, 62
mode, 62–63, 107
models, 52
    in linear regression, 171–88
    in logistic regression, 209–16
"monkey business," 63, 79. *See also* "spin"
multi-category variable, 39
multiple regression, 155, 172–73, 184–88
    adjusted multiple *R*-squared, 188
multiplication, 296
multivariate analysis, 157
    interaction effect, 158, 160
    intervening variable, 158, 161
    spurious relationships, 157, 160
multivariate relationships, 42

natural log, 209
natural log of the odds ratio, 207
natural log transformation, 164
nominal (level of measurement), 32
non-spurious relationship, 42
normal curve, 74, 88, 94–95
    as continuous probability distribution,
        106–7
    distribution of values, 108
    mean, mode and median in, 107
    sampling distributions and, 109, 127
null hypothesis, 87–88, 127–28, 134–41, 144–
        46, 153, 192, 196
    algorithm for testing, 142
    tips for setting up, 140
number line, 287

"objectivity," 40
observation, 51
odds ratios, 156–57, 206–07
"on the average." *See* ANOVA
one sample *t*-tests, 140, 146, 217, 244
operationalized variables, 39–40

reliability, 40
    validity, 40
operations, 296–301
ordered pairs, 308–10
ordinal (level of measurement), 32
ordinary least squares (OLS)
    linear coefficients, 173
    regression line, 154, 171

p-values, 137–39, 144. See also significance
parameters. See population parameters
Pearson correlation coefficient, 154, 164–71,
        222
    algorithms and formulas, 223–24
percentages
    math review, 21–22, 292–94
percentages in the direction of the IV, 191, 193,
        201, 235
percentile distributions, 69, 78
pie charts, 70–71
place-level correlations, 44
population
    definition, 45
population mean, 88
population parameters, 88–89, 94, 106
population proportion, 88
predictor variables, 153
probability, 88, 95, 97–126
probability distribution. See sampling
        distribution
probability sample, 96
proportional reduction in error (PRE)
        measures, 176, 237–41
proportions, 192
pseudo-R-squared, 210–11

qualitative data, 35
quantitative data, 35

R-squared, 174–76, 180, 188, 288
    algorithms, 229
random number generator, 96
random samples, 89, 124
    simple random samples, 47, 95–97, 100,
        109
random variable, 102
Randomness (Bennett), 96
range, 65

regression analysis, 154–55, 163–88, 217, 222
    beta weight or standardized regression
        coefficient, 173
    bivariate regression, 173, 224–31
    coefficient of determination, 164, 174–76,
        228–31
    correlation coefficient, 164–71
    multiple regression, 172, 184–88
    slope, 172
    Y-intercept or constant, 172
regression coefficients, 172–74, 210–11
regression line. See under ordinary least squares
        (OLS)
reliability (of operationalized variables), 40
row and column totals (marginals), 190, 192,
        195

sample means, 92. See also sample statistics
sample size, 115–16, 123–25, 134, 145, 197
sample statistics, 46, 109–13, 121
samples, 46
    definition, 45
    simple random samples, 47, 95–97, 100,
        109
sampling
    biased, 47, 96
sampling distribution, 29, 93, 95, 104, 113–20,
        124, 126
    distribution of sums, 101–3
    expected value, 87
    normal curve, 106–12
    of a proportion, 121–22
    standard deviation, 65–67, 87–88, 113, 120
    t-distribution, 126
sampling error, 47, 90, 95, 111, 155
scatterplot, 154, 164. See also regression
        analysis
scientific notation, 304
significance, 115, 144, 152, 208
    chi-square test of, 191–96, 200
    level of, 135–36
    statistical significance, 136, 138–39
    testing R-squared for, 176, 180
simple random sample, 47, 95–97, 100, 109
skew, 109, 164
    formula for, 75
slope, 172–74
"spin," 58, 64. See also "monkey business"